Private Acts in Public Places

Private Acts in Public Places

A Social History of Divorce in the Formative Era of American Family Law

Richard H. Chused

University of Pennsylvania Press

Philadelphia

Library of Congress Cataloging-in-Publication Data

Chused, Richard H., 1943–
  Private acts in public places: a social history of divorce in the formative era of American family law / Richard H. Chused.
    p.   cm.
  Includes bibliographical references and index.
  ISBN 0-8122-3202-X (alk. paper)
    1. Divorce—Law and legislation—United States—History—19th century.   2. Divorce—Law and legislation—Maryland—History—19th century.   3. Divorce—United States—History—19th century.   4. Divorce—Maryland—History—19th century.   5. United States—Social conditions—To 1865.   I. Title.
KF535.C48   1994
346.7301'66—dc20
[347.306166]   94-1335
                                                                                                    CIP

Dedicated with love to my wife, Elizabeth Langer,
and our sons, Ben Chused and Sam Langer.

Contents

1. Introduction

Before 1841, divorce was a legislative affair in Maryland. Those wishing to divorce sought the aid of representatives in the House of Delegates of the General Assembly, who filed petitions in the lower house seeking passage of private acts ending the marriages of their constituents. Between 1790 and 1850, the state legislature passed 549 divorce acts and three acts of annulment.[1] During the 1841 legislative session, Maryland's courts gained authority, concurrent with the legislature, to sever marital bonds.[2] Only in 1851, after the new state constitution's provision barring legislative divorce took effect, was the General Assembly ousted from day-to-day oversight of family life.[3]

The first private divorce bill passed after the Revolutionary War was obtained in 1790 by John Sewell, of Talbot County, Maryland.[4] The act's preamble instructs us that his wife, Eve Sewell, was convicted in county court of adultery for bearing a mulatto child. Mother and child were condemned to servitude. The General Assembly granted John a divorce, taking care in the legislation to protect the legitimacy of the white children of John Sewell born before Eve's conviction.[5] Statements confirming the legitimacy of children were common in the early private divorce acts, most of which were adopted on adultery grounds. Of the fifty legislative divorces or annulments passed between 1790 and 1815, thirty-nine, or 78 percent, had clauses protecting the legitimacy of children of the severed marriages.[6]

Though Eve's behavior must have been widely condemned, John struggled for more than two years to obtain his divorce. He first petitioned for a private bill at the 1788 session. The effort failed in the House of Delegates by a 34 to 22 vote despite a statement from the committee considering Sewell's petition that "sufficient evidence has been adduced to establish . . . [the facts] as represented" and a recommendation that "an act ought immediately to pass annulling the said marriage agreeably to the prayer of the said petition."[7] As John Sewell discovered, the General Assembly was reluctant to grant divorces to anyone during the last decade of the eighteenth-century.

More than five decades after the Sewell divorce, by a simple, unedifying one-line statute, "Eliza Gibson, of the city of Baltimore" was "divorced from her husband, Edmund D. Gibson, a vinculo matrimonii."[8] Obviously, significant changes had occurred between the Sewell and Gibson divorces. Petitioners were generally rural and male before 1800. By mid-century significant numbers of urban women were seeking legislative assistance.[9] In 1850, the presence of an "immoral" wife was not the obvious or only factor sparking the passage of private divorce bills. Middle-class and urban pressures worked to expand the scope of divorce.[10] By 1840, the acts often were ludicrously simple, and consideration on the floor of the legislature was frequently fast and uneventful.

The simple, often opaque, quality of many of the mid-nineteenth-century private divorce acts,[11] however, hides some major conflicts. Though the extant legislative records usually reveal little controversy, severance of nineteenth-century marital ties was sometimes as fiery and unpleasant as our own contemporary experience. During the first half of the nineteenth century, romantic expectations for marriage increased, domestic obligations of wives expanded, and the number of husbands working outside the home to provide their families with economic support rose. Each of these developments created the potential for new forms of bitterness when marriages dissolved. Heavenly romance could convert to hatred; women's changing roles upset traditional men; and failure of husbands to support their families left freshly domesticated wives with few options for survival. Acrimony about children also heightened the unpleasantness of some legislative divorce disputes. By the 1820s youngsters, often viewed in colonial times as economic assets of fathers, were thought by many to be malleable creatures needing intellectual, moral, and emotional guidance to become productive adults. Nineteenth-century disputes about their supervision, therefore, might slip into arguments about the respective worth of mother and father.

Disappointed expectations, economic difficulties, personal anger, and the status of children were not the only causes of legislative controversy. Though the private bill debates, taken one at a time, usually reveal little of note, the totality of legislative trends, such as rates of bill failure or the frequency of amendment proposals, provides clues to the cultural, political, and religious debates in society at large. Legislative conflicts rooted in strands of political, economic, religious, and cultural thought were often more important than the facts of any particular case, even in the midst of open and tumultuous family discord. In addition, many spouses petitioned the legislature for a divorce not to escape the depredations or offenses of a mate still living in the household, but to gain their economic and social freedom from a relationship which had *de facto* ended at an earlier time. Whether these petitions were filed by an abandoned woman, a deserted man, or separated spouses cooperating in efforts to end their relationship, opposition to the divorce had to be manufactured by the General Assembly. Such parties were unlikely to create discord on their own. The significant increase between 1800 and 1840 in both the divorce rate and the proportion of legislative petitions granted by the General Assembly[12] confirms that mobility, consensual divorce,[13] desertion,[14] and urban disarray were increasing in Maryland, as in the Northeast and West.[15] The legislative divorce process, therefore, could not be conflict-free. The wish to help those in desperate straits conflicted with traditional attitudes opposing divorce. Though careful factual scrutiny of divorce bills was sometimes frustrated by the clever preparation of individuals or couples cooperating in the presentation of their case to the General Assembly, the domain available for conflict was spacious—roomy enough to allow political, economic, religious, and cultural disputes to influence many family law debates.

Maryland presents an especially important laboratory for exploration of divorce in the formative decades of the republic. We can watch the vagaries of the legislative process unfold in a place that was enormously diverse in its religious, cultural, commercial, and political leanings. The history of Maryland's legislative divorce process brings to light new data on large cultural rifts—North and South, East and West, urban and rural, settled and frontier—that have long been the subject of historical inquiry, but rarely have been explored in a single data base useful to both social and political historians. Southern culture dominated areas west of the Chesapeake; shipping and agricultural interests controlled the Eastern Shore; Baltimore was a metropolis of national importance; the north central area surrounding Baltimore looked more to the North than the South for its cultural values; and the western panhandle evolved much like neighboring areas in the Northwest Territory.[16] The state is a rich venue for exploring and altering our understanding of the now generally accepted notion that, during our early history, divorce was accessible to many in the North and few in the South.[17] Recounting the Maryland legislature's work will bring these conflicts to life.

During the earliest days of the republic, images of the family were central organizational features of political, religious, and economic understandings throughout the nation. Husbands and fathers served as a fulcrum for religious activity and distribution of political authority, simultaneously controlling the civic activities of their households and voting to send their landed peers to government service. The late eighteenth-century "corporate economy" of the Northeast, Mary Ryan teaches us,[18] created similar devotional customs, with men serving as intermediaries between God and family, salvation and politics. Common law coverture, or marital property, rules gave husbands a like role, controlling both the economic relationships between the family and the outside world and the distribution of resources within the family itself.[19]

While many early Maryland households also may have been highly integrated "corporate" entities analogous to Ryan's corporate family, the variety of cultural motifs in the state made for a quite diverse set of family models. During the late eighteenth century, the Maryland General Assembly was dominated by landed and slaveholding elites surrounding the Chesapeake. Both the divorce rate[20] and the passage rate[21] for legislative divorce petitions were lower in Maryland after the Revolutionary War than in the Northeast. On the surface at least, Maryland conformed to the general Southern pattern of granting divorces more reluctantly than other regions at the turn of the nineteenth century.[22] But contrasting cultural forms similar to those found in the Northeast began to influence areas of the state, especially around Baltimore and in the western panhandle, after 1800. New tensions developed in Maryland family law as the nineteenth century progressed.

During the first half of the nineteenth century, contests about political, religious, and economic roles of husbands and wives were prevalent throughout the North and West. Debates about limiting suffrage to male property owners emerged early in the century. Civic responsibility came to be shared among a larger class; property restrictions on male voting waned.[23] As men moved out of the home to work, women gained recognition as teachers of domestic, cultural, and religious values.[24] In many areas of the country, and in parts of Maryland, both spouses acquired new roles. Husbands and fathers, while retaining their position as political governors, became breadwinners. Wives and mothers, while continuing their household chores, became teachers and moral beacons. Faith also became more democratic. Salvation for many became an individual decision to be made rather than an outcome to be imposed by God. Women, deprived of political and economic power, often were attracted to this devotional message and integrated its teachings into their family life. Since salvation required good deeds on earth, maintenance of an observant family became an essential good deed for women. Throughout, however, patriarchal families remained central, as a place for faithful religious observance, a site for inculcation of cultural values, and a training ground for adult exercise of civic responsibility.

Modification of marital property rules throughout the nation during the first decades of the nineteenth century, like changes in political and religious structures, left the essential features of the patriarchal family intact. Upon marriage, common law rules used in much of the nation during the Revolutionary War era gave a husband ownership of almost all of the personal property of his wife as soon as he reduced it to his possession. In addition, he also gained management rights over her real property for the life of the marriage. Upon the birth of a child, control over the wife's real property was extended to the lifetime of the husband. While early nineteenth-century reforms allowed some deserted women to regain their property or their economic independence and married women's property acts precluded attachment of a wife's property by creditors of her husband, men retained control over the central economic features of intact families.

Family formation rituals also changed after the Revolutionary War. Arranged marriages virtually disappeared. Romance emerged as a basis for mate selection. But such "freedom" did not reduce the impetus to marry. Family remained as a solid source of status and cultural location. The attractions of power remained for men; the promise of economic security attracted women; the legitimation of sexual behavior attracted both. In stark contrast with the present day, when images of rock-solid, politically attuned, churchgoing families often seem little more than nostalgic symbols called to duty by desperate politicians, early nineteenth-century adults expected to marry, raise a family, develop a family economy, and stay together 'til death did they part.

Many of these developments influenced Maryland. Property restrictions on male access to the franchise were eased early in the nineteenth century,[25] religious revivalism swept parts of the state,[26] and married women's property law reforms were passed.[27] But the traditional Southern undertones of much of Maryland society inevitably made debates about family discord prominent features of judicial and legislative discussions in the state. A number of forums existed for these family law debates. Though coverture rules employed by common law courts prevented spouses from contracting directly with each other,[28] chancery courts enforced separation agreements in which husbands reposed assets in trustees for the benefit of their estranged wives. Couples therefore had the ability to privately settle many of their domestic differences.[29] Maryland's chancery courts also had authority throughout the period to grant alimony to women whose husbands engaged in adultery or cruelty and refused to establish trusts for their separated wives.[30] In addition, the 1829 session of the General Assembly enacted legislation granting courts authority to appoint commissioners to receive evidence and draft reports for use by divorce committees of the legislature.[31] Other general divorce bills regularly came before the state legislature for debate. And, as already noted, the legislature passed a number of private divorce acts before 1851, when such matters fell completely into judicial hands.[32]

By mid-century, Southern influence over divorce standards waned but did not disappear. Citizens of Maryland were filing petitions seeking passage of private divorce acts at a rate of more than seventy per year. Maryland's legislative divorce rate was comparable to the judicial rates in other areas of the country.[33] The rising influence of nonslaveholding western settlers, Eastern Shore farmers and traders, and Baltimore urbanites fueled a steady rise in the state's divorce rate. Watching this story unfold in a legislative arena provides dramatic evidence of regional and class differences in attitudes toward family law. Traditional, more aristocratic, Southern delegates continually voted against private divorce bills in large numbers, while representatives from other areas voted the opposite way.[34]

Telling stories about divorce in a political, legislative environment, placing the intact family at the focal point of cultural life is ironic history at its best. Tales of failure become the vehicle for expounding upon both ideal and flawed images of family culture, economic life, religious devotion, politics, and law. Recent social history literature has only begun to pry open this complex story.[35] Norma Basch's work is a particularly good explication of Northeastern judicial divorce in the mid-nineteenth century.[36] She carefully instructs us that the development of divorce was not a simple tale of women claiming new realms of autonomy in a world of disappointed romantic expectations. For many women, divorce only formally ended a marriage terminated earlier by a deserting husband. The courts enabled them to reconstruct their economic lives and, perhaps, to remarry. Those women with property of their own fared much better than those without, since alimony was of little use to women deserted by impoverished husbands. For the departed men, divorce served to sanction their leaving. In a nice reconstruction of prior work describing the rise of divorce as a claim by women for autonomy from the constraints of family culture,[37] Basch paints a more interesting, complex picture in which the arrival of divorce freed deserting men to seek out new mates. "Men," Basch writes, "created de facto divorces, women sought out legal ones."[38] The nineteenth-century history of divorce in the Northeast, therefore, is not a linear story of gradual liberalization in the face of changing cultural norms and social pressures. Divorce, like much of women's legal history, was laden with double-edged consequences.[39] Women, Basch tells us, might obtain some autonomy by divorce, but only at the expense of being labeled a failure in the moral education of their spouses. And the freedom from family constraints resulting from divorce was frequently tempered by economic insecurity, if not by abject poverty.

The complexities of electoral politics undergirding the private act divorce process add new dimensions to this tangled family law story. Many classic jurisprudential texts discuss the development of judge-made common law norms as a gradual, intensely fact-based creation of "rules."[40] We were told that these rules, while always subject to modification in new factual situations, gave guidance to the community at large and shaped the contours of legal debate. *Stare decisis* (the homage paid to the wisdom of prior decisions), it is assumed in such scholarship, restrained quixotic changes in the rules, making it easier to report on trends in legal attitudes and to predict the future behavior of courts. While many now dispute this simplistic, apolitical view of judicial behavior, there is a grain of truth to the notion that courts, constrained by the need to resolve specific disputes, often act cautiously, paying some deference to prior history and decisions. To whatever degree the image of courts as gradualist institutions reflects reality, it is clear that the Maryland General Assembly did not feel bound by many court-like restraints in its review of divorce petitions. The legislative process itself left much room for manipulation, both by those seeking divorces and those occupying the corridors of power. Resolution of factual controversies was not trial-like. And, most importantly, the apparent substantive "rules" of legislative divorce changed often, sometimes in quite remarkable, abrupt, and surprising fashions. The beginning and the end of Maryland's nineteenth-century divorce story was a bit like those in other places, but the body of the story is remarkably different.

The basic structure of the private act process was quite simple. Those seeking legislative divorces filed petitions stating their grievances and requests for relief with the General Assembly. Leave to file a petition was almost always sought by a member of the House of Delegates from the county or region in which the petitioner lived. Senators rarely initiated a divorce bill. Since members of the House of Delegates were at their homes scattered throughout the state during most of the year when the legislature was not in session, it was fairly easy and, absent great controversy, relatively inexpensive to initiate the divorce process.[41] A visit with a delegate, perhaps followed up by the signing of an affidavit, could start the ball rolling. Each member of the House would simply bring divorce papers with him to each session. Though the famous and wealthy sometimes used the legislative divorce process, many of the cases involved middle-class or impoverished families.[42]

Until the House of Delegates established a standing divorce committee in 1822, ad hoc committees were designated to review each petition and present a report or bill for review by the entire body. The delegate seeking leave to file the petition virtually always served on the ad hoc committee reviewing it. Evidence was generally not taken, though counter-petitions and affidavits were sometimes filed. Committee decisions on divorce petitions were rarely accompanied by reports stating reasons and opinions for the proffered recommendations. The process followed by divorce committees was often one-sided, especially in cases in which one spouse was no longer in the area or wished her or his spouse's petition to be well received. By 1840 there was clearly some room for cooperative couples wishing to divorce to proceed in an "uncontested" manner.[43] Delegates interested in divorce also made their mark. Whether devotion to a cause, retribution for a slight, or performance of a personal favor motivated their interest, delegates were free to seek membership on committees reviewing divorce petitions, to work their will without the need to publicly state their reasons, and, as with all legislative disputes, to work the corridors of power.

In such an environment transformation of political party alignments or enlargement of the franchise had marked impacts on legislative family law policy. Those seeking divorces often found themselves at the mercy of larger political shifts. Expansion of the franchise and the rise of the Republican Party at the turn of the nineteenth century, for example, loosened the constraints on divorce prevalent in the largely aristocratic pre-1800 General Assembly. Before 1805 all the legislative divorces were obtained by men. Although some women sought a divorce, they were all turned aside. This pattern changed in 1806. For the next decade, women petitioned for divorce more often than men, and with somewhat greater success.[44]

Political, combined with religious, events led to another abrupt change in legislative divorce patterns in 1816. Only *a vinculo*, or complete, divorces had been granted during the prior twenty-five years.[45] That is, all prior parties to divorces were permitted to remarry after their legislative divorce act was passed; they were freed "from the chains" of marriage. But after the Federalists, led by Roger Brooke Taney, a Catholic, regained control of the Maryland Senate in 1816, the legislature refused to pass *a vinculo* divorces. For the next decade, only *a mensa et thoro*, or partial, divorces were enacted. These acts freed men and women "from the obligation to share bed and board," but they could not remarry. While this hints of a conservative reaction in family law once the lively post–Revolutionary War debates on the role of women faded from view,[46] the change in policy led the legislature to initiate a number of other changes that were not so traditional. New types of provisions appeared in the private acts, such as *feme sole* protections permitting women living apart from their husbands under partial divorces but still "bound by the chains of marriage" to participate in economic transactions otherwise precluded by marital property rules. Some women regained property they brought to their marriages or obtained other economic awards. Such benefits allowed women to escape from the more egregious depredations of departed husbands. In addition, the rate of success for women petitioning for legislative relief rose.[47] Child custody provisions also became central features of the legislative debates during this time.[48] The era, therefore, was traditional in some ways and reformist in others.

From 1826 until the Maryland General Assembly first adopted general divorce legislation at its 1841 session,[49] the proportion of complete divorces among the enacted private bills gradually rose. There were disputes over the granting of complete divorces, with the State Senate sometimes blocking the adoption of *a vinculo* bills and insisting on the passage of partial divorces. The last partial divorce was passed in the 1840 legislative session. After 1841, the legislature fitfully attempted to get out of the divorce business, leaving a batch of simple *a vinculo* divorces, much like that granted to Eliza Gibson, in its wake. During the few years before the state adopted its first general divorce act, more than seventy petitions for private bills were filed in each session.[50] After adopting its first general divorce act, the legislature got out of the private bill business for a few years. Most assumed that the general act adopted in 1841 had ended the legislative divorce process. Pressures to continue granting private divorces, however, arose from many parties, including a state governor, who could not obtain relief under the narrow divorce act governing judicial decision making. Divorce petitions had returned to a high level by the time Maryland's 1850 state constitutional convention opened its deliberations[51] and, with minimal debate, inserted a provision in the new constitution banning legislative divorce.

Though divorce petitions did cast a burdensome pall over the legislature after 1840, the disappearance of legislative divorce a decade later is not just a classic tale of frustration over individuated decision making leading a legislative body to push controversies into a judicial branch designed to handle one-on-one disputes.[52] Despite the increasing pressure to grant divorces as the nineteenth century evolved and the palpable need to resolve the status of women left in legal limbo by departed men, those sitting in Maryland's General Assembly before 1850 were extremely reluctant to pass general divorce legislation. Such reluctance was quite remarkable, since a significant number of legislators voted in favor of private bills granting divorces on grounds the same officials refused to allow in general legislation. Individual plights of woe were one thing; broad approbation of divorce through reformist general legislation was quite another.

This is actually not an unusual phenomenon, though examples of it in nineteenth-century legal history have not previously been noted. Some of those adjudicating individual disputes—whether judges or legislators—inevitably empathize with the plight of breathing human beings laying their problems before them for resolution. Such empathy will lead to results in individual cases that are not possible when general principles come under discussion. The history of the twentieth-century is littered with examples of this political dynamic. Individuals could obtain birth control devices from under drugstore counters, even as legislators refused to repeal broad regulatory limitations on their advertisement and distribution.[53] Individual use of condoms was one thing; running the gauntlet of the political and religious right to propose lifting controls on distribution was quite another. Individuals seeking abortions in trying circumstances evoked sympathy from politicians who professed opposition to freedom of choice. Sherri Finkbine's widely publicized efforts to abort a thalidomide-affected fetus in the 1960s was one thing; general repeal of restrictions on abortion was quite another.[54] In like manner, the mid-nineteenth-century denouement of the divorce story in Maryland found a traditional, rather than reformist, coalition pushing the General Assembly out of the divorce business. By the 1840s, those favoring liberal divorce preferred to maintain the legislature's right to grant divorces; those preferring a traditional family with restrictive access to divorce voted to ban private divorce bills and push family conflicts into the courts under narrowly drawn general legislation. The final result was a quite conservative divorce statute, left largely intact until 1937.[55]

Nonetheless, the shift of divorce to the courts was a significant historical event. It symbolized the lessening role of families as a central organizing force of religion, politics, and the economy. Industrial concerns, work places, markets, schools, and churches were all focal points for the exercise of power and the training of citizens. Family was becoming "private," and the resolution of "private" family matters in the "public," politically charged legislature was losing its aura of propriety. Eventually it became acceptable to contend that leaving divorce in legislative hands was "obviously" wrong "because it would occupy too much time, and because it is properly a judicial act."[56] This book tells the convoluted story of how traditional politics made divorce "properly a judicial act."

Notes

1. *See* Table 1 in Appendix 1. Between 1790 and 1851 one or both members of at least 1,100 couples filed 1,386 petitions for divorces. Seventy-two couples filed three or more times. It is possible that I missed a few petitions or acts. The possibility of inaccuracies in the indexes for each year of the legislative journals and session laws cannot be eliminated. The early journals were often unindexed. The year a divorce is granted is normally described in both the tables and the text by reference to the date on which the legislative session in which the divorce was passed actually began, not the date the private act was formally adopted. Most sessions began late in one year and continued into the following calendar year.

2. An Act to Give to the Chancellor and the County Courts as Courts of Equity, Jurisdiction in Cases of Divorce, ch. 262, 1841 Md. Laws (Mar. 1, 1842). Complete divorce grounds were limited to impotence at the time of marriage, adultery, abandonment for five years, and grounds traditionally available to annul a marriage, such as bigamy. Additional grounds were listed for a partial divorce—cruelty of treatment, excessively vicious conduct, abandonment, and desertion. In other states, these grounds often served as a basis for obtaining a complete divorce. The courts also were granted authority to award alimony and property to wives, and custody and child support to either spouse.

3. In 1851, section 21 of a new state constitution forbade the General Assembly from granting private divorces.

4. This was almost surely the first Maryland divorce. Other searches of Maryland legislative records have also failed to turn up an earlier one. *See* M. K. MEYER, DIVORCES AND NAMES CHANGED IN MARYLAND BY ACT OF THE LEGISLATURE, 1634–1854 (1970). Riley contends it was the first post–Revolutionary War legislative divorce in the South. G. RILEY, DIVORCE: AN AMERICAN TRADITION 35 (1991).

5. An Act for Annulling the Marriage of John Sewell, of Talbot County, and Eve his Wife, ch. XXIV, 1790 Md. Laws (Dec. 21, 1790). Although the word "annulling" is used in the title of the Sewell divorce act, it was not an annulment. The body of the legislation contains *a vinculo* divorce language, that is, language breaking "the chains" of marriage. In addition, the setting is one not traditionally handled by designating a marriage void at its inception.

6. Only seven, or less than 2 percent, of the 502 divorces adopted later contained such language. This change occurred for two reasons. As Chapter 4 makes clear, only divorces from bed and board were passed by the legislature between 1816 and 1826. The legitimacy of children is not cast in question by such divorces since the parents may not remarry. After 1826, when complete divorces reappeared, no one felt that the legitimacy of children was at risk because of divorce.

7. VOTES AND PROCEEDINGS OF THE HOUSE OF DELEGATES OF THE STATE OF MARYLAND. NOVEMBER SESSION, 1788, at p. 68 (1789). (This series of volumes, which covers the entire period of this study, will be cited as [date] HOUSE JOURNAL at [page], with the appropriate year in which the legislative session began and the page reference provided. Similar citations will be given for the VOTES AND PROCEEDINGS OF THE SENATE OF THE STATE OF MARYLAND, using the form [date] SENATE JOURNAL at [page].)

8. An Act to Divorce Eliza Gibson, of the City of Baltimore, from Her Husband, Edmund D. Gibson, ch. 558, 1849 Md. Laws (Mar. 9, 1850). *A vinculo matrimonii* means "from the chains of marriage." Other divorces were granted *a mensa et thoro*, or "from bed and board." The latter technically left the parties married—free to live apart, but unable to remarry.

9. By 1840, about 40 percent of all those petitioning the legislature for divorces and half of the couples actually divorced by private bills involved people from Baltimore City. *See* Tables 6 and 7 in Appendix 1. Before 1805 those filing petitions with the state legislature were usually male. That changed after 1805. About three-fifths of the petitioners were women from 1805 on. *See* Table 8 in Appendix 1.

10. *Compare* L. FRIEDMAN, A HISTORY OF AMERICAN LAW 500 (1985). And *see* Table 9 in Appendix 1, showing that Baltimore had a higher divorce rate than the rest of the state.

11. The legislative record is quite sparse. Maryland's General Assembly, like virtually every other nineteenth-century legislature, failed to archive its papers. This problem is one of the major reasons why private bills have been so rarely studied in the historical literature. Petitions, committee reports, and bill files were routinely destroyed. Although Maryland newspapers sometimes reported on legislative events, they apparently were not interested in divorce. A search through many papers failed to produce any useful information. Despite the lack of extensive legislative records, a few sources exist for studying the legislative divorce process. First, some court records of alimony and commission proceedings remain. They are, of course, interesting in their own right. In addition, they sometimes shed light on actions of the General Assembly, especially when the litigants were the same as those seeking legislative relief. Second, legislative journals, though not word-for-word transcripts of floor proceedings, provide a number of clues about the divorce process. Most of the journal entries are mundane reportage of bill and

petition filings, committee appointments, committee conclusions, and floor votes. Once in a while, committee reports were explicated, amendments explained, and debates summarized. The litany of routine procedural items recorded in the journals for each bill, together with the acts themselves, produced a useful computer data base. Information on the passage rate of bills, gender of petitioners, and residence of the parties, among other useful items, was retrieved and analyzed. From time to time, the journals also provided details about proposed amendments or other facets of floor debates on particular bills. Finally, there is a scattering of useful data in library, manuscript, and pamphlet collections.

12. *See* Tables 2 and 9 in Appendix 1. Baltimore City divorce rates were higher than in the state at large after 1800. Divorce rates for 1850 cannot be figured from the data in this study since both courts and the legislature granted divorces between 1842 and 1851. While I know the number of legislative divorces, I do not know the judicial divorce rate. The legislative data demonstrate that the number of divorce petitions filed in the legislature and the number of private divorce bills actually adopted declined markedly immediately after the courts obtained divorce jurisdiction in 1842.

13. "Collusive" divorce, while not common before 1850, was not unknown. *See* FRIEDMAN, *supra* note 10, at 207–208. Some friendly divorces certainly passed Maryland's General Assembly during the first half of the nineteenth century. *See* the discussion in Chapter 7.

14. The number of Maryland women receiving outpensions (payments to women unconstrained by obligations of servitude or debt imprisonment) in the opening decades of the nineteenth century increased significantly, especially in the cities. C. McKenna, *Women, Welfare and Work in Maryland: A Historical Survey of the First Two Hundred Years* 25–29 (1982) (Student paper on file with author).

15. Norma Basch, in her recent article on divorce in New York and Indiana, *Relief in the Premises: Divorce as a Woman's Remedy in New York and Indiana, 1815–1870*, 8 LAW & HIST. REV. 1 (1990), paints a striking portrait of the women and men left behind by migrating spouses.

16. In this study, these regions are broken down into the following counties:

North Central Region: Baltimore, Frederick, and Harford Counties
Eastern Shore Region: Caroline, Cecil, Dorchester, Kent, Queene Annes, Somerset, Talbot, and Worcester Counties
Southern Region: Anne Arundel, Calvert, Charles, Montgomery, Prince Georges, and Saint Marys Counties
Western Region: Allegany and Washington Counties

17. *See* FRIEDMAN, *supra* note 10, at 204–206.

18. M. RYAN, CRADLE OF THE MIDDLE CLASS: THE FAMILY IN ONEIDA COUNTY, NEW YORK, 1790–1865, at 22–43 (1981).

19. R. Chused, *Married Women's Property Law: 1800–1850*, 71 GEO. L. J. 1359, 1361–1372 (1983).

20. M. Schultz, in *Divorce in Early America: Origins and Patterns in Three North Central States*, 25 SOC. Q. 511, 518 (1984), reports that the divorce rate for a sample of counties in Illinois, Missouri, and Ohio was 8 per 100,000 in 1810, 4 in

1820, 9 in 1830, and 14 in 1840. For the early decades of the nineteenth century, Maryland's rates were consistently lower, although those for Baltimore City alone crept closer to the Schultz findings. By 1840, the statewide rate rose to just under 7 per 100,000 and the rate in Baltimore to more than 18. *See* Table 9 in Appendix 1.

21. Schultz, *supra* note 20, at 520, also reports that 48.1 percent of legislative divorce petitions were adopted in 1820, 59.0 percent in 1830, 62.3 percent in 1840, and 67.1 percent in 1850. Maryland's passage rates were somewhat lower, though as with divorce rates, passage rates rose to levels comparable to those in Northern states by 1840. By then about half of the legislative divorce petitions led to divorce acts. *See* Table 2 in Appendix 1.

22. Statutes granting courts authority to issue divorces were adopted later in the South than in the Northeast. Passage of legislative divorces, though more common in the South than others areas, probably did not occur often enough to equalize regional divorce rates in the first half of the nineteenth century. RILEY, *supra* note 4, at 25–29, 34–44; M. Schultz, *Divorce in the South Atlantic States: Origins, Historical Patterns, and Recent Trends*, 16 INT'L. J. SOC. FAM. 225, 245 (1986). The best study of divorce in the South is J. Censer, *"Smiling Through Her Tears": Ante-Bellum Southern Women and Divorce*, 25 AM. J. LEG. HIST. 1 (1981).

23. See R. Steinfeld, *Property and Suffrage in the Early American Republic*, 41 STAN. L. REV. 335 (1989).

24. L. KERBER, WOMEN OF THE REPUBLIC: INTELLECT & IDEOLOGY IN REVOLUTIONARY AMERICA 269–288 (1980).

25. R. BRUGGER, MARYLAND: A MIDDLE TEMPERAMENT, 1634–1980, at 160–166 (1988).

26. *Id.* at 147–151.

27. Chused, *supra* note 19, at 1365–1381, 1399.

28. The often-stated ground for this and other rules was that husband and wife were one entity. Since an entity may not contract with itself, spouses were unable to make legally binding agreements. The most commonly used statement of this "logic" may be found in ch. XV, part III on the law of husband and wife in BLACKSTONE'S COMMENTARIES, an English treatise first published in 1765. The most prominent early American edition of Blackstone, edited by St. George Tucker, Professor of Law at the College of William and Mary, was published with heavy commentary in 1803 in Philadelphia.

29. *See* M. SALMON, WOMEN AND THE LAW OF PROPERTY IN EARLY AMERICA 66–76 (1988).

30. Section XIV of An Act Concerning Marriages, ch. XII, 1777 Md. Laws provided "[t]hat the Chancellor shall and may hear and determine all Causes for Alimony, in as full and ample Manner as such Causes could be heard and determined by the Laws of England in the ecclesiastical Courts there." Ecclesiastical courts allowed bed and board divorces for adultery or cruelty. This statute confirmed a long-standing practice in the state. M. SALMON, *supra* note 29, at 62–63; G. MAY, DIVORCE LAW IN MARYLAND: INTERIM REPORT OF THE STUDY OF DIVORCE LITIGATION IN OHIO AND MARYLAND 3–6 (1932).

31. An Act for Taking Testimony in Cases of Applications for Divorce, ch. 202, 1829 Md. Laws (Feb. 27, 1830).

32. From 1842 to 1849, divorces emanated from both the courts and the legislature. There was no 1850 legislative session while the state constitutional convention was in session.

33. *See* Schultz, *supra* note 20, at 518; Schultz, *supra* note 22.

34. *See* Table 13 in Appendix 1, showing that for most time periods delegates from the South favored private divorce bills at lower rates than delegates from other areas.

35. For general summaries of divorce law before and just after the Revolutionary War, see G. RILEY, *supra* note 4, at 1–129; M. SALMON, *supra* note 29, at 58–80; N. M. BLAKE, ROAD TO RENO: A HISTORY OF DIVORCE IN THE UNITED STATES 34–96 (1962); L. C. HALEM, DIVORCE REFORM: CHANGING LEGAL AND SOCIAL PERSPECTIVES 9–26 (1980). For studies of particular jurisdictions in the same eras, see Basch, *supra* note 15; S. Cohen, *The Broken Bond: Divorce in Providence County, 1749–1809*, 44 R.I. HIST. 67 (1985); S. Cohen, *"To Parts of the World Unknown": The Circumstances of Divorce in Connecticut, 1750–1797*, 11 CAN. REV. AM. STUD. 275 (1980); N. Cott, *Divorce and the Changing Status of Women in Eighteenth-Century Massachusetts*, 33 WM. & MARY Q. 586 (1976); N. Cott, *Eighteenth Century Family and Social Life Revealed in Massachusetts Divorce Records*, 10 J. SOC. HIST. 20 (1976); C. DAYTON, WOMEN BEFORE THE BAR: GENDER, LAW, AND SOCIETY IN CONNECTICUT, 1710–1790, at 284–376 (1986) (Thesis, Princeton U.); T. Meehan, *"Not Made Out of Levity": Evolution of Divorce in Early Pennsylvania*, 92 PA. MAG. HIST. & BIO. 441 (1968).

36. Basch, *supra* note 15.

37. *Contrast*, FRIEDMAN, *supra* note 10, at 501–502 (1985); C. DEGLER, AT ODDS: WOMEN AND THE FAMILY IN AMERICA FROM THE REVOLUTION TO THE PRESENT 168–169 (1980).

38. Basch, *supra* note 15, at 8.

39. *Compare* the attractions of married women's property laws to traditional men, discussed in R. Chused, *The Oregon Donation Act of 1850 and Nineteenth Century Federal Married Women's Property Law*, 2 LAW & HIST. REV. 44, 69–73 (1984), and radical reformers.

40. *See, e.g.*, E. LEVI, AN INTRODUCTION TO LEGAL REASONING (1948).

41. The ease of gaining access to members of the House of Delegates suggests that the legislative divorce process was not any more expensive, and maybe less expensive, than the judicial divorce process.

42. Divorce broadened into a largely middle-class remedy in many areas in the nineteenth century. *See* FRIEDMAN, *supra* note 10, at 500–501.

43. *See id.* at 207–208.

44. *See* Tables 3 and 8 in Appendix 1. These data show that the proportion of women petitioners jumped from 33 percent to 60 percent after 1804, and the passage rate for women from zero to 26 percent.

45. *See* Table 1.

46. *See, e.g.*, the discussion of this era in KERBER, *supra* note 24, at 269–288.

47. *See* Table 3 in Appendix 1, showing that the passage rate for women petitioners jumped from 26 to 45 percent.

48. *See* Table 4 in Appendix 1 for data on the timing of custody, name

change, and property distribution issues in enacted private bills. Between 1816 and 1825, 15 percent of the acts contained child custody provisions. No custody provisions appeared in earlier legislation. About half of the 1816–1825 acts also contained provisions on the rights of husbands in the property of wives. These data confirm other work showing that child custody and property issues emerged as serious issues early in the nineteenth century. *See, e.g.,* M. GROSSBERG, GOVERNING THE HEARTH: LAW AND THE FAMILY IN NINETEENTH CENTURY AMERICA 234–285 (1985); J. Zainaldin, *The Emergence of a Modern American Family Law: Child Custody, Adoption and the Courts, 1796–1851,* 73 NW. L. REV. 1038 (1979); N. BASCH, IN THE EYES OF THE LAW: MARRIAGE AND PROPERTY IN NINETEENTH-CENTURY NEW YORK (1982); Chused, *supra* note 19, at 1404–1409 (1983).

49. An act to give to the Chancellor and the County Courts as Courts of Equity, jurisdiction in cases of Divorce, ch. 262, 1841 Md. Laws (Mar. 1, 1842). The act provided for complete divorces only for adultery, impotence, marriages unlawful from the beginning (such as marriages between relatives), or abandonment from the state for five years. Cruelty was a ground for bed and board divorce. The abandonment ground was amended a few years later to reduce the period to three years and to remove the requirement that the departed spouse be out of state.

50. Seventy-eight petitions were filed in the 1838 session, 73 in 1839, 74 in 1840, and 75 in 1841, the year the general legislation was adopted.

51. No private bills were enacted during the 1842, 1843, and 1844 legislative sessions, and only 11 petitions were filed during those years. Then the filings and adoptions began to grow again, with 43 petitions filed in the 1847 session and 71 in 1849.

52. *Contrast* Friedman, *supra* note 10, at 206.

53. *See* E. CHESLER, WOMAN OF VALOR: MARGARET SANGER AND THE BIRTH CONTROL MOVEMENT IN AMERICA (1992).

54. *See* K. LUKER, ABORTION AND THE POLITICS OF MOTHERHOOD 62–91 (1984); E. R. RUBIN, ABORTION, POLITICS, AND THE COURTS: *ROE V. WADE* AND ITS AFTERMATH 29–55 (1982). Thalidomide, an experimental sedative, was distributed in samples by physicians in the United States. When taken during pregnancy, it caused major deformities of the arms and legs of the baby. Newspaper reports of the birth defects led Ms. Finkbine to seek an abortion. Her complex attempts during 1962 to abort a fetus after learning she had taken thalidomide produced quite different reactions in the public press from those of the myriad right-to-life demonstrations of the past two decades. Finkbine's plight was widely and often sympathetically reported in the press. *See* the coverage of the Finkbine story in the N.Y. TIMES, July 25, 1962, at 22; July 26, 1962, at 25; July 31, 1962, at 9; and Aug. 19, 1962, at 69. She eventually flew to Sweden to obtain an abortion when Arizona authorities refused to allow it. D. Tarka, *Thalidomide: The Drug Companies' Fallacy* (1991) (Student paper on file with the author). After abortion was legalized, the ability to empathize with individuals disappeared in a stormy moral, ethical and religious debate.

55. Maryland adopted a voluntary separation ground in 1937, the first major change in divorce law since the mid-nineteenth century. Matysek v. Matysek, 128 A.2d 627, 631 (1957).

56. This statement was made by Edward Otis Hinkley of the Baltimore Bar in an appendix to an 1855 edition of the new Maryland Constitution. THE CONSTITUTION OF THE STATE OF MARYLAND, REPORTED AND ADOPTED BY THE CONVENTION OF DELEGATES ASSEMBLED AT THE CITY OF ANNAPOLIS, NOVEMBER 4TH, 1850, AND SUBMITTED TO AND RATIFIED BY THE PEOPLE ON THE FIRST WEDNESDAY OF JUNE, 1851, at 78 (E. O. Hinkley ed., 1855).

2. Miscreant Women and Male Divorce: Family Discord Before 1805

Introduction

Others have written of the emergence of divorce in the North as a remedy for women during the eighteenth century.[1] Hundreds of divorce petitions were filed in Connecticut and Massachusetts courts before the Revolutionary War.[2] Dozens of petitions were filed with the Pennsylvania legislature in the same period.[3] In each of these studies,[4] the author noted that marriage was frequently thought of as an economic relationship before the Revolutionary War, that children were sometimes treated as economic rather than psychological members of the family, that love as a marital ideal was just emerging, that the notion of breaching romantic "obligations" was not mature enough to justify widespread divorce, that the economic dependency of women on their husbands led them for reasons of self-preservation to seek legislative or judicial remedies more often than men, and that complaints of desertion were much more likely to come from women than men.[5]

Nancy Cott, in her classic study of divorce in Massachusetts, noted that the significant increase in the numbers of divorces after the Revolutionary War, particularly for women claiming their husbands committed adultery,[6] made it "tempting to propose . . . that the republican ideology of the Revolutionary era ushered in a 'new deal' that recognized the injustice of the double standard, evened obligations of marital fidelity, and made redress within marriage more accessible to women."[7] But Cott warned that the changes probably were "more in men's political intentions than in their desire for sexual justice." Rejection of the "vice" and traditionally "loose sexual standards" of Britain's upper-class men in favor of a republican ideology emphasizing "virtue" and "marital fidelity" as foundations for the strong families needed to train future citizens did not necessarily mean that women's marital status would be dramatically improved.

Legal responses to family discord in post-Revolutionary War Maryland were quite different from those in Cott's New England. While "virtue" and "vice" were of political concern to those serving in the Maryland legislature before 1800, use of such rhetoric was not accompanied by either a rise in the divorce rate or the emergence of divorce for women. And save for cases of adultery by women deemed particularly odious, divorce was also unavailable to men. In contrast to much of the Northeast, however, Maryland couples willing to settle their differences privately and live apart could adopt separation agreements.[8] As a result, most judicial and legislative pleas by women for economic or marital relief involved either uncooperative husbands or men who had deserted. Assistance for such women, attainable only through an alimony proceeding or a private legislative act, was difficult to obtain. The greatest similarity between early Massachusetts and Maryland arose in the handling of children. Offspring were rarely mentioned in the early Maryland divorce acts, though virtually all of the disputes involved couples with children.[9] Their fate depended upon post-marital economic arrangements rather than on a vision of their psychological best interests. Custody did not become a contestable issue until childhood emerged as a distinct part of the economic and psychological life cycle, until children were seen as requiring the nurture and care of mothers to become responsible, republican, adult citizens.

There are plausible explanations for the differences between family law in Massachusetts and Maryland after the Revolutionary War. Family property rules and alimony processes differed in the two states; those in Maryland made it easier for spouses wishing to separate to arrange for independent economic lives. Prevailing religious practices in Massachusetts were less hostile to divorce. Racial concerns placed constraints on the development of Maryland's family law after the Revolutionary War. And the structure of Maryland's government established obstacles to the early passage of divorce legislation.

Regional Differences and the Impact of Chancery Courts

Regional differences in family property law before the Revolutionary War era were stark. The South, with conservative policies on divorce, "lent particularly strong support to private separation agreements,"[10] while the North allowed divorce, but restricted married women's property rights. Maryland had a long chancery tradition supporting the creation of married women's separate trust estates and the legality of separation agreements.[11] Although eighteenth-century common law rules gave a wife's personal property to her husband if he reduced it to his possession and subjected her real estate to lifetime management by her spouse, chancery courts in England, Maryland,[12] and other parts of the South allowed both personal and real property to be reposed in separate trusts for the use and benefit of married women. Married couples wishing to live apart could arrange their economic lives by placing assets in such a trust. Separate trusts for married women and separation agreements were not as warmly received in Massachusetts, Connecticut, and Pennsylvania.[13] Chancery courts were not fully established in Massachusetts until 1857.[14]

The regional differences arose out of important political and religious currents. New England Puritans viewed sin as a failure to perform good works on earth, not a breach of any promise made to God. Similarly, marriage was a civil contract rather than a covenant with God.[15] And the Puritan family, under the strict patriarchal guidance of a husband, was a crucial place for the performance of good works. Acts threatening family unity challenged central features of the Puritan community's religious and political organization. Adultery, therefore, was both a sin and a breach of a civil agreement. It was better, in such a structure, to ease the establishment of new, functional civic and religious units by permitting divorce than to require the continued existence of unworkable families.

The Puritans, once released from the strictures of English culture, established new religious, political, and legal norms for family life. Complete divorces were granted for adultery and abuse, and partial ones for cruelty and desertion.[16] Confirming Cott's warning that the availability of divorce to women did not necessarily lead to greater sexual justice, Marylynn Salmon concluded that the devotion of New England Puritans to a patriarchal ideal not only led to divorce, but also to reductions in the marital property rights of wives. Any actions that caused conflicts between spouses and "worked against the patriarchal ideal"—whether it was adultery by a husband, a claim for greater economic rights by a wife, or the use of separation agreements—were subject to criticism. "The rules of law adopted in Connecticut and Massachusetts assumed that families would be loving, considerate, and interdependent. Protective strategies for wives and widows could be reduced because they were viewed as unnecessary, restrictive, and perhaps even destructive of family harmony."[17]

By contrast, Maryland and other Southern states imitated significant parts of English family and property law before the Revolutionary War. Those comprising Southern elites at the turn of the nineteenth-century were immigrants or descendants of immigrants who came here because of financial pressure more than political or religious repression. New arrivals sought large estates, servants, and slaves to gain riches unavailable in Europe. Many did so, Salmon opines, "at the price . . . of their dignity," leaving them feeling "inferior to the English in culture, lifestyle, politics and law." One form of solace was to "adhere as closely as possible to English forms."[18]

The areas of Maryland east and south of Baltimore surrounding the Chesapeake Bay were heavily influenced by Southern cultural norms and English legal forms. Their population was also largely Catholic and Anglican, adding to the general reluctance to approve divorce.[19] Even when divorce did arrive in Maryland, its legislative focus partially mirrored English practice. Parliament was the only source for a *vinculo* divorces in Britain before the middle of the nineteenth century. Parliamentary divorce, as in Maryland before 1805, was also extremely difficult to obtain. A divorce plaintiff was required to secure both a tort award in a criminal conversation action against a man who had sexual intercourse with the plaintiff's wife and a bed and board divorce from the Anglican Church before seeking parliamentary action.[20] Only 325 private divorce acts were passed in England between 1670 and 1857, mostly benefiting the English upper crust. Many of the divorces were granted to Englishmen residing in India or other British colonies.

While there is no evidence that those seeking a legislative divorce in Maryland before 1805 had to first run an ecclesiastical divorce gauntlet, there is evidence that a criminal court conviction for adultery was sometimes required.[21] Indeed, the rigors of the early legislative private bill process led Maryland's women, even those desperately in need, to seek alimony in the courts rather than a divorce in the legislature. The existence of alimony jurisdiction in Maryland's chancery courts, like the use of separation agreements, made it possible for a few women, victimized by their husbands' adultery or physical cruelty, to gain a modicum of economic relief without the need to divorce. In most states, including Massachusetts, alimony was a part of the divorce process. Court jurisdiction to hear alimony cases independently of a divorce proceeding did not exist.[22] To the extent Maryland's women viewed marriage as an economic relationship, alimony awards without divorce provided a measure of satisfaction to wives quite similar to that obtained in bed and board divorces granted by other states. To some extent this outcome was mirrored in Massachusetts, where the availability of alimony in bed and board divorce settings reduced the frequency of complete divorces granted to women in comparison with men.[23]

Although the economic relief available in an alimony proceeding was quite narrow,[24] the award of maintenance payments by a court gave a small measure of legitimacy to the status of a wife separated from her husband.

Men were in a different position. Since, unlike the New England states, Maryland did not adopt general divorce legislation after the Revolutionary War, men wishing to rid themselves of their wifely support obligations could only flee or seek redress through adoption of a private divorce bill. Thus, before 1805 most of those petitioning the Maryland legislature for divorces were men and only petitions filed by men were granted. A complete search for alimony cases in the same time period would certainly confirm that many more women than men sought some form of marital relief in Maryland before 1805.[25]

The legality of separation agreements and the existence of a judicial alimony process does not fully explain the differences between early Maryland and those Northern states adopting divorce legislation shortly after the conclusion of the Revolutionary War. The basic shape of family law for women in the two areas was different. The inability to completely divorce had significant consequences. Maryland women could seek neither greater security nor renewed community respect by marrying a new husband. Alimony awards in Maryland only provided maintenance payments to women and left them economically, if not physically or emotionally, entangled with their husbands. Women unable to find their husbands, of course, got nothing. But any earned income obtained by a wife, whether she received alimony or not, was still subject to her husband's control.[26] Even long-absent spouses could reappear and claim dominion over their wives' assets. Division of property, settlement of dower claims, or return of property brought to marriage by women was not possible in an alimony proceeding. Even Massachusetts women obtaining only bed and board divorces could hope to resolve more of their economic woes before the Revolutionary War; and they could, if abandoned by their husbands, seek the status of *feme sole* trader under legislation passed in 1787.[27] Not until 1805, when the General Assembly first opened the legislative divorce door to women,[28] could wives, especially those with uncooperative or absent husbands, dare to hope for resolution of their family law woes.

The Impact of Race on Early Legislative Divorce

Even the divorces granted to men before 1805 by the Maryland legislature were quite different from their counterparts in New England. Racial concerns dominated the early Maryland divorce debates. Adultery, if sanctioned as a ground for severing family ties, threatened to undermine the long-standing acceptance of sexual encounters between white men and slave women. Permitting women to complain about private liaisons across racial lines would have removed the ability of men to control the form of their public family ties. While such concerns arguably led South Carolina to prevent divorce altogether in order to protect men,[29] the punishment of women breaking racial taboos may have stimulated the passage of the earliest Maryland divorces.

John Sewell's divorce of his wife after the birth of a mulatto child was a prototype for Maryland private acts passed before 1805.[30] Three other quite similar measures were approved, one each in the 1794, 1801, and 1803 sessions.[31] The behavior of Eve Sewell and her three contemporaries presented imposing threats to the extant sexual order. The first divorce act not involving charges of interracial sexual activity, passed at the 1797 session, was granted to William Barroll for repeated acts of adultery, prostitution, and desertion by his wife.[32] Though there is nothing in the extant information on this divorce suggesting that Lucretia Barroll had sexual liaisons with African-American men, the possibility may not be ignored.[33] All of these acts were laden with preambles explicating the sins of the married women as adequate justification for the then unusual step of severing marital ties. Not until 1805 did the General Assembly pass a divorce bill without clearly stating that one of the parties to the marriage committed adultery.[34] Private divorce did not become a plausible remedy for women in terrible marriages until the 1806 session, when Pamela Sampson convinced the legislature that her husband was a deranged drunkard.[35]

The "Marriage" of Electoral and Divorce Reform

Despite the cultural differences between early Maryland and New England, regional variation in family law may not be fully understood by simply positing that traditional cultural, economic, racial, industrial, and urbanization differences between North and South led to different legal norms.[36] Some traditional Southern influences were obviously at work in Maryland, but other structural features of Maryland's governance also inhibited the development of family law reforms. Maryland was a complex mixture of urban and rural settings, with significant political and cultural divisions. Southern cultural mores did not dominate all areas. By 1790, for example, Baltimore was the fourth largest city in the United States, smaller only than Philadelphia, New York, and Boston. A decade later it was larger than Boston. Its port bustled with activity.[37] Other parts of the state, especially the Eastern Shore and south, were much more Southern, with large slave populations, more poverty, and soil in some areas washed out from tobacco farming.[38] The Eastern Shore and south also had their differences. The former was largely Anglican and Methodist, with some Quaker and Presbyterian congregations. It had a commercially oriented elite living along the shore, but reliance on tobacco had declined by the Revolutionary War era. Southern Maryland, mostly Anglican and Catholic, continued as a tobacco-producing area well into the nineteenth century. Slave populations there were more stable than on the Eastern Shore, where both white and black populations fell.[39] And the sparsely populated western agricultural areas looked much more like frontier areas in the upper Midwest, producing a wide array of foodstuffs, and had a diverse ethnic and religious population.[40]

The General Assembly, established under the Maryland Constitution of 1776, was dominated in its early decades by wealthy rural elites from the Eastern Shore and southern regions. That was surely the intention of those who drafted the charter. Each county, regardless of population, was entitled to four members in the annually elected House of Delegates; Baltimore and Annapolis received only two each. Thus the Eastern Shore and southern regions elected 73 percent of those serving in the House of Delegates even though in 1790 they had only 58 percent of the white population.[41] This made legislative pressure for family law reform emanating from Baltimore a bit easier to suppress.

Every five years the Senate was indirectly selected by a specially elected body. Senators had to possess property worth one thousand pounds. The governor was also selected indirectly by a joint vote of the House of Delegates and the Senate. White men could vote if they owned fifty acres or had thirty pounds in cash.[42] But voting for delegates to the House and for the senatorial electors was *viva voce*. Men would gather to vote and publicly state their preferences. Those living some distance from the voting site were at an obvious disadvantage. The property qualifications for holding office and voting, the indirect selection of senators and governors, the public nature of the process, and the selective location of polling places made the system perfect for insuring control of the General Assembly by the privileged.[43]

As a result the legislature was dominated by seaboard gentry on many questions during its first two decades. Interesting regional alliances sometimes emerged, as when debtor-creditor controversies were debated. Baltimore commercial interests and Eastern Shore patricians generally sided with creditors. Delegates from other areas often sided with debtors.[44] When allied, Baltimore and Eastern Shore delegates needed only a few other votes to adopt legislation. In bad economic times, however, those favoring debtors would sometimes prevail.[45] Political and religious controversy, however, made it difficult for the same commercial alliance between coastal patricians and urban entrepreneurs to dominate divorce debates. By the end of the eighteenth century, these changing voting blocs became part of the matrix swirling around the creation of the Federalist and Republican parties. A political structure relying upon prominent individuals then gave way to more formally organized political groups.

The structure permitting Maryland's nonurban elite to control legislative politics on many questions was in place almost two decades before Baltimore began its explosive growth and commercial development. Some electoral reforms were adopted at the turn of the nineteenth century, but significant changes in the structure of the Maryland executive and legislative branches did not occur until 1838. That year's session of the General Assembly, gathered just three years before adoption of the first general divorce act, granted more populous areas somewhat greater representation in the House of Delegates. The governor and all senators became subject to direct election.[46] Four decades earlier, at the turn of the nineteenth century, emerging party rivalries, together with the general cultural interest in new forms of republican "citizenship," led the General Assembly to adopt election reforms and eliminate property requirements for voters in state elections. It is likely that Republicans supported the measures in an attempt to bolster their fortunes in the state, but by 1800 even Federalists felt the pressure to remove property restrictions on voting and rid Maryland of the *viva voce* voting system. Both changes went into effect in 1802.[47] A decade later the suffrage reforms were extended to federal elections, and property requirements for those holding office were repealed.[48] Within a few years after the earliest of these electoral reforms, the private bill divorce process showed significant signs of change, especially for women.[49]

Pre-1805 Legislative Divorces

The combined influences of traditional family property law, Southern cultural norms, and a closed electoral system left divorce in the hands of traditionalists until middle-class urbanites and other reformist Marylanders gained enough electoral influence to alter the status quo. In this environment, men had great difficulty obtaining a divorce and women who applied for divorces were unsympathetically treated. Though only five of the twenty-one husbands seeking legislative divorces before 1805 obtained them, none of the eleven wives succeeded in their quests for marital freedom.[50] The depth of opposition to divorce is made palpable by the details of some of the tales of family woe laid before the General Assembly.

Grizelda Hannah of Baltimore sought a divorce and *feme sole* status during the 1788 legislative session, but her petition, like those of most of the other women, never emerged from committee.[51] Two years later she filed a petition seeking only economic relief, stating that her husband, David, "possessed of a considerable real estate," had left her and gone to Germany. She asked for an act "to prevent her said husband from disposing of, or in anywise conveying, the property away to her prejudice."[52] The committee investigating her petition reported that they believed her story "to be true," but that "the interference of the legislature, in order to redress the injury complained of, would be improper."[53]

Anna Maria Sewell found herself in a similar situation. She first applied for a divorce in 1787, but the House of Delegates was not even willing to refer her petition to a committee for investigation.[54] Her 1790 petition did make it to committee, but the resulting report was unfavorable.

> The committee to whom was referred the petition of Anna Maria Sewell, report . . . that [she] . . . and her husband have for a considerable time past lived separate from each other, and that a continuance of their connexion will not probably contribute to that happiness which it was originally intended to secure. And it further appears . . . that the conduct of Mr. Sewell . . . has been truly represented in the petition.
>
> The committee are of opinion, that the dissolution of the marriage contract is an extremely delicate subject, and ought to be justified by powerful reasons before it is determined on. In many governments the judiciary has the power of granting them under particular circumstances; and in others, where no ordinary tribunal is competent to adjudge them legislative interference has been frequently obtained; but in the present case, the committee can see no reason sufficiently strong to induce the legislature to interpose. They may think it hard that the matrimonial union should be perpetuated where the affections have been withdrawn, or where either of the parties has ceased to pursue the welfare of the other, but still it cannot but occur to them, that to destroy so sacred a connexion upon grounds of such a nature, would be dangerous as a precedent, and unwarrantable in itself. The committee are therefore of opinion, that the prayer of the petition ought not to be granted.[55]

The House of Delegates concurred in the committee's judgment.

On the rare occasions when women did obtain some relief, they were left in marital limbo. Prior to 1790, when the legislature granted its first divorce to John Sewell, women probably knew it was hopeless to seek such a remedy. Thus in 1782 Lilly Blair applied only for property relief. She had married Alexander Hamilton in 1758. At the marriage her father and brother gave her new husband some property without any provisions, such as might be created by an equitable separate estate for a married woman, to protect Lilly in case her husband deserted or died first. Hamilton, a sailor, was later reported lost at sea. Lilly then married Charles Blair. The trap was closed when Alexander Hamilton reappeared with a new wife from "foreign parts."[56] For his "misconduct," the state took all of Hamilton's property, including that given to him by Lilly's father and brother. The legislature, in a private bill, then gave Lilly twelve slaves and a life estate in some of the land given to Hamilton by her family.[57] That action, however, left her still married to Hamilton and an adulteress with Charles Blair.

Mary Gwinn first sought a divorce rather than property relief. Her divorce petition was filed with the legislature in 1790, but a bill in her favor was never reported out of committee.[58] She did not obtain any relief until a private act was passed at the 1808 session. It reported that she had married John Gwinn in the belief that her first husband, whose whereabouts were unknown, was a bigamist. The act legitimated the children of Mary and John, designated the children as heirs of Mary and John as if Mary's first husband had died before Mary, and permitted Mary to sue and be sued in any case at law or equity.[59] This legislation provided Mary with the ability to defend her children's right to inherit significant amounts of property she had brought to her first marriage—rights never obtained by Lilly Blair. But Mary never obtained a divorce.

Thus, before 1805, the General Assembly held firmly to the principle that women could pursue only economic remedies. Not until 1805 did the legislature display any willingness to permit a woman to resolve her ambiguous marital status. Susannah Alexander found herself in straits similar to those of Mary Gwinn. She married John Muskett on April 6, 1805,[60] after hearing a "well founded" report that Archibald Alexander was dead. Susannah and Archibald had lived apart for some time under the terms of a separation agreement entered into because of the "misconduct" of Archibald. Both Susannah, who was caring for six children, and Archibald petitioned for divorce. After a significant legislative struggle, Susannah's petition was granted. The House of Delegates initially turned down the bill on a 26 to 21 vote.[61] It passed 31 to 17 only after an amendment removed language confirming the legality of Susannah's marriage to Muskett.[62] Thus, like Lilly Blair and Mary Gwinn, she was left with the legal status of a fornicator. But at least the divorce gave her the ability to go through a marriage ceremony to legitimate her family status. That is exactly what she did on January 9, 1806, about three weeks after her legislative divorce was passed.[63]

Passage of divorces for men before 1805 was inhibited by imposition of very strict requirements on proof that wives had committed adultery. Although the standards, if any, underlying the adoption of private divorces in later years were frequently left unstated in the legislative record, several explicit statements were placed in the early journals. In 1794, for example, Moses Lecompte requested a divorce, complaining that his wife had committed adultery with a mulatto slave.[64] His divorce bill failed 35 to 21 after the committee entertaining the petition found "the facts therein stated supported by depositions accompanying the same, but as it does not appear to your committee, that the wife of the said petitioner was convicted of adultery in any court of law in this state, your committee submit to the house the propriety of passing a law to divorce the petitioner from his said wife."[65]

Susannah Alexander's 1805 divorce verifies that the British-like requirement of a court conviction for adultery did not last long. But the need for strong proof of adultery turned up in other cases described in the pre-1800 legislative journals. Auguste Buard obtained a favorable committee report in the House of Delegates in the 1796 session after its members found that his wife Sofia had "married" Lewis Bullay of Philadelphia.[66] But his bill was never adopted. Charles Heron's petition in the 1798 session probably lacked any proof of adultery, his committee reporting that:

> [T]he said Charles has given notice of his intention to petition this assembly for an act to divorce him from his wife, but as the granting of a divorce involves in it a question serious and important both in a moral and political point of view, your committee are at a loss what report to make thereon. They have no doubt as to the truth of the facts stated in his petition, and as his situation must be wretched and miserable in the extreme, your committee, in order to bring the question before the house, report it as proper to grant the law he prays for.[67]

The report was never acted upon.[68] Finally, Samuel Veazey's 1802 petition also failed for lack of proof of adultery. The committee reviewing his case reported "that although the facts stated in the petition may be correct, and of course render his case peculiarly unfortunate, still there is not sufficient testimony of his wife's infidelity to her marriage bed to warrant the legislature in passing an act of divorce in his favour."[69]

Though these tidbits of legislative history make it quite likely that, before 1805, adoption of a divorce bill was dependent on very strong proof of adultery by wives, there were indications of dissent from this "rule." The obvious cases involving women convicted of adultery after having mulatto children usually led to divorce acts, but dissension surfaced in some other cases. Roll call votes were demanded in four cases in which bills were not passed, and the House passed three bills that died in the Senate. There was some sign of legislative disagreement in more than one-fifth of the bills that did not pass between 1782 and 1804.[70] Tables 10 and 11 in Appendix 1 report data on legislative controversies surfacing in debates over enacted and non-enacted bills. The overall rate of floor debate contention was similar in the two settings,[71] but it took on quite different forms at different times. During the debates on bills eventually enacted into law, legislators were more likely to call for roll call votes or proffer amendments. This makes sense, for bills doomed to defeat weren't worth the time it took to vote or amend. The most notable exception to this trend was in the early divorce debates, when roll calls were called for only when bills were defeated. As Table 11 shows, 14 percent of the divorce bills defeated before 1805 met their fate only after a roll call vote. Some delegates must have felt either that the tally was likely to be close or that those wishing to ;. .. divorces should be forced to publicly state their views. Both are plausible, since the divorces actually adopted before 1805 all involved allegations of interracial adultery or prostitution, faults generally viewed with displeasure.

Legislative traditionalists made their feelings known in cases like that of Moses Lecompte by casting votes against divorces even when proof of adultery was strong. Reformist delegates, however, expressed concern about the House of Delegates' refusal to grant divorces except in the most flagrant cases of adultery by women. Those reviewing Charles Heron's petition deemed his marriage "wretched and miserable in the extreme." Samuel Veazey's situation was described as "peculiarly unfortunate." For these delegates it was difficult to understand why private acts granting property relief to Lilly Blair and Susannah Alexander passed while divorces to men in pathetic marriages failed.[72]

Though nothing in the extant historical record suggests that any delegates were concerned about the potentially calamitous connections between the disabilities imposed on married women by common law rules of coverture and their inability to divorce,[73] the marital controversies coming before them certainly accentuated these problems. The lawyers among the House of Delegates, if not others, must have known of the limitations of existing judicial remedies for married women in economic difficulties. While Maryland equity courts had the authority to grant alimony to women, the remedy was narrow in scope and of little utility to poor women.[74] Even for those with some means, the alimony statute limited relief to situations in which English ecclesiastical courts normally granted bed and board divorces.[75] Thus, if a wife could "shew, either that her husband has been guilty of adultery, or cruel treatment of her" she might be able to obtain alimony.[76] Even if alimony was due, however, the remedy was a separate maintenance—payment of support rather than a setting aside of assets to cover payment of dower or a division of property brought to marriage by a husband or wife.[77]

An early reported case decided in the courts tells the story of Mrs. Wallingsford, a once wealthy woman who failed to regain control of property she brought to her marriage with a man of little means, even though she alleged and proved her husband forced her out of the house and left her destitute. She only had a right to sue for support during their joint lives in an amount dependent upon the wealth of the husband.[78] And this limited right required that the husband be found and that control of his assets be retained, both difficult tasks.[79] Impoverished women were therefore not the only ones left economically trapped in bad marriages. Once-wealthy women also found themselves without either support or the ability to seek security in a new marriage. This was particularly devastating to women who brought substantial amounts of personal property to a marriage. While a husband gained management rights over his wife's real property for his life, there was the possibility that she would regain her land if she survived her estranged spouse. Personal property reduced to possession by a husband, however, was permanently lost to a married woman. By the turn of the nineteenth century, growth of commercial forms of wealth other than real estate, such as notes evidencing indebtedness or other forms of commercial paper, made more palpable the limitations of alimony relief.

Though there were ritual qualities to many of the alimony court filings,[80] some wrenching stories emerge from behind the formal curtain of the pleading process. Women routinely alleged that husbands deserted and left them without any means of support[81] or "without any cause whatsoever" turned them out of doors.[82] More elaborate case chronicles, like that of Sally and John Armstrong, who married in New York City in 1803, are compelling. A few months after their marriage, Sally alleged in her alimony pleadings, John sold all of their property and, promising to follow, sent her, pregnant, to Philadelphia. She did not hear from him for six months. "[H]aving heard by accident that the said John Armstrong went to Baltimore she followed him from Philadelphia."[83] He then moved to Alexandria, Virginia, and back to Baltimore. Sally followed, and in order to help her gain access to her husband, changed her name to Sarah McDowell. Long arm statutes permitting suits against nonresidents of a state carrying on activity there did not exist;[84] Sally therefore had to find her husband rather than sue him in her home state. And her name change was apparently part of a more general attempt at disguise. Necessity, it appears, led some women to take extraordinary measures. She eventually found him and "applied to him to be decreed as his wife, but that the said John Armstrong positively refused, either to receive her as his wife, or afford her any of the smallest assistance, altho he is in good circumstances and well able to do it." After five months of trailing her husband with a new child in tow, she finally sued for alimony. The Baltimore Court of Chancery, however, dismissed her claim because she did not sue with the aid of a "next friend." "In the present case," the court said, "the husband cannot give a bond to his wife."

The "next friend" requirement was one of a broad set of common law rules barring married women from independent participation in the civil legal system. They could not contract, sue, or be sued without the permission of their husbands. Save for intimate personal items, a husband took ownership of any personal property of his spouse once he reduced it to his possession. A woman's real property was subject to the management and control of her spouse. The only ameliorative exceptions to the common law rules required husbands to support their wives and provided women married to men holding real property some prospect of economic well-being in their widowhood through the institution of dower.[85] Wives were in "coverture"—covered, merged, and, at least rhetorically, protected by their men. A husband responding to an alimony complaint by giving a bond in favor of his wife, according to the common law structure, would be performing the useless act of giving a bond to himself. Since husband and wife were one legal entity, a "contract" requiring a husband to provide security to a wife payable upon the happening of an event was a contradiction in terms. Exceptions to the rules arose, particularly at equity, where women obtained the right to the use and transfer of real and personal property held in separate trust estates. Maryland's alimony statute created another circuitous exception, permitting a woman to sue in the chancery court with the aid of a male "next friend," usually a close relative, to whom the husband could write a bond. Thus the court's dismissal of Sally Armstrong's complaint was perfectly in tune with then extant norms. The result of her case, however, was a particularly grim reminder of the traditional contours of Maryland family law in 1805. Economically distressed, far away from home, and lacking "next friends," Sally Armstrong was sent away by a court with no apprehension that common law coverture rules and legislative restrictions on access to divorce operated unfairly upon this stranger to Maryland.

Notes

1. For general summaries of divorce law before and just after the Revolutionary War, see G. RILEY, DIVORCE: AN AMERICAN TRADITION 1–129 (1991); M. SALMON, WOMEN AND THE LAW OF PROPERTY IN EARLY AMERICA 58–80 (1988); N. M. BLAKE, ROAD TO RENO: A HISTORY OF DIVORCE IN THE UNITED STATES 34–96 (1962); L. C. HALEM, DIVORCE REFORM: CHANGING LEGAL AND SOCIAL PERSPECTIVES 9–26 (1980). For studies of particular jurisdictions in the same eras, see N. Basch, *Relief in the Premises: Divorce as a Women's Remedy in New York and Indiana, 1815–1870*, 8 LAW & HIST. REV. 1 (1990); S. Cohen, *The Broken Bond: Divorce in Providence County, 1749–1809*, 44 R.I. HIST. 67 (1985); S. Cohen, *"To Parts of the World Unknown": The Circumstances of Divorce in Connecticut, 1750–1797*, 11 CAN. REV. AM. STUD. 275 (1980) [hereinafter Cohen, *Conn. Divorce*]; N. Cott, *Divorce and the Changing Status of Women in Eighteenth-Century Massachusetts*, 33 WM. & MARY Q. 586 (1976) [hereinafter Cott, *Mass. Divorce*]; N. Cott, *Eighteenth Century Family and Social Life Revealed in Massachusetts Divorce Records*, 10 J. SOC. HIST. 20 (1976); C. DAYTON, WOMEN BEFORE THE BAR: GENDER, LAW, AND SOCIETY IN CONNECTICUT, 1710–1790, at 284–376 (1986) (Thesis, Princeton U.); T. Meehan, *"Not Made Out of Levity": Evolution of Divorce in Early Pennsylvania*, 92 PA. MAG. HIST. & BIO. 441 (1968).

2. Cohen, *Conn. Divorce, supra* note 1, at 275, reported that 839 divorce petitions were filed in Connecticut between 1750 and 1797. DAYTON, *supra* note 1, at 305, found 133 divorce complaints in New Haven County alone; of the 122 cases for which results are known, divorces were obtained in 111. Cott, *Mass. Divorce, supra* note 1, at 587, reported on 229 divorce petitions filed between 1692 and 1786.

3. Meehan, *supra* note 1.

4. The most lucid accounts are found in Nancy Cott's two classic articles on Massachusetts, cited *supra* note 1.

5. In part this reflected the economic dependence of women. But the English legal system had no history of granting bed and board divorces to women for

adultery by men. When Massachusetts began to recognize male adultery as a divorce ground after the Revolutionary War, more women began to use it successfully. Cott, *Mass. Divorce, supra* note 1, at 605.

6. Dayton, in her study of New Haven, Conn., divorce cases, also found a significant increase in the rate of filing after 1770. She attributes the increase less to changed expectations about marriage or increased feelings of independence than to acceptance of the court remedy as a workable device, the appearance of a cadre of lawyers, and the reduction of scandal associated with divorce. DAYTON, *supra* note 1, at 300–304.

7. Cott, *Mass. Divorce, supra* note 1, at 605.

8. Before the adoption of married women's property law reforms beginning in the 1830s, husbands and wives could not enter into standard contracts with each other. However, in those (mostly mid-Atlantic and Southern) states that followed the English chancery court tradition allowing equitable separate estates to be held by married women, a husband could repose property in a trust and instruct the trustee to pay his wife a maintenance. The enforceability of such agreements in Massachusetts was in doubt until the middle of the nineteenth century. For more on this phenomenon, *see* SALMON, *supra* note 1, at 71.

9. When children were mentioned it was only to note that as the product of an interracial relationship they had been sold into servitude. Such language only reemphasized the economic contours of childhood for family law purposes.

10. SALMON, *supra* note 1, at 71.

11. *See id.* at 9–11, 90.

12. *See id.* at 71. Some of the early divorce acts adopted in Maryland also make reference to pre-existing separation agreements. *See*, for example, the discussion of the Alexander *infra* at the text accompanying note 60.

13. SALMON, *supra* note 1, at 6–10; R. Chused, *Married Women's Property and Inheritance by Widows in Massachusetts: A Study of Wills Probated Between 1800 and 1850*, 2 BERKELEY WOMEN'S L. J. 42, 48–58 (1986).

14. Chused, *supra* note 13, at 50.

15. R. PHILLIPS, PUTTING ASUNDER: A HISTORY OF DIVORCE IN WESTERN SOCIETY 134 (1988).

16. SALMON, *supra* note 1, at 60.

17. *Id.* at 7–9.

18. *Id.* at 10.

19. Catholics played an important role in the early history of Maryland. Several families were deeply involved in the governance and development of the colony. Though many of their civil rights were terminated late in the seventeenth century, they were restored during the Revolutionary War era. In addition, significant numbers of Catholics immigrated to Baltimore during the first half of the nineteenth century. *See* R. BRUGGER, MARYLAND: A MIDDLE TEMPERAMENT, 1634–1980, at 37–38, 120–122, 147–148 (1988). It is not surprising, therefore, to see Catholics emerge in important positions in Maryland and wield their influence in family law. *See*, for example, the description in Chapter 4 of the role Roger Brooke Taney played while a senator in restricting the availability of *a vinculo* divorce.

20. PHILLIPS, *supra* note 15, at 227–241.

21. *See* the discussion of the Moses Lecompte divorce petition *infra* at the text accompanying note 64.

22. J. P. Bishop, Commentaries on the Law of Marriage and Divorce 443 (1852).

23. Salmon, *supra* note 1, at 68–69.

24. Alimony awards provided only for payments of maintenance. *Feme sole* status was not awarded and wives did not regain control over property they brought to the marriage.

25. Gathering a complete collection of chancery court records of family discord is not possible. Many collections of court files are not yet indexed. Some county records are destroyed. The Maryland Hall of Records has computer indexes to records for the Maryland Chancery Court, which sat in Annapolis. This court, unlike the courts sitting in each county seat, had statewide jurisdiction. The Hall of Records' staff has also computerized many of the records from the Baltimore area, generally only for cases filed after 1814. These relatively new research tools produced a number of useful files and data. The computer data base at the Maryland Hall of Records, for just the Maryland Chancery Court sitting in Annapolis, contains entries for 10 alimony cases filed between 1790 and 1806, and 10 more for the period 1806–1815. The total number of alimony filings for all of the state's chancery courts must have been significantly larger. Table 3 in Appendix 1 shows that only 11 women and 21 men petitioned the legislature for divorces between 1782 and 1804.

26. Virtually all personal property of a married woman was owned by her husband once he reduced it to his possession. There is more discussion of the common law rules of coverture *infra* at the text accompanying note 73.

27. *See* Salmon, *supra* note 1, at 49–53.

28. *See* the discussion of the Alexander divorce *infra* at the text accompanying note 60.

29. *See* Salmon, note 1 *supra* at 65.

30. An Act for Annulling the Marriage of John Sewell, of Talbot County, and Eve his Wife, ch. XXIV, 1790 Md. Laws (Dec. 21, 1790). Before 1805, the General Assembly often described its reasons for granting divorces in preambles to private acts. It is therefore much easier to understand the contours of the earliest Maryland divorces than those adopted several decades into the nineteenth century.

31. An Act for Annulling the Marriage of Schoolfield Parker, of Worcester County, and Sarah his Wife, ch. III, 1794 Md. Laws (Dec. 26, 1794); An Act Annulling the Marriage of John Crist, of Frederick County, and Susannah his Wife, ch. LXV, 1801 Md. Laws (Dec. 31, 1801); An Act Annulling the Marriage of Joseph Bray, of Anne-Arundel County, and Anne his Wife, ch. XCIV, 1803 Md. Laws (Jan. 7, 1804).

32. An Act Annulling the Marriage of William Barroll, of Kent County, and Lucretia his Wife, ch. XXVII, 1797 Md. Laws (Jan. 20, 1798). Lucretia Barroll was also "seized of considerable real and personal estate, which by mutual consent has been lately settled, by deeds duly executed, in a just and proper manner, in the judgment of the committee." 1797 House Journal at 70.

33. Though the Barrolls had children, the General Assembly said nothing about their status in the Barroll private divorce bill. That probably meant that William Barroll gained control over them. Nor is there any indication that Eve Barroll gave birth to any mulatto children.

34. An Act Annulling the Marriage of Archibald and Susannah Alexander, ch. XXIII, 1805 Md. Laws (Jan. 25, 1806). Susannah Alexander married John Muskett after hearing a "well founded" report that Archibald Alexander, from whom Susannah had been voluntarily separated for many years, had died. When Alexander later turned up alive, he and Susannah both applied to the General Assembly for a divorce. The legislature complied, taking care to preserve the legitimacy of her children. But even with this bill, the possibility of adultery by the husband was high. The preamble of the act reports that Susannah and Archibald had lived apart for some time under the terms of a separation agreement entered into because of the "misconduct" of Archibald.

35. An Act annulling the marriage of George Sampson and Pamela Sampson, ch. XXXIX, 1806 Md. Laws (Jan. 3, 1807). Though, as note 34 confirms, Susannah Alexander petitioned for a divorce bill which was adopted in the prior session, her husband, who was probably guilty of adultery, had also filed a divorce petition in that same session. Pamela Sampson was the first woman to successfully obtain a divorce without the presence of either a male petition or proof of male adultery.

36. Others have also noted the differences in divorce rates between North and South. *See* M. Schultz, *Divorce in the South Atlantic States: Origins, Historical Patterns, and Recent Trends*, 16 INT. J. SOC. FAM. 225, 244 (1986).

37. BRUGGER, *supra* note 19, at 132, 133, 141.

38. *Id.* at 158–160.

39. W. H. RIDGWAY, COMMUNITY LEADERSHIP IN MARYLAND, 1790–1840: A COMPARATIVE ANALYSIS OF POWER IN SOCIETY 16–18 (1979).

40. *Id.* at 17.

41. *See* Table 12 in Appendix 1.

42. The property requirements were low for the time, but they did exclude tenant farmers and other poor people. N. RISJORD, CHESAPEAKE POLITICS, 1781–1800, at 73 (1978).

43. RIDGWAY, *supra* note 39, at 6–8.

44. RISJORD, *supra* note 42, at 73–81, 138–156.

45. *See, e.g.*, BRUGGER, *supra* note 19, at 137.

46. A brief description of this story may be found in F. F. WHITE, THE GOVERNORS OF MARYLAND: 1777–1970, at 111–113 (1970). The 1838 changes did not come close to modern "one person, one vote" standards. *See* Table 12 in Appendix 1.

47. BRUGGER, *supra* note 19, at 160–166; RISJORD, *supra* note 42, at 495–500.

48. BRUGGER, *supra* note 19, at 166.

49. It was not entirely coincidental that these reforms emerged after the two figures dominating rivalries in the early General Assembly, Charles Carroll and

Samuel Chase, no longer wielded much legislative influence. Carroll retired from politics in 1800 after the election of Jefferson. Chase was appointed to the Maryland Supreme Court in 1791, and the United States Supreme Court in 1796. RISJORD, *supra* note 42, at 74, 352, 464–465. Their rivalries are nicely described in BRUGGER, *supra* note 19, at 134–136. Carroll was a wealthy Catholic who "devoted his life to the preservation of the status and powers of the elite," denouncing "every political upheaval of the age, from the tenant riots of the Revolution to the election of Jefferson," and retiring in fear of the subversion of "our social order and the rights of property." RISJORD, *supra* note 42, at 74. Chase was the son of an Anglican minister, an entrepreneur and speculator. He sided with debtors while in economic difficulties in the 1780s, but ended up as a Federalist when his economic fortunes improved. RISJORD, *supra* note 42, at 74–81, 349–351, 464–465.

50. *See* Table 3 in Appendix 1.

51. 1788 HOUSE JOURNAL at 6.

52. 1790 HOUSE JOURNAL at 3.

53. 1790 HOUSE JOURNAL at 10.

54. 1787 HOUSE JOURNAL at 151. During this period neither the House of Delegates nor the Senate had standing committees to entertain divorce petitions. Ad hoc committees were appointed to review each petition. The committees usually had at least one member from the county in which the petitioner resided.

55. 1790 HOUSE JOURNAL at 29.

56. The exact meaning of this language is not revealed in the historical record. It is certainly possible that the stern response of the state occurred because Hamilton returned with a woman of color.

57. An Act for the relief of Charles Blair and Lilly his wife, lately called Lilly Hamilton, ch. XIV, 1782 Md. Laws. The transfer of assets obtained by Blair in this act was not available in an alimony action. Only monetary payments based on the income and property of the husband could be obtained. *See* Wallingsford v. Wallingsford, 10 Md. (6 H. & J.) 398 (1825).

58. 1790 HOUSE JOURNAL at 11.

59. An ACT for the relief of Mary Gwinn, of Frederick County, ch. LXIII, 1807 Md. Laws (Jan. 20, 1808).

60. Dielman-Hayward File, Md. Hist. Soc'y. The Dielman-Hayward File is a collection of biographical references about Maryland residents gleaned from newspapers, family genealogies, and other materials. The Maryland Historical Society Library is in Baltimore.

61. 1805 HOUSE JOURNAL at 39.

62. *Id.* at 40–41.

63. The report of her marriage to Muskett is in the Dielman-Hayward File, Md. Hist. Soc'y. Her legislative divorce from Alexander was passed on December 20, 1805. 1805 HOUSE JOURNAL at 56.

64. 1794 HOUSE JOURNAL at 7.

65. *Id.* at 63.

66. 1796 HOUSE JOURNAL at 27.

67. 1798 HOUSE JOURNAL at 66.

68. A similar fate befell Ann Gross, who obtained leave to bring in a bill

after a favorable committee report. Her bill never appeared on the House floor. *See* 1799 HOUSE JOURNAL at 88–89, 100.

69. 1802 HOUSE JOURNAL at 18.

70. *See* Table 11 in Appendix 1.

71. The tables show that some form of legislative controversy emerged just less than one-fifth of the time for both enacted and non-enacted bills.

72. Other property relief acts were also adopted in this time period. *See, e.g.*, An ACT for the relief of Margaret Razer, of Frederick-town, in Frederick County, ch. VIII, 1802 Md. Laws (Jan. 8, 1803); An ACT for the benefit of Elizabeth Webster, of the City of Baltimore, ch. LXVII, 1806 Md. Laws (Jan. 3, 1807).

73. *See* L. KERBER, WOMEN OF THE REPUBLIC: INTELLECT & IDEOLOGY IN REVOLUTIONARY AMERICA 137–184 (1980); R. Chused, *Married Women's Property Law: 1800–1850*, 71 GEO. L. J. 1359, 1372–1384 (1983).

74. For the text of the alimony statute, see note 30 in Chapter 1.

75. Since alimony was normally not available in English religious courts independently of the divorce process, the Maryland statute conferring authority to issue alimony decrees upon chancery courts was construed to cover only settings in which ecclesiastical courts issued partial divorces. Wallingsford v. Wallingsford, 10 Md. (6 H. & J.) 398 (1825); Helms v. Franciscus, 2 Bland ch. 519, 543 (1830). *See also* BISHOP, *supra* note 22, at 439–447. English courts did not permit *a vinculo* divorces at this time.

76. Helms v. Franciscus, 2 Bland Ch. at 543.

77. Wallingsford v. Wallingsford, 10 Md. (6 H. & J.) 398 (1825).

78. *Id.*

79. Many alimony court files from Maryland's chancery courts contain requests by women for issuance of a writ of *ne exeat*, originally used in the ecclesiastical courts to force husbands about to depart the jurisdiction to post bonds. Wives had to file an affidavit that their husbands were about to leave. Though this may have become a routine practice, a counter affidavit could frustrate the ability of a wife to control the movement of her husband. *See* Bayly v. Bayly, 2 Md.Ch. 326 (1847); 2 J. STORY, COMMENTARIES ON EQUITY JURISPRUDENCE AS ADMINISTERED IN ENGLAND AND AMERICA 686, 691 (1836).

80. For a description of means of accessing alimony files *see supra* note 25. The files often gave no clues about the final litigation outcomes. But they did reveal some routine practices and a few interesting stories.

81. *See, e.g.*, Esther Hall v. Lawrence Hall, Md. Hall of Records, Ch. Ct. Chancery Papers, Document Group 17, Call No. 898-2571, Series S 512-2650, Location 1/36/3/51 (Queene Annes County, 1793). Cases in the Maryland state archive's collection used hereinafter are cited as [Case Name], [Name of Document Group], MdHR [Document Group Number], [Call Number], [Series Number], [Location] ([County], [Year]).

82. *See, e.g.*, Anne Connally v. William Connally, Ch. Ct. Chancery Papers, MdHR 17, 898–884, S 512–920, 1/36/1/6 (Anne Arundel, 1795).

83. Bill of Complaint, Sally Armstrong v. John Armstrong, Ch. Ct. Chancery Papers, MdHR 17, 898–54, S 512–50, 1/35/5/15 (Baltimore City, 1805). The narrative in this paragraph comes from this file.

84. Every state now has statutes allowing suits to be brought against non-resident parties having some significant connection with the state. The Sally Armstrongs of today may usually file their divorce cases where they live and serve their estranged husbands with the court papers by mail or, if they cannot be found, by publication in the local press.

85. Dower traditionally created a life estate in one-third of the real property held by a husband at any time during marriage. Conveyance reforms made it relatively easy for a wife to sell her dower interest when her husband wished to transfer his property, and other late eighteenth- and early nineteenth-century changes sometimes limited the impact of dower. *See* SALMON, *supra* note 1, at 141–184.

3. Political Reform and Family Law at the Turn of the Nineteenth Century

Introduction

Thomas Jefferson's rise to power at the turn of the nineteenth century was accompanied by gradual alterations in the face of Maryland politics. The 1800 elections gave the Republicans a fragile majority in the House of Delegates, while Federalists retained control over the indirectly elected Senate and governorship.[1] The election reforms of 1802, combined with the rising popularity of Republicans, swept the Federalists from power in Maryland by 1806.[2]

Significant shifts in the legislative divorce process arrived with the Republicans. Divorce petitioners responded to the changing political winds. Only one petition was filed in both 1803 and 1804. The numbers rapidly rose thereafter, with five in 1805, eleven in 1806, eighteen in 1807, sixteen in 1808, and twenty-nine in 1809. The petitions were almost always filed by a member of the House of Delegates from the county in which the parties resided.[3] The serving of constituents with marital difficulties must have had a significant impact on the two delegates from the city of Baltimore,[4] which contributed more than a third of the petitioners after 1804.[5]

Unhappy Maryland citizens clearly were reading the legislative tea leaves. The General Assembly's voting patterns presented striking evidence of a change of mood. Before 1805, delegates from all regions of the state tended to vote against divorce bills, though that trend was least pronounced on the Eastern Shore and most pronounced in the southern regions of the state.[6] Between 1805 and 1815, the proportion of delegate roll call votes cast in favor of divorces rose to about one-half. That shift in voting preferences meant that more people could expect to obtain legislative relief after rather than before the turn of the nineteenth century. The adoption in 1805 and 1806 of the first divorces granted to women had a particularly dramatic effect. The proportion of those seeking legislative relief who were female leaped from a third to 60 percent.[7] Private acts were passed divorcing about a quarter of these women, while the passage rate for men actually fell a bit after 1804.[8]

It was not just serendipity that the Republican Party emerged as a political force in Maryland at the same time that restrictive private bill divorce processes were eased. Taking the reins of power as a party of reform, some, though certainly not all, of its members were quite willing to displace family as well as political traditions. Some Republicans from Baltimore willing to vote for divorces, for example, replaced more traditional delegates. Jefferson himself empathized more with the plight of those seeking marital relief than did the Federalists running Maryland in earlier times. When Dr. James Blair sought his aid in 1771 to obtain a legislative divorce in Virginia, Jefferson took on the case despite much evidence that success was unlikely.[9] Blair's early death mooted the case, but the notes Jefferson prepared in anticipation of the 1772 session arrayed a number of arguments justifying divorce on grounds other than adultery. One prophetic notation captured a central feature of the early nineteenth-century changes in Maryland divorce practice. Divorce, Jefferson wrote,

> [r]estores to women their natural right of equality. Cruel to confine Divorce or Repudiation to husband who has so many ways of rendering his domestic affairs agreeable, by Command or desertion, whereas wife confined & subject.[10]

Equality for Jefferson did not connote sameness, but relative importance. Though the willingness of Maryland's General Assembly after 1804 to divorce a few women opened new avenues of relief to wives, it hardly created a family law based on Jeffersonian equality. Most women in disagreeable marriages or left behind by deserting men still found little sympathy in either court or legislature. The reforms emerging in the Republican era were timid ones at best.

Indeed, Republican ascendancy does not fully explain even the modest shifts in divorce policy that occurred shortly after the turn of the nineteenth century. Not all Republicans favored changes in divorce policies; nor did all Federalists oppose them. Just as evangelical religion affected segments of both the Federalist and Republican parties,[11] divorce preferences crossed party lines. Voting preferences were not uniform throughout either the state or areas dominated by the Republicans. Delegates from Republican-dominated commercial areas in Baltimore, Annapolis, and the Eastern Shore voted in favor of private divorce bills most of the time between 1805 and 1815, but they did not always have enough allies to overcome the opposition from other Republican regions, especially in the south.[12] In the 1805–1815 era a total of 1,517 votes were cast by delegates on divorce bills. Only 43 percent (649 of 1,517) of these votes were cast by delegates representing Baltimore, Annapolis, and the Eastern Shore counties. Sixty-one percent of these votes from the more commercial areas of the state were in favor of divorces. But other areas of the state cast a similar percentage (58 percent) of their votes against divorces. Since they held the balance of power in these votes, they could outvote Baltimore, Annapolis, and the Eastern Shore in close cases.

Party loyalty, weak at best in the early nineteenth century, could not overcome a variety of other cultural constraints and structural limitations on the distribution of legislative power. Commercial interests in Baltimore and the Eastern Shore, for example, quite naturally favored some divorces. For many entrepreneurs, it made little sense to tie up a man's assets in continued obligations to support a broken family; nor was it rational to preclude women with assets from using them free of constraints imposed by a misbehaving husband. Southern delegates, however, imbued with Anglican traditions and afraid of creating chinks in the armor of paternal control, voted against divorces at a high rate. Legislative malapportionment amplified the impact of these regional variations. The allocation of delegates in the House remained incongruent with population levels through much of the nineteenth century. The southern region, for example, elected a third of the delegates with only 20 percent of the population in 1810.[13] In family law debates, Eastern Shore and Baltimore delegates, though able to control the legislature on many other issues after the turn of the nineteenth century, could not always overcome the artificially strong representation in the House of Delegates of southern counties with traditional social values. Just as votes on debtor-creditor issues began to run in favor of debtors during bad economic times before 1800,[14] so too did urban and Eastern Shore delegates have difficulty controlling family law debates after the turn of the nineteenth century.

The mild reformist tone of Maryland's early nineteenth-century family law debates was further emphasized by the dearth of serious legislative debate about general divorce legislation. No general divorce bill was given serious attention until 1824.[15] Adoption of a general act was out of the question until social changes and further electoral and legislative reforms created a more hospitable environment for family law reform. The voting patterns in the House of Delegates demonstrate that representatives of upper-class and commercial interests favored divorce more than those from rural counties with less well-defined economic elites at the turn of the nineteenth century. But they also exemplified the uneasy balance of family law power between commercial and traditional, sometimes religiously motivated, voices. While Northern states were busy working out the details of their late eighteenth-century divorce reforms, Maryland still was working out conflicts among its various cultural models.

Legislative Divorce Reform: Cruelty and Male Adultery Grounds for Private Acts

The tone of limited reform found in the period 1805–1815 was set by two divorces adopted during the 1805 and 1806 legislative sessions. Both Susannah Alexander[16] and Pamela Sampson[17] divorced their husbands, apparently without any strong proof of adultery. The preamble to the Alexander bill referred mysteriously to the "misconduct" of Archibald as an impetus for the couple's agreeing to a separation agreement. But the primary basis for passage of the legislation appeared to be Susannah's reliance upon reports of Archibald's death to undertake a second marriage. Pamela Sampson's divorce was the first to be clearly based on a ground other than adultery. The legislature inserted a preamble stating that George and Pamela's marriage was "incompatible with the happiness of the conjugal union, which every day, if possible, increased, owing to intoxication, which deranged his mind; that the said Pamela is entirely dependent on her friends and neighbors for a support for herself and infant child." Rather than continuing prior practice by limiting relief to a declaration that Pamela Sampson was a *feme sole*, the General Assembly divorced her from George.[18]

The Sampson divorce was an event of some moment in the history of Maryland family law. The apparent practice of the post–Revolutionary War General Assembly to grant divorces only when a wife committed adultery, was swept aside in circumstances akin to those supporting divorces for intemperance or mental cruelty. No allegations of violence or adultery appeared in the Sampson record, even though the legislature mentioned adultery in the preamble of several other divorces enacted after Sampson's.[19] Indeed, the Sampson case apparently drew some public attention, for a memorial from Bishop Claggett and the Convention of the Protestant Episcopal Church of Maryland, written less than five months after the Sampson act's adoption, was filed with the General Assembly early in the following legislative session. The communication, "suggesting the impropriety of granting divorces,"[20] was the only general memorial on the subject filed with the Assembly during the entire history of private family law legislation in Maryland.

The annual convention of the Protestant Episcopal Church was held in Baltimore from May 20–22, 1807. At the convention it was,

> [r]esolved that a committee be appointed to draught and present a memorial to the next general assembly of the state, respectfully remonstrating against the practice of granting divorces on slight and insufficient grounds; and praying that, in future, no dissolution of marriage be sanctioned by the legislature, except in cases, in which the woman, in a court of law, have been convicted of the crime of adultery.[21]

Although this was the only public decree on divorce issued by the church, two other letters with references to the subject from members of the General Assembly to Bishop James Kemp survive.[22] Both indicate that at least through the 1820s the church leadership maintained a stable and quite conservative policy which, as in Britain, permitted bed and board divorce only in cases of adultery by wives.

In 1801 Charles Goldsborough, representing Dorchester County in the General Assembly, wrote to the then Reverend James Kemp:

> [T]here are many petitions before the House, & some very extraordinary ones. Among them are six or seven applications for divorces, some by husbands & some by wives, and I am informed there is a petition . . . presented by a married man who has had children by another man's wife praying that his family name may be given to them & they enabled to inherit his estate.[23] Thus it seems to be supposed that these are liberal times, not to be fettered by the commands of ancient ways, or old fashioned prejudices.[24]

Goldsborough, who during the 1802 session voted against a private bill to divorce Robert and Henrietta Ingram,[25] was surely writing to one of conservative sympathies. For, twenty years later, Richard Carroll, a senator from the Western Shore,[26] wrote to Bishop Kemp:

> I have this day received your letter of the 9th on the subject of divorce. I am decidedly of your opinion on the subject, tho not derived from the same source as your own, which is the first and greatest authority.
>
> Many applications have been made this session. One or two which in my opinion ought to have been granted in the way suggested by you, but the Senate uniformly reject all. Voted in favour of one myself,[27] and had I then the information on the particular case, which I obtained afterward, I certainly should not have voted as I did. It was however lost, as it should have been.

It is a subject of grave difficulty and delicacy to legislate upon. Although adultery is perhaps the only justifiable ground of granting a divorce, yet, even in that instance we have known, I have myself known of instances, where both the parties have been guilty of it and the fact known to both, and have afterward come together and perhaps lived happily.

It is after all, a subject the control and direction of which had better perhaps be left in the hands of him who ordereth all things for the best, under whose superintending care and management, good may grow out of evil.[28]

Four bed and board divorces were passed during the 1820 session after this letter was written. Other bills calling for *a vinculo* divorces were defeated before Carroll wrote to Kemp. This makes Carroll's reference to the granting of divorces "in the way suggested by you" understandable as a preference for bed and board divorce.

Though the position of the Episcopal Church and other religious organizations disapproving complete divorces was well known,[29] the 1807 memorial from Bishop Claggett did not have any immediate effect. Most of the private divorce acts did not contain informative preambles after 1805.[30] But women continued to obtain divorces during the following ten years, and it is clear from both legislative and nonlegislative sources that some of the cases involved divorce grounds other than adultery. Religious opposition had not yet gained sufficient strength to cause political embarrassment to those "favoring" immorality by voting for complete divorces.[31]

For example, the preamble of the private act divorcing Anne Hoskyns from her husband, John Henry Hoskyns, reveals that John committed forgery and fled the state, leaving Anne with three infant children, one a cripple. All of his property was seized by creditors.[32] The legislature noted sympathetically that Anne Hoskyns,

would be able by her own labor and industry to support herself and her said children, but is prevented from attempting that desirable object from the certainty that her little earnings and the property with which her friends might entrust her is liable to be seized by the creditors of her husband, and subject to his controul and disposal; to prevent which she has prayed her marriage with the said John Henry Hoskyns may be annulled.[33]

Rather than grant her *feme sole* status, the only possible outcome before 1800, Anne Hoskyns obtained a divorce.

She was in famous company. Elizabeth Patterson Bonaparte, the wife of Napoleon's youngest brother, Jerome Bonaparte, was divorced in the 1812 session by the most famous of Maryland's private acts. Jerome met and, it is said, swooned over Elizabeth in 1803.[34] After the signing of carefully drawn antenuptial agreements, her father reluctantly consented to a marriage. Napoleon, however, refused to recognize the union, even though performed by the highest Catholic prelate in the United States. Upon Jerome's return home in 1805, Elizabeth was denied entry to France. Napoleon failed to obtain an annulment of the marriage from Pope Pius VII, but French authorities were more compliant. As the price for Jerome's consent to the annulment of his marriage with Elizabeth, Napoleon agreed to marry him off to Princess Catherine of Württemberg and make him king of Westphalia. Meanwhile Elizabeth went to England and gave birth to a child. Some years later she obtained a divorce from the Maryland legislature.[35] Though Jerome Bonaparte may have been an adulterer, assuming Maryland did not recognize the French annulment, this highly charged story was about political desertion more than marital infidelity.[36] Indeed it is interesting that Elizabeth waited until 1812—a time more sympathetic to her plight than the year she was denied entry to France—to seek release from her marital vows.

The Bonaparte act was not the only one passed between 1805 and 1815 which granted a divorce to the wife of an arguably adulterous husband. Though granting divorces to women on the grounds of their husbands' adultery began decades before in New England,[37] it was a new experience for Maryland. In addition to the sensational Bonaparte case, the legislature granted adultery-based divorces to less prominent women such as Elizabeth Burk[38] and Phoebe Taylor.[39] Thomas Burk was sentenced to death in 1809 for the rape of an eleven-year-old girl. He escaped from jail the day before his execution, never to be heard from again.[40] The General Assembly passed an act divorcing the Burks during its 1809 session. The rape of a child made it difficult for the General Assembly to turn aside Elizabeth Burk's plea for help. Adoption of the act did not suggest that the General Assembly was about to sever the marital ties of all women with adulterous husbands, any more than the Sampson act implied that cruelty was on the verge of becoming a path to mass divorce. The door, however, was opened and left ajar.

Despite the passage of a few acts expanding the limits of the traditional "rule" permitting divorce only when wives deviated from the straight and narrow, the General Assembly was still very reluctant to pass private bills. Less than a fourth of the divorce petitions filed between 1805 and 1815 were granted by the legislature.[41] Situations we now find egregious hardly caused a ripple. Thus, Kitty Emory, after two tries, obtained a private divorce from Peregrine, whom she alleged beat her and perpetrated a "horrid outrage" upon a young female slave. Peregrine confessed to treating Kitty badly when he was drunk.[42] But Mary Sergeant, who made more "prosaic" complaints in an alimony petition, never obtained a divorce. In her court pleading she alleged,

> Altho your complainant was then and always has been of good name, form and reputation among all her neighbors and always conducted herself most virtuously, modestly and discreetly,[43] yet the said Samuel Sergeant, wantonly and without any cause whatever, kept his own irregular appetites. On or about the month of June which was in the year 1810, rejected, discharged, repudiated and turned out of doors your complainant together with her two children.[44]

In the 1807 session, the ad hoc committee reporting on her petition for a divorce recommended against its adoption.[45] In 1810 and 1811, bills got to the floor but never passed.[46]

Mary Cartwright also failed to win a divorce. The petition she filed in the 1813 session to divorce Abraham Cartwright never got out of committee.[47] In a chancery petition filed just after the General Assembly failed to act on her divorce bill,[48] she alleged that due to "some unhappy differences" they had in 1799 agreed to live apart for the rest of their lives under the terms of a separation agreement. Taking advantage of Maryland's long-established tradition supporting the validity of married women's separate estates, the agreement established for Mary's benefit a trust managed by three men. Though such arrangements did not help women married to uncompromising or deserting men, trust settlements were a convenient way for couples wishing to separate to settle their economic differences. Women could gain some economic security; men could free themselves of additional maintenance and support obligations; and both could be rid of contact with unwanted spouses. Equity agreements were used with increasing frequency as the nineteenth century unfolded.[49] All went well, according to Mary Cartwright's petition, until the last of the trustees died. Abraham then began to seek control over her separate estate. Mary sought the appointment of new trustees and an injunction prohibiting interference with her property. The alimony statute did not give the chancery court authority to grant such relief.[50] The court, however, did take steps to protect one of its own equitable creatures, the married woman's separate estate.[51] If divorce for cruelty was available, it was obviously limited in scope; Mary Cartwright was left to struggle with the quirks of equity law.

Rumbles of Discontent: Legislative Controversy and Social Discord

The Sampson, Hoskyns, Bonaparte, and Burk divorce acts indicated that some segments of Maryland's political establishment, willing to allow divorce for male adultery, certain egregious forms of physical or even mental cruelty, and gross intoxication, were on the verge of moving significantly beyond traditional family law. There is a great deal of evidence that over the course of the nineteenth century, cruelty emerged as a basis for divorce in all sections of the country, including the South.[52] But the Maryland private acts freeing Pamela Sampson and Anne Hoskyns from their marital vows were passed very early in the history of this movement. These acts, as well those based upon male adultery, were likely to draw the attention of family law traditionalists. Though the family law reforms of this era were not dramatic, it is not surprising that alarm bells rang in certain quarters.

Legislative controversy over family law, in fact, was pervasive. In addition to the previously noted memorial from the Protestant Episcopal Church Convention, roll call votes on private divorce bills occurred with greater frequency between 1805 and 1815 than in any other era. The totality of recorded votes cast in the House of Delegates divided almost evenly between those in favor of and opposed to divorces.[53] A raft of close tallies revealed a significant amount of cultural disarray on the divorce question.[54] An incredible 44 percent of all adopted acts emerged from legislative debate only after a roll call vote was taken.[55] Rumbles of discontent with both the process used to evaluate divorce petitions and the practice of relying on the General Assembly to obtain divorces also surfaced.

Struggles with process appeared in a couple of settings. In an intriguing situation, Mary and George Moore filed a petition seeking a divorce for Henry Moore, allegedly a lunatic. Alice Moore, Henry's wife, filed an opposing petition asking that the marriage be confirmed. This may have been a property squabble, since the proposed bill discussed the care of both his person and his estate. The legislature was puzzled about how to handle this fact-intensive dispute. The House of Delegates turned itself into the equivalent of a courtroom, taking the unusual step of asking the attorneys for the parties to appear to argue their cases. The bill did not pass.[56] In another effort to deal with procedural problems, Mr. Peter Emerson, representing Calvert County during the 1811 session, made the first attempt to appoint a standing committee to entertain all divorce petitions. His motion failed.[57] These episodes opened what turned out to be a continual series of struggles over the procedural and evidentiary rules governing the legislative divorce process.

Two abortive attempts also were made in each house of the General Assembly to debate general divorce bills between 1809 and 1815.[58] Though passage was impossible, their emergence befit the times. There is much in our history to confirm that public controversy about divorce and family structure arises when widespread debates about basic cultural issues are occurring. Politics and religion are too intertwined with images of family and spousal roles to permit one arena to escape discord when another is in flux. Political and religious realms in Maryland were rife with controversy between 1805 and 1815. The end of the revolutionary political era did not come quietly. Maryland's Federalists fell from grace while Jefferson held the presidency, returned to favor briefly after 1812, and then disintegrated as a political force.[59] Methodist, Presbyterian, and Baptist evangelical congregations grew dramatically,[60] amid major public confrontations over the morality and ethics of various churchmen.[61] Collective concerns about morality and vice were often voiced.[62] Legislative and judicial treatment of divorce mirrored the more general currents of social discord. Reformers readily supported divorces for the likes of Mary Cartwright, who found herself in "unhappy circumstances." A few, such as Mr. Worthington of Baltimore City, who proposed the 1809 general bill,[63] were even willing to codify divorce standards. And, of course, those with the traditional views of Bishop Claggett bemoaned the appearance of new forms of divorce. Though the legislature withstood the most conservative onslaughts of public opinion in this era, it was not evident that this would continue indefinitely. As Brugger has noted in his definitive general history of Maryland, "[a]fter 1815 no American state portrayed as vividly as did Maryland the contrast between slavery and steam power, past and future, convention and change—between what Ralph Waldo Emerson called the party of memory and the party of hope."[64]

Emergence of Children as a Family Law Consideration

Shifts also appeared in the treatment of children. For the first time, their status became a special concern of the General Assembly. In an unusual case, Peter Rouck's attempt in 1811 to divorce his wife Mary failed. But in the same session, another act passed legitimating the children of Peter Rouck by Eve Cassell and those of Jacob Kershner by Mary Rouck.[65] Either both Roucks had had affairs with others or they were caring for children from other relationships who joined their marital household. It is possible that a primitive form of recrimination was operating in this case, precluding either party from obtaining a divorce because each was guilty of adultery.[66] The decision to legitimate the children rather than divorce the parents was the first clue that the legislature was prepared to think about the economic position of children apart from the marital status of their parents. While many of the divorces passed before the Rouck petition contained clauses protecting the legitimacy, and therefore the inheritance rights, of children born to the divorcing parents,[67] this was the first time that parents were left in marital confusion while the children's inheritance rights were guaranteed.

The Rouck case, in an interesting way, confirmed the blossoming of childhood as a culturally distinct period of human development. Legislative willingness to adopt the provisions protecting the Rouck children was probably increased by the focus on inheritance rights. Traditional views that sons provided productive labor for their agricultural families during their youth and continued their fathers' enterprise as adults had already been modified. By 1810, primogeniture was gone and all children, rather than just sons, were typical intestate successors. It was therefore not a major policy shift to guarantee that property held by a woman, either as an heir of her father or a survivor of her husband, should pass through standard family lines.

Other cultural forces easing the shift to protection of children's inheritance rights were also at work. Improved agricultural efficiency created a child labor surplus in many areas of the country.[68] Children left their homes for other job venues with greater frequency, making the sale of the family farm rather than its transfer to the eldest son an attractive alternative. The development of nonagricultural jobs in a money economy and the settlement of Western territories also created incentives for children to leave their homes. The productive capacity of children was reduced and the cost of raising them increased as education became widely accepted as a prerequisite to full participation in political, religious, economic, and family life. Family life is in this list for important reasons. As women took over educational obligations and household management, they too needed education. Reason emerged as a socially constructed rather than innate characteristic. As logic and thoughtfulness became measures of success, the value of teaching those characteristics grew. All these factors helped demarcate childhood as a special time. In the context of divorce, such demarcation made child custody a matter of great importance. As inheritance issues gave way to concern about nurture, women sought and obtained control of their children with increasing frequency. Only a few years after the Rouck debate, custody clauses began to appear in many private divorce acts. During the period 1816–1825, discussed in the next chapter, one-seventh of the private divorce acts contained custody clauses.[69]

Notes

1. The Republicans obtained a 40 to 37 majority, but could not control the House on close questions. There were three independents, and party discipline was poor. D. M. BROWN, PARTY BATTLES AND BEGINNINGS IN MARYLAND 225 (1961) (Thesis, Georgetown Univ.); L. M. RENZULLI, MARYLAND: THE FEDERALIST YEARS 217–218 (1972).

2. Republicans gradually increased their control over the reins of Maryland state government between 1800 and 1806, when an indirect quinquennial Senate election was held. RENZULLI, *supra* note 1, at 227–237.

3. In 1809, for example, all but two of the petitions were filed by a delegate from the petitioner's home district. The other two were filed by delegates from a neighboring county.

4. Note that all the counties in the state had four delegates at this time. The town of Annapolis, like the city of Baltimore, had only two.

5. *See* Table 7 in Appendix 1. The proportion of Baltimore petitioners reached a peak of 41 percent between 1837 and 1841.

6. *See* Table 13 in Appendix 1. The regional differences in voting patterns before 1805 are *not* statistically significant. Since the number of votes in this era was small, and the regional variations in outcomes were not large, there is a high chance the data could be random. Nevertheless, the data trends are intriguing, particularly the lower rate of support for divorce in the south than on the Eastern Shore.

7. *See* Table 8 in Appendix 1.

8. *See* Table 3 in Appendix 1. The passage rate for women stayed above that for men during a 32-year period extending from 1805 to 1837. The passage rates for

petitioners from Baltimore did not consistently differ during the study period from the rates for other petitioners. *See* Table 2 in Appendix 1.

9. *See* F. Dewey, *Thomas Jefferson's Notes on Divorce*, 39 WM. & MARY Q. 212, 213–214 (1982).

10. *Id.* at 219. This note, Dewey suggests, was taken "from Montesquieu who says it is tyrannical to permit husbands to repudiate their wives without granting the same right to women."

11. W. H. RIDGWAY, COMMUNITY LEADERSHIP IN MARYLAND, 1790–1840: A COMPARATIVE ANALYSIS OF POWER IN SOCIETY 14 (1979).

12. *See* Table 13 in Appendix 1.

13. *See* Table 12 in Appendix 1.

14. N. RISJORD, CHESAPEAKE POLITICS, 1781–1800, at 73–81, 138–156 (1978).

15. General divorce bills were filed in nine sessions between 1809 and 1823. No significant actions were taken on any of them. Serious debate began in 1824 when the House passed a bill that the Senate rejected. *See* the table of General Bill Proposals in Appendix 2.

16. An Act Annulling the Marriage of Archibald and Susannah Alexander, ch. XXIII, 1805 Md. Laws (Jan. 25, 1806).

17. An Act annulling the marriage of George Sampson and Pamela Sampson, ch. XXXIX, 1806 Md. Laws (Jan. 3, 1807).

18. One other divorce adopted at the 1807 session also may have involved a nonadultery situation. The Senate defeated a bill passed by the House of Delegates divorcing Brittania Marshall from her husband Thomas. The House then sent a message to the Senate:

> THE bill which originated in our house . . . has been returned, and we are sorry to find that it has not met with the concurrence of the senate. The peculiar situation of the person applying for the aid of the legislature, has induced us to return the bill for the reconsideration of your body, with a hope that upon further reflection it will meet with the concurrence of the senate.

1807 HOUSE JOURNAL at 37. The exact nature of Brittania Marshall's "peculiar situation" was not revealed, though the language suggests it might have involved another case of mistaken reliance on reports of a dead husband as a basis for a second marriage. The Senate did in fact reconsider and pass the bill. An Act annulling the marriage of Brittania Marshall, of Dorchester county, ch. XXX, 1807 Md. Laws (Jan. 15, 1808).

19. An act annuling the marriage of Joseph Boyd, and Elizabeth Boyd his wife, ch. CIII, 1807 Md. Laws (Jan. 20, 1808) (adultery by Elizabeth Boyd); An Act Annulling the Marriage of Ephraim Furniss, and Polly his Wife, of Somerset County, ch. LXVII, 1809 Md. Laws (Jan. 6, 1810) (birth of mulatto child); An Act annulling the Marriage of Thomas Taylor, and Phoebe his wife, ch. LII, 1809 Md. Laws (Dec. 23, 1810) (adultery by Thomas Taylor).

20. 1807 HOUSE JOURNAL at 59.

21. JOURNAL OF A CONVENTION OF THE PROTESTANT EPISCOPAL CHURCH IN THE STATE OF MARYLAND HELD IN THE CITY OF BALTIMORE FROM MAY 20, TO MAY 22, 1807, at p. 6. A committee composed of the Rev. Dr. Bend, Dr. Kemp, Mr. Davis, Mr. Dorsey, and Mr. Heath was appointed to prepare the memorial.

22. James Kemp was elected Claggett's successor as bishop of the Protestant Episcopal Church of Maryland at the 1814 convention in a bitter contest between traditional churchmen favoring Kemp and more evangelical factions favoring George Dashiell. *See* T. D. BILHARTZ, URBAN RELIGION AND THE SECOND GREAT AWAKENING: CHURCH AND SOCIETY IN EARLY NATIONAL BALTIMORE 126–128 (1986).

23. This case is described in C. N. EVERSTINE, THE GENERAL ASSEMBLY OF MARYLAND 1776–1850, at 241–242 (1982).

24. Letter from Charles Goldsborough to the Rev. James Kemp (November 19, 1801), Collection of the Archives of the Episcopal Church of Maryland in Baltimore.

25. 1802 HOUSE JOURNAL at 97. The vote was 41 to 16 against the bill.

26. Before 1838, Senators represented only two districts, the Eastern Shore and the Western Shore.

27. I have no record of a Senate roll call vote during the 1820 session. This reference may be to a committee or voice vote.

28. Letter from Richard Carroll to Bishop James Kemp (January 12, 1821), Collections of the Archives of the Episcopal Diocese of Maryland in Baltimore.

29. The Catholic Church position that divorce was unacceptable was standard at the time.

30. Much of the legislation of the period 1805–1815 was quite routine. We know very little about the bills other than the simple language adopted by the General Assembly. A typical act of the time is An Act annulling the Marriage of Ezekiel Walker and Anne Margaret Walker, of the City of Baltimore, ch. LXX, 1810 Md. Laws (Dec. 23, 1810), which read:

> BE IT ENACTED, *by the General Assembly of Maryland,* That the marriage of the said Ezekiel Walker, and Anne Margaret Walker his wife, heretofore solemnized, be, and the same is hereby declared to be, absolutely, and to all intents and purposes, null and void; and the said Ezekiel Walker, and Anne Margaret Walker his wife, are hereby declared to be divorced *a vinculo matrimonii;* provided always, that nothing herein contained shall be construed to illegitimate the children of the said Ezekiel Walker, and Anne Margaret Walker his wife, born prior to the passage of this act.

31. *Compare* the discussion, in Chapter 4, of the era beginning in 1816, when more conservative elements gained control of the Maryland Senate and halted the adoption of *a vinculo* divorces.

32. Elizabeth Taylor was in a similar economic pickle because of the desertion of her husband Vincent. The legislature, at its 1812 session, noted that he had gone to sea nine years earlier and left Elizabeth impoverished with four children. When Elizabeth received a small inheritance, Vincent's creditors threatened

seizure. The legislature intervened and granted her a divorce. This preamble also states that Elizabeth "has just cause to believe that he has since his departure again married." Thus, this bill was in part about adultery. But the primary story, like that of Anne Hoskyns, was about an absconding husband and father. An act annulling the marriage of Vincent P. Taylor, and Elizabeth his wife, ch. 168, 1812 Md. Laws (Dec. 29, 1812).

33. An act to annul the marriage of John Henry Hoskyns and Anne his wife, ch. 181, 1811 Md. Laws (Jan. 7, 1812).

34. Madame Bonaparte's reputation lends some credence to the story. Benjamin W. LeCompte, a member of the 1812 House of Delegates representing Dorchester County, sent a copy of Bonaparte's petition to Mrs. Josiah Bayly, along with a note commenting that the "question on the law will not be taken until after the Coltz Ball at which Madame Bonaparte is to appear & exert the blandishments of her beauty & address to induce a favorable impression on the legislature." LeCompte was also careful to say that he abhorred all French alliances, "matrimonial or political and will cheerfully consent to their severance whenever they can be, with justification, or even a plausible appearance of justice." Finally, he indicated that two women—Mrs. Barney and Mrs. Caton—"are industriously electioneering in her behalf." This is the only indication I have that any lobbying was ever done in a divorce case, although it must have happened from time to time. This correspondence is in the Md. Hall of Records, Sharf Collection, MdHR S1005, Call No. 19,999-110-066, Loc. 1/5/8/78 (Dec. 12, 1812).

35. 1 DICT. AMER. BIOG. 428–429 (1936); An act annulling the marriage of Jerome Bonaparte, and Elizabeth Bonaparte of the City of Baltimore, ch. 130, 1812 Md. Laws (Dec. 15, 1812).

36. The debate in the House of Delegates focused only on the form of the preamble and the title of the bill, with particular concern voiced about designating Jerome Bonaparte as King of Westphalia. 1812 HOUSE JOURNAL at 9–10. Delegate LeCompte also noted his displeasure with the French in his correspondence on the matter. *See supra* note 34.

37. *See* N. Cott, *Divorce and the Changing Status of Women in Eighteenth-Century Massachusetts*, 33 WM. & MARY Q. 586 (1976)

38. An act annulling the marriage of Thomas Burk, and Elizabeth his Wife, of Frederick County, ch. XIII, 1809 Md. Laws (Jan. 6, 1810).

39. The Taylor divorce is cited *supra* note 19. In this case all that is known comes from the preamble, which stated that Thomas Taylor was guilty of adultery.

40. 1 T. J. C. WILLIAMS, HISTORY OF FREDERICK COUNTY MARYLAND, at 179 (1910).

41. *See* Table 3 in Appendix 1.

42. Kitty Higson's marriage to Peregrine Emory on May 8, 1806, was reported in the May 13, 1806, edition of the *Easton Star*. Dielman-Hayward File, Md. Hist. Soc'y. Other details of this case are known from a bill Kitty filed in the Maryland Court of Chancery seeking alimony from Peregrine after their final separation in 1808. Kitty E. Emory v. Peregrine Emory, Ch. Ct. Chancery Papers, MdHR 17, 898-1628, S 512-1697, 1/36/1/73 (Queene Annes, 1808). Kitty filed petitions in the 1809 and 1815 legislative sessions. The 1809 bill passed the House, but

failed in the Senate. 1809 HOUSE JOURNAL at 78; 1809 SENATE JOURNAL at 32. She
won her divorce the second time, but only by a 30 to 27 roll call vote in the House
of Delegates. 1815 HOUSE JOURNAL at 126–127. An act annulling the marriage of
Peregrine Emory, and Kitty E. Emory of Queen Anne's County, ch. 60, 1815 Md.
Laws (Jan. 8, 1816).

43. This sort of allegation was common in the alimony petitions I read.
Mary Sergeant was also represented by counsel in her case.

44. Mary Sergeant v. Samuel Sergeant, Baltimore County Court Chancery
Papers, MdHR 40, 200–143, 2/15/11/36 (Baltimore, 1819).

45. 1807 HOUSE JOURNAL at 11.

46. 1810 HOUSE JOURNAL at 59; 1811 HOUSE JOURNAL at 133. Multiple attempts to obtain divorces were fairly common. Some couples showed up as many
as six times. Some of these mutliple application cases are discussed in Chapter 6.

47. The divorce petition was reported to the floor on January 24, 1814. 1813
HOUSE JOURNAL at 83.

48. Her chancery petition was filed on March 23, 1814.

49. See R. Chused, Married Women's Property Law: 1800–1850, 71 GEO. L. J.
1359, 1379–1381 (1983).

50. See Wallingsford v. Wallingsford, 10 Md. (6 H. & J.) 398 (1825).

51. Mary Cartwright v. Abraham Cartwright, Chancery Court Chancery Papers, MdHR 17, S 512-1059, 1/36/1/21 (Baltimore County, 1814). It turned out that
Mary Cartwright also gained her marital freedom. There is a notation in the chancery court file that, at some unknown time, Abraham Cartwright died and that
Mary had settled her claim with his estate.

52. R. PHILLIPS, PUTTING ASUNDER: A HISTORY OF DIVORCE IN WEST-
ERN SOCIETY 450–461 (1988); R. GRISWOLD, FAMILY AND DIVORCE IN CALI-
FORNIA, 1850–1890, at 19–20 (1982); J. Censer, "Smiling Through Her Tears": Ante-
Bellum Southern Women and Divorce, 25 AM. J. LEG. HIST. 1 (1981).

53. See Tables 10, 11, and 13 in Appendix 1. If the data for the 1805–1815 time
period in the first column of Tables 10 and 11 are combined, 14 percent (31 of 197)
of all divorce petitions led to roll call votes.

54. About two-fifths (10 of 26) of the roll call votes taken in the House of
Delegates between 1805 and 1815 were decided by six votes or less. These votes
would have shifted in result if four delegates had switched sides. Only about a
quarter (6 of 23) of the votes after 1815 were that close.

55. See Table 10 in Appendix 1. Roll call votes were taken on only 7 percent
(38 of 507) of bills enacted throughout the rest of the study period.

56. 1811 HOUSE JOURNAL at 90, 172.

57. He moved to appoint a divorce committee "to whom all petitions of a
similar nature shall be referred." 1811 HOUSE JOURNAL at 45.

58. The first attempt came in the 1809. 1809 HOUSE JOURNAL at 13. The
other attempts are reported at 1815 HOUSE JOURNAL at 45, 56, 62, 64; 1811 SENATE
JOURNAL at 289, 307; and 1815 SENATE JOURNAL at 124, 125, 149. The terms of these
various bills are not known.

59. RENZULLI, supra note 1, at 211–321. L. S. DEMAREE, MARYLAND DUR-
ING THE FIRST PARTY SYSTEM: A ROLL-CALL ANALYSIS OF THE HOUSE OF

DELEGATES, 1789–1824, at 172 (1984) (Thesis, U. Mo. Columbia), reported that the Federalists controlled 56 of 80 seats in the 1816 House of Delegates, 45 in 1817, 35 in 1818, 30 in 1819, 32 in 1820, 19 in 1821, 15 in 1822, and only 7 in 1823. The last Federalist strongholds were mostly in the southern counties, especially Montgomery, Charles, and Saint Marys. *Id.* at 211–216.

60. BILHARTZ, *supra* note 22, at 83–99.

61. *Id.* at 38–51.

62. *Id.* at 52–64.

63. 1809 HOUSE JOURNAL at 13. Mr. Worthington served only one year in the House of Delegates and did not participate in any roll call votes on divorce bills. It is therefore not possible to define his family law views.

64. R. BRUGGER, MARYLAND: A MIDDLE TEMPERAMENT, 1634–1980, at 187 (1988).

65. 1811 HOUSE JOURNAL at 64, 147, 173.

66. In the traditional fault-based divorce law extant in most areas of the country before 1970, a divorce plaintiff alleging fault by his or her spouse could be barred from obtaining a divorce if the plaintiff was also guilty of some fault. Two parties at fault were left to stew in their own juices by this recrimination rule.

67. Between 1790 and 1815, 78 percent (39 of 50) of the private divorce acts contained clauses protecting the inheritance rights of children.

68. *See* W. Rasmussen, *The Mechanization of Agriculture*, 247 SCI. AM. 76 (1982); Chused, *supra* note 49, at 1362.

69. *See* Table 4 in Appendix 1.

4. Religious and Political Maneuvering: The Disappearance of *A Vinculo* Divorce, 1816–1825

The Rise of Partial Divorce

Family law changed abruptly at the 1816 session of the General Assembly. Only two divorces were passed, compared to eight the prior year. And the language of both of these bills was dramatically different from all previous enactments. Martha Graham and Ann Neilson obtained divorces from their husbands, Augustus Graham and Hugh Neilson, but they were only "from bed, board and mutual cohabitation." Every divorce passed in the preceding twenty-five years had been *a vinculo matrimonii*. And in identical language, not seen in prior divorce acts, Martha Graham and Ann Neilson were granted *feme sole* authority "in as full and ample a manner as if she . . . had never been married" to sue and hold property "without the molestation, interference, hindrance or consent, of her said husband."[1] For the next decade, the General Assembly refused to adopt any complete divorces. The policy change had one quite dramatic consequence—those obtaining legislative divorces before 1816 could remarry, while those securing relief during the following decade could not.

The demise of complete divorce in 1816 demonstrates the intimate connections between family life, religion, electoral politics, and the structure of the Maryland General Assembly. Both the Sampson divorce,[2] passed during the 1806 session when the Republicans gained legislative ascendancy, and the change in divorce policy occurring in 1816, when the Federalists regained control of the Senate, occurred after dramatic shifts in Senate membership. Indirect Senate elections occurred every five years. Election year turnover in that body was very substantial. The party gaining a majority among the electors chosen to pick senators routinely appointed its own members to most of the fifteen Senate seats.[3] Swift political transitions and reluctance to serve for more than one term controlled the makeup of the upper house. In the Senate taking office in 1806, ten of the fifteen members were new. In 1811, that grew to twelve. The 1816 and 1821 Senates were completely new; there were no holdovers. There were three holdovers in 1826, one in 1831, and none in 1836. In a larger body elected directly every year, such as the House of Delegates, membership changes were more gradual. Turnover was significantly lower each year in the Maryland House than it was each fifth year in the Senate. Almost half of the delegates were new in the 1806, 1811, and 1816 sessions. But there were also a number of people who served in that body for many years, and leadership roles turned over less rapidly than the membership at large. Even though the possibility of policy change was high in the House of Delegates, it lacked the quinquennial volatility of the Senate. Institutional memory was therefore a more potent force in the House than in the Senate.

Though alterations in divorce policy occasioned by membership flux in the legislature were sometimes sudden,[4] the changes were not outside the boundary lines of standard family law rhetoric. The Senate's preference for partial divorce certainly mirrored the predilection of many segments of early nineteenth-century Maryland society. The rumbles of dissent from the adoption of divorces that arose before 1815 became the majority's discourse in the following decade. This tumult in legislative family law mirrored a number of conflicts then troubling Marylanders.

International and domestic conflict dominated the second decade of the nineteenth century in Maryland. Major clashes occurred there during the War of 1812. The Battle of Baltimore is still celebrated by "The Star-Spangled Banner." Commerce and trade were severely disrupted. Church schisms arose over political affiliations, theological differences, and allegations of sexual impropriety by ministers.[5] The best-known incident of alleged ministerial indiscretion began in 1815 when George Dashiell, leader of St. Peter's Episcopalian Church in Baltimore, was charged with making improper advances to the wife of a parishioner. Dashiell, an evangelical preacher, had lost a bitter contest to James Kemp for the post of bishop of the Protestant Episcopal Church of Maryland just one year earlier.[6] Kemp's victory and Dashiell's scandal suggest that traditional religious influences were still strong and resilient. The Dashiell affair became a *cause célèbre* over the next two years.[7] Church trials, pamphlets and court proceedings captured the public eye. The era also witnessed a dramatic increase in evangelical activity and revivalism,[8] the rise of numerous reform, educational and temperance societies,[9] and the appearance of a variety of moral crusades against theaters, slavery, and, of course, divorce.[10]

Given the disarray caused by war and widespread social upheaval, it is easy to understand why many Marylanders wished to see both a speedy and successful conclusion to the fighting with Britain and greater stability in social and family circles. Indeed, bitter denunciation of Republican war policies by antiwar New England Federalists did not sit well with many Federalist Party members in Maryland. In 1812, a vengeful, Republican-led riot against a band of antiwar Federalists in Baltimore led voters to oust many Republicans from the General Assembly in favor of moderate, Federalists who were not bitterly antiwar. While the Federalist Party faded in other areas of the country, it took control of the House of Delegates and remained a political power there through the 1815 elections.[11] Sympathetic voters also supported the moderate Federalists when selecting senatorial electors in 1816. Under the leadership of Roger Brooke Taney, chosen as an elector and then approved as a senator, the Federalists wrested control of the State Senate from the Republicans indirectly elected five years before.[12]

The political upheaval allowed previously dissenting views to dominate family law debates. Divorce certainly was not the only domain of early nineteenth-century family law to be subjected to vigorous debate. Jamil Zainaldin, for example, has traced the ebbs and flows in early child custody law across the nation.[13] But it is rare to see a policy change as abrupt and dramatic as that displayed in the Maryland legislative divorce process. Roger Brooke Taney, best-known as a Supreme Court Chief Justice and author of the infamous opinion in the *Dred Scott* case,[14] was one of the new senators who went about altering Maryland's legislative family law after 1815. Though his wife Anne Key Taney, Francis Scott Key's sister, was Episcopalian, Taney was Catholic.[15] Roger and Anne apparently had a good understanding about their respective faiths. Biographers report their marriage was a happy one.[16] His traditional family law views had a profound impact.

As far as we know, divorce was not a subject Taney spoke about publicly. But certain conclusions can be drawn from the extant historic record. Taney's actions as a state senator from 1816 to 1821 were perfectly consistent with the Catholic Church's opposition to *a vinculo* divorce. Recorded roll call votes show that Taney voted in favor of several partial divorces.[17] In the 1818 session, for example, he voted in favor of the Fitzhugh divorce after it was amended to a bed and board bill and supported the bills partially divorcing Elizabeth Morgan and Mary Louisa Hall. He also introduced a bill for the relief of Phoebe Cresap which was eventually adopted as a private bed and board divorce act.[18] But he never went on record favoring a complete divorce bill. For example, Stephen Lewis petitioned the House of Delegates for a divorce from his wife Betsy during the 1818 session.[19] On December 15, the House passed a bill divorcing them *a vinculo matrimonii* after a motion to amend the legislation to a partial divorce failed.[20] Early in 1819, the Senate defeated the bill in a 9 to 6 roll call vote, with Taney voting against it.[21] The House then sent the Senate the following message:

> We return you the . . . [Lewis bill] which was rejected by your honourable body a few days past; and we hope that you will agree to reconsider and pass the same. We are well convinced, that if your honorable body shall agree to pass any bill for a divorce "a vinculo matrimonii," that you will pass this bill, but if you cannot consent to pass this bill as it now is, and will agree to pass it "a mensa et thoro," we beg leave to state that this house will assent to such change being made in the bill.[22]

In response, the Senate postponed consideration of the complete divorce bill and, with some disdain, refused to acquiesce in the House preference for divorcing the Lewises *a vinculo*:

> The senate have refused to reconsider the bill for the benefit of Stephen Lewis, of Worcester County, for reasons that will appear obvious to the members of the house of delegates, return you the same, every object desired in your message is accomplished by another bill herewith sent down.[23]

The new partial divorce bill was then passed by the House.[24] Other bills for complete divorce also had difficulty in the Senate, some failing and others passing as bed and board acts.[25] During the following session another bill followed the Lewis path, with Taney voting against the legislation before it was finally passed as a partial divorce.[26] And in some cases, women petitioning for divorces had to be satisfied with property relief alone; these cases echoed the plight of Lilly Blair almost forty years earlier.[27]

Such results, of course, could not come with only Taney's support. As the generally recognized leader of the moderate Federalists,[28] he wielded significant influence over his political allies. Taney was a member of the electoral body that selected the Senate in 1816,[29] and he obviously played a role in developing the slate of candidates eventually picked to become senators. It therefore is not surprising that most of his aristocratic, Federalist Senate colleagues had similar attitudes about the family. Data gleaned from the legislative journals demonstrate that after 1815 the Senate was the stumbling block to passage of divorces in general and *a vinculo* divorces in particular. Fifteen percent of all the petitions filed between 1816 and 1825 were approved in the House of Delegates only to die in the Senate.[30] Put another way, in nearly one-fourth of the petitions not leading to a divorce act, the House of Delegates passed a bill that failed in the Senate.[31] Only once in that decade did the House refuse to pass a bill passed by the Senate. The extent of Senate opposition to divorce was significantly higher in this time period than in any other.[32] And when floor amendments to change bills from complete to partial divorces were reported in the journals, they were more likely to occur in the Senate.[33]

The depth of Senate opposition to complete divorce after 1815 is best told by the cases of Joseph Price and Thomas Knock. In the preamble to the Price divorce, the legislature stated that "Sarah Price has eloped from his bed and board, without any just cause or provocation on the part of her said husband, and has taken up and lives with a black man, in a state of open and disgraceful adultery." Though Sarah Price lost her dower rights in property acquired by Joseph after the adoption of the private act,[34] only a bed and board divorce was granted.[35] Thomas Knock obtained the same relief after his wife "was delivered of a colored child."[36] Price and Knock fared worse than the few men who managed to obtain complete divorces for similar reasons in the 1790s!

The shift to partial divorces did have some ironic results. Legislators with traditional family ideologies were more willing to vote for bed and board, as opposed to *a vinculo*, bills. Delegates from the southern region of Maryland, who tended to oppose private divorces throughout the first half of the nineteenth century, voted for them more often during the 1816–1825 period than at any other time.[37] Southern delegates cast roll call votes in favor of divorce bills 52 percent of the time between 1816 and 1825. The highest rate of affirmative votes in any other era was only 38 percent. Indeed, it became easier for women to gain both divorces and economic relief after partial divorces became the standard.[38] Requests for roll call votes in the House took a nose dive after 1815,[39] perhaps because everyone knew the futility of pursuing certain issues as long as the Senate stubbornly declined to pass *a vinculo* bills. But when roll calls occurred, the proportion voting in favor of what were usually bed and board divorce bills rose dramatically from 50 to 61 percent.[40] The voting changes meant that more bills passed at the behest of both husbands and wives.[41] Reform-minded delegates, who surely thought it better to pass partial divorces than none at all, were joined by some traditionalists in passing these bed and board acts.

Though Taney did not return to the Senate in 1821, the general tenor of divorce legislation remained the same for the following five years, a period of continuing political turmoil and realignment. No *a vinculo* acts were passed. During the 1825 session, a committee reviewing the petition of Eleanor Foreman reported to the House of Delegates,

> that they deem it inexpedient to introduce a bill such as would meet the wishes of the petitioner. There are but few reasons which could be urged to induce them to report a bill a vinculo matrimonii; and Mrs. Foreman having been divorced from bed and board, only two sessions since, the committee think that quite as much as her case merits, they therefore recommend that the petitioner have leave to withdraw her petition.[42]

Although petitioners could hope to gain only partial divorces, the grounds the legislature acted on favorably were similar to those operating in 1806 when the Sampsons were divorced. The few tidbits of legislative history available reveal that both adultery and cruelty or ill usage sufficed as grounds. During the 1822 session, the standing divorce committee filed this report with the House of Delegates:

> The committee to whom were referred sundry petitions praying for divorces, beg leave to report—That they have had the same under their consideration, the subject committed to them was one of a peculiarly delicate character, and required from them all the considerations which they could bestow on it. It is a subject which has frequently commanded the attention of the legislature of *Maryland*, and divorces have often been granted by it. Your committee believes also, that there are cases in which legislatures may interpose to dissolve the tie of marriage, laid down a principle which should govern them in their decision on the cases presented to them, that, whenever the fact of adultery was established by such proofs as could not be resisted, they would recommend such cases to the favorable consideration of the house. In conformity to this decision, they present the cases of Everiste Maury, Theophilus Russel and George Yeaman. Your committee had before them other cases, which, not coming under the principle laid down, they return to the house subject to its disposition, remarking at the same time, if the proofs had been sufficiently strong, some of them would have been recommended for partial divorces.[43]

This report implies that the 1822 House of Delegates approved divorces only for adultery, but a report filed in the next session condoned divorce for other reasons. The committee reviewing the petition of Elizabeth Shaw for a divorce noted,

> [I]t appearing that no ground of ill usage to the petitioner whatever is stated, no allegation of a breach of the marriage contract adduced, but symply

against the moral character of her husband, as manifested by his conduct before marriage. Your committee believe the said conduct no special violation of the marriage contract, and that the said petitioner having undertaken to enter into the same with her said husband, "for better or worse," has no claim to the interference of the legislature, therefore recommend that the petitioner have leave to withdraw her petition.[44]

These two reports may mirror different understandings about divorce grounds operating in two different sessions of the General Assembly. But whether the House of Delegates changed its view of divorce from year to year, the two committee statements present the contours of a debate much like that in earlier decades about the wisdom of divorcing couples for grounds other than adultery. The major difference, of course, was that the discourse was about partial rather than complete divorce. Although the House of Delegates did approve some complete divorces during the sessions in which these reports were prepared, everyone must have known they would never be passed by the Senate.[45]

The committee statements also echoed the traditional ecclesiastic grounds used to support alimony petitions in Maryland's chancery courts—adultery and cruel treatment.[46] The power of revivalist and other contemporary religious movements with traditional views of the family must have had an influence on the General Assembly after 1815. Taney's position of power gave him room to impose his Catholic views on the General Assembly. After he left the Senate, religious influences were still at work. The House divorce committee for the 1824 session, reporting on the petition of Elizabeth Shaw, noted that they

> have carefully examined the prayer of the petitioner, and are unanimously of opinion that it is improper to interfere in a case such as her's. The marriage ceremony at all times ought to be viewed as it really is, solimn—and to legislate without being justified by the divine law, is what we ought to avoid.[47]

Even as religious concerns contributed to the elimination of complete divorces from Maryland's legislative agenda, evangelical movements claimed greater empathy with individualistic and romantic notions of family life attractive to many women. A number of historians have argued that religion was feminized in this time period.[48] Women's religious and moral reform organizations grew and flourished. As some began to think of the decision to marry in romantic terms, religious movements developed individualistic theories of redemption for men and women, initiated both home- and school-based religious education relying heavily on women, characterized the domestic roles of women as divine, and chastised women failing to fulfill their "chosen" roles.

In such a context it is plausible that some religiously motivated legislators, both the evangelicals and those bound by traditional Catholic or Anglican beliefs, would decline to pass *a vinculo* divorces while paying close attention to the post-divorce status of women.[49] Though the core of traditional theological opposition to divorce was not yet open to change, the shape of remedies granted to women divorced from bed and board was not as tightly controlled by religious dogma. Thus, for traditionalists, marriage, even if redefined with modern romantic expectations, was still a covenant with God as well as spouse. Complete release from such an agreement was impossible. God could not completely forgive a woman whose family failed to meet the new images of domesticity. But the new individualistic interpretations of religious movements and the enlarged divinity of women's marital, political, and educational roles validated increased legislative attention to abdication of expected family roles by men and the post-divorce economic status of women.

It makes sense, therefore, that the proportion of petitioners obtaining relief from the legislature rose dramatically between 1816 and 1825, and that women were particularly successful. Only 18 percent of the male petitioners procured divorces between 1805 and 1815; 32 percent were successful in the next decade. The comparable figures for women were 26 percent before 1816, and 45 percent during the following ten years.[50] In addition, many of the bed and board private bills adopted between 1816 and 1825 contained provisions about the post-divorce economic lives of both spouses and children.

Partial Divorce and the Economic Interests of Marriage

There is some irony in describing how the moral and religious overtones of the Taney and post-Taney era may have led some in the General Assembly to undertake more detailed consideration of the economic interests embedded in marriage. But this renewed attention to an older idea—that marriage was largely defined as an economic relationship rather than a romantic alliance—now resonated in a different context than it did in 1790. Alimony defined the upper limits of a disappointed wife's economic remedies after the Revolutionary War. By the Taney era, many segments of society, including some with quite traditional family attitudes, agreed that women separated from their husbands needed more than the minimal protections afforded by the alimony statute. The Senate, at least in theory, could have demanded a return to the eighteenth-century no-divorce-for-women rule. But, given the economic difficulties during and after the War of 1812, the growth of urban areas, and the departure of men for the newly opened frontiers, that was unlikely. Although *a vinculo* divorces were refused, bed and board arrangements allowed the legislature to resolve the economic contours of some unsalvageable marriages when alimony relief was inadequate.

In fact, the shift to partial divorces *required* the General Assembly to pay more attention to economic issues. When parties divorced *a vinculo*, marital property regimes terminated automatically. A completely divorced woman usually lost to her husband the personal property she brought to the marriage,[51] surrendered dower rights, and forfeited her right to maintenance and support, but she regained both the real property she brought to the marriage not lost to her husband's creditors and the right to participate in the economy as a *feme sole*. Bed and board divorces left spouses economically entwined. Given the grounds usually supporting a legislative divorce—adultery and cruelty—and the status of many women involved in marital disarray—abandoned or without means of support—these entanglements frequently needed to be regulated, if not loosened or severed. Limitations on the economic power of husbands were therefore commonly adopted between 1816 and 1825.[52] Table 4 in Appendix 1 signals the dramatic arrival of property provisions. No acts contained provisions on the rights of husbands in the property of wives before 1816, while about half contained such clauses between 1816 and 1825. Virtually all the acts of this period contained financial provisions. Of the eighty-nine divorce acts passed between 1816 and 1825, only ten lacked some sort of provision limiting the rights of a spouse in the property of the other or the obligation of one spouse to pay the debts of the other. The link between bed and board divorces and property provisions was more apparent after 1826, when the legislature began again to pass complete divorces. Bed and board divorces enacted after 1826 were almost four times more likely to contain economic provisions than contemporaneously adopted *a vinculo* acts.[53] The bed and board divorce path also was more likely to be granted to women than to men. Some women may have preferred such an outcome. For a partial divorce preserved the rights of a wife to seek alimony, payment of her debts,[54] and other economic rights from her husband, while a complete divorce cut her off from such economic security.

The appearance of economic provisions in many private divorce acts occurred at a time when a number of legal provisions limiting the roles of married women were under scrutiny. During the first decades of the nineteenth century, widows in some jurisdictions obtained additional rights to control the devolution of their husbands' estates, abandoned or deserted women regained some control over their economic lives, imprisonment of women debtors was largely ended, and poor laws were altered to modestly improve relief for women left without any means of support.[55] The same dislocations creating pressure on the Maryland legislature to grant divorces—urban growth, husbands leaving for the frontier, economic difficulties, war and expanded cultural understandings of political equality—caused changes in other legal constraints on the economic and social roles of women.

Terms of the limitations on husbands' economic interests varied some from divorce act to divorce act, particularly after 1821. Language in some of the acts inferred there would be retroactive effects; others quite explicitly stated that alterations in prior economic arrangements were precluded. Despite the linguistic differences, it is not clear that results changed much. The terms of the potentially retroactive property provision most commonly used in this period, for example, voided "all the right and title which the said [husband], by virtue of his marriage with the said [wife], had acquired to any property which she is or may become entitled to in any way or manner whatever."[56] There are no reported cases construing the meaning of this provision, and the legislative journals contain no explanatory material. As to real property brought to a marriage by a wife, the husband surely lost his management rights under such an act. But personal property reduced to possession by a husband prior to the adoption of the divorce was not "property which she is or may become entitled to." Such a construction of the language would result in a bed and board divorce having the same basic effect on a husband's property as an *a vinculo* severing of marital ties.

A few acts had limitations in the *feme sole* sections similar to this:

> *Provided*, nothing in this act contained shall be so construed as to invalidate any act or acts which the said William Harding may have lawfully done, respecting any property obtained by virtue of his marriage with the said Elizabeth Harding before the passage of this act.[57]

Others only removed husbandly rights in property acquired by wives "after the passage of this act."[58] The quoted provision arguably affirmed the validity of any encumbrances imposed on a wife's real property by a husband during their marriage. A different outcome might have been derived from a potentially retroactive provision, but such a reading was not required. Even the acts limiting alterations in marital property rights to property acquired after an act's passage would have no effect if the parties had little or no property.

It is therefore difficult to read any far-reaching conclusions into the terminology of the property provisions limiting husbands' economic rights. The likelihood that any acts adopted in this period had substantial retroactive effects is small. Many restrictions on husbands may have reflected little more than the obvious need to deal with women's economic status when the divorce was from bed and board. Several other important possibilities, however, are worth noting. First, bed and board divorce acts without any provision limiting the rights of wives in husbands' property left dower rights intact. Thus, the standard *feme sole* language found in most acts, unless accompanied by other provisions, left women with the right both to retain their future property and earnings and to claim dower if they survived their partially divorced spouses. Restrictions on wives' interests in husbands' property were adopted with increasing frequency after 1825, but there were always some bills limiting only husbands' rights.[59] Second, a number of acts contained provisions limiting the property rights of both husbands and wives, as if the legislature wished to sever all or most economic ties between divorcing men and women. Indeed, this became standard in the period 1826–1836, when more than 60 percent of bed and board divorce acts contained provisions dealing with the property of both husbands and wives.[60]

The shift to adoption of economic provisions dealing with the property of both spouses also infers that the tendency to use property rules as punishment devices probably declined after 1826. That idea is consistent with the contemporaneous reemergence of *a vinculo* divorce allowing those breaching marital vows to escape from marriage despite their misbehavior. Some legislators apparently understood the economic futility of leaving offending spouses, particularly women, destitute. Nonetheless, there were still a few bed and board acts limiting only the rights of wives in husbands' property or lacking property provisions of any sort. In such settings, as well as in some of the cases where limitations were imposed only on husbands, the legislature may have used the economic terms of divorce legislation to make moral judgments about particularly deviant spouses.[61] Credence is lent to this theory by differences in private acts initiated by the petitions of husbands and wives. Although the number of acts is a bit low to allow for statistically significant conclusions, all of the acts limiting only the rights of wives in husbands' property were initiated by petitions filed by men. Similarly, the proportion of acts limiting the rights of husbands in wives' property falls noticeably in cases in which wives petitioned the legislature.[62] It is also possible, however, that the acts limiting the property rights of only one spouse reflected the departure of that spouse from the area or hid settlements in which husbands agreed to establish trusts for the benefit of their wives.[63]

In sum, the variety and frequency of economic provisions in the post-1815 divorces embodied quite basic shifts in attitudes about family culture. The economic provisions were surely practical. Women exiting a marital home needed some economic footing in order to avoid reliance on public or private charity. Men presumably wished their real property to be free of the encumbrance of dower. But these provisions were also dramatically different from the alimony rules operating before 1800. Economic rewards and punishments were handed out under a new set of understandings. While complete reliance on alimony to "solve" the economic problems of wives in domestic trouble left women entangled in the economic lives of their husbands, most women obtaining partial divorces after 1815 gained some measure of economic independence from their husbands. Increased reliance upon women as educators, moral beacons, child supporters, and participants in urban commercial life necessitated a redefinition of post-marital status. Rising petition rates, especially by women, confirmed that family status was in the midst of some redefinition. Legislative deliberations about both family roles and marital economic expectations covered a much larger array of questions at this time than in the period just after the Revolutionary War.

Child Custody

In a similar fashion, children emerged as a focus of legislative attention. Cultural and religious understandings about children, like those about their mothers, became more attuned to individual characteristics and needs. Redemption, as a choice to be made rather than a fate to be endured, required education, understanding, and motivation. Complementing concepts of republican citizenship in the political arena, children required moral and religious molding, development, and care. Sunday schools be-

gan to appear in Baltimore beginning in 1816.[64] As more men left the
family home to work, women took on the roles of caretaker, educator,
home "pastor," and moral role model. And as more men deserted their
wives, either physically or emotionally, the Maryland legislature responded
with provisions in divorce acts awarding child custody to women.[65] The
legislative links between women and their children were strong. Of the
eighty-one custody provisions in this study, only one gave children to a
man.[66] Virtually all custody awards were made when the divorce petition
was filed by a wife rather than a husband. Between 1816 and 1836, 93 percent (56 of 60) of the custody awards came after petitions were filed by
women.[67] Court review of legislative custody determinations was apparently rare. Papers for only one such dispute are known to exist.[68]

It is most unlikely that lack of child custody awards to fathers meant
that children always lived with their mothers after divorce. In the late eighteenth century, legal norms left children of divorce with their fathers.[69] It
is therefore logical to assume that the legislature felt a need to say something about child custody only if they wished to change the extant legal
norm. If this assumption is correct, the presence of custody awards to
women after 1820 yields a measure of the scale and rate of change, rather
than a picture of revolution in family law. This theory is given some support by the legislative data. Custody awards appeared in significantly fewer
acts after 1836 than before. By the middle of the century it was likely either
that women were the presumptive custodians of children of divorce or
that parents were settling custody issues before seeking adoption of a private act. The Warfield divorce, together with the simplicity of virtually all
later divorce acts, suggests that most of the details of marital breakup
were being privately arranged. Gradual acceptance of a new custody norm
and settlement agreements both reduced the need for legislative intervention.

The first custody award appeared in the act divorcing Adelaide and
Bradley Lowe adopted in the 1822 session.[70] Their short marriage began
in 1819.[71] Before the act's adoption, the legislature reported, the parties
agreed to articles of separation "sanctioned and approved of by the family and friends of the said Adelaide." Adelaide was designated a *feme sole*
and given the "care, custody, guardianship and controul of Enoch Lewis
Lowe, the infant son . . . [of the parties] until . . . [he] shall arrive to the
age of twenty-one years." She was also given the authority to appoint a
guardian for Enoch by deed or will. Bradley, however, was excused from

paying "for the support or maintainance of the said Adelaide V. Lowe or the said Enoch Lewis Lowe." The consequences of this last provision are ambiguous. If the parties' separation agreement contained child-support provisions or a monetary settlement large enough to support the child, the act served merely to preclude reliance on the statutory alimony provisions. But it is also possible that Adelaide and her child were left, at least in part, to find economic support from family or friends.[72] Two more custody awards were made during the following session.[73] Such awards continued at a high level through the 1830s.[74]

Notes

1. An act for the relief of Ann Neilson of Baltimore County, ch. 155, 1816 Md. Laws (Jan. 29, 1817); An act for the relief of Martha Graham of Frederick County, ch. 213, 1816 Md. Laws (Feb. 3, 1817).

2. An Act annulling the marriage of George Sampson and Pamela Sampson, ch. XXXIX, 1806 Md. Laws (Jan. 3, 1807). Note that Susannah Alexander's divorce, adopted during the 1805 session, a year before the Senate turned over, did not represent as significant a change in divorce policy as the Sampson case because there was some evidence of adultery by Archibald Alexander.

3. C. N. EVERSTINE, THE GENERAL ASSEMBLY OF MARYLAND 1776–1850, at 463 (1982).

4. Shifts in Senate membership did not always cause dramatic changes in divorce policy. The loss of Federalist control of the Senate in 1821, for example, did not lead to any dramatic shifts, although the property provisions of the acts developed more diversity.

5. T. D. BILHARTZ, URBAN RELIGION AND THE SECOND GREAT AWAKENING: CHURCH AND SOCIETY IN EARLY NATIONAL BALTIMORE 38–51 (1986).

6. *Id.* at 126–128.

7. *Id.* at 47–49.

8. *Id.* at 83–99.

9. *Id.* at 100–116.

10. *Id.* at 55–57.

11. The Federalists held a slim majority in the House after the 1815 elections and faded rapidly as a political power after the 1816 elections. By 1818, the party was only an insignificant minority in the House of Delegates. L. M. RENZULLI, MARYLAND: THE FEDERALIST YEARS 314–318 (1972).

12. *Id.* at 305–316; R. BRUGGER, MARYLAND: A MIDDLE TEMPERAMENT, 1634–1980, at 178–179, 196–197 (1988).

13. J. Zainaldin, *The Emergence of a Modern American Family Law: Child Custody, Adoption and the Courts, 1796–1851*, 73 NW. L. REV. 1038, 1052–1074 (1979).

14. Dred Scott v. Sanford, 60 U.S. (19 How.) 393 (1857).

15. Taney was also an adviser to Archbishop Ambrose Marechal of Baltimore. B. C. STEINER, LIFE OF ROGER BROOKE TANEY: CHIEF JUSTICE OF THE UNITED STATES SUPREME COURT 85 (1922).

16. C. B. SWISHER, ROGER B. TANEY 49–51 (1935).

17. 1818 SENATE JOURNAL at 23, 36.

18. *Id.* at 16, 23, 29.

19. 1818 HOUSE JOURNAL at 9.

20. *Id.* at 15.

21. 1818 SENATE JOURNAL at 22.

22. 1818 HOUSE JOURNAL at 67. Nothing is known about why the House of Delegates thought the Lewises were such good candidates for a complete divorce.

23. 1818 SENATE JOURNAL at 29.

24. 1818 HOUSE JOURNAL at 82.

25. The House refused to amend the Brotzman divorce bill to a partial divorce, (1818 HOUSE JOURNAL at 20), but the bill did not pass the Senate. The Perkins bill was amended in the Senate to a partial divorce and eventually was passed. 1818 SENATE JOURNAL at 17, 28. The same pattern repeated itself in other sessions.

26. 1819 SENATE JOURNAL at 29, 36. This activity led to the partial divorce of Thomas and Ann Ward in their second attempt to get divorced. Three more tries were made to obtain a complete divorce, which they finally got in the 1831 session, 14 years after their first petition was filed with the legislature.

27. For example, Susannah Teas petitioned for a divorce in the 1819 session. 1819 HOUSE JOURNAL at 68. The legislation that finally emerged did not divorce her, but she did regain *feme sole* status. An Act for the relief of Susanna Teas, of Washington County, ch. CXXX, 1819 Md. Laws (Feb. 7, 1820). *See also* An Act for the relief of Catherine McKiernan, of Washington County, ch. LXXVIII, 1820 Md. Laws (Jan. 25, 1821).

28. SWISHER, *supra* note 16, at 53–81.

29. RENZULLI, *supra* note 11, at 305–316; BRUGGER, *supra* note 12, at 178–179, 196–197.

30. *See* Table 14 in Appendix 1.

31. *See* Tables 11 and 14 in Appendix 1.

32. *See* Table 14. In general, the Senate was much more likely to block passage of bills than was the House. Between 1782 and 1836, 73 bills passed one house but did not get through the other. Of these bills, 97 percent (71 of 73) passed only in the House of Delegates. But from 1837 to 1850, when elements in both houses began to urge adoption of a general divorce bill and recusal from the private act business, 55 bills passed only in one house. 73 percent (40 of 55) passed only the House of Delegates; the rest passed only the Senate.

33. The number of reported amendments was too low to create any statistically significant tables. But the general trends are worth reporting. Between 1816 and 1836, the journals reported 11 motions in the House of Delegates and 15 in the Senate. The House voted only once to change a total divorce bill to a partial one. Five other attempts to do so failed. Four motions to amend a partial divorce to a complete one passed; one such motion failed. In the Senate, 13 of the 15 motions

were to change a complete divorce to a partial one; seven of these motions passed. Only two tries were made to change a bill to a complete divorce; one passed and one failed. Putting the general sentiments of these results together, the House of Delegates made decisions favoring *a vinculo* divorces in nine of the eleven amendment cases. The Senate made decisions favoring *a mensa et thoro* divorces in eight of its fifteen cases. From 1837 to 1841, the outcomes in the two houses were in greater parity. The House and Senate both adopted amendments making bills complete divorces, with the House passing nine and the Senate eight. The House also reduced six bills to partial divorces; the Senate reduced five. For an example of Senate practices, *see supra* text accompanying notes 19–24 relating the saga of the Lewis divorce.

34. It is intriguing that even though Sarah Price was a pariah in her time, she retained dower rights in pre-divorce property. The reluctance to adopt retroactive property rules was relaxed only for a short period between 1826 and 1832. *See* the discussion in the next section of this chapter.

35. An Act to annul the Marriage of Joseph Price, and Sarah his Wife, ch. LIX, 1820 Md. Laws (Jan 18, 1821).

36. An act to divorce Thomas Knock and Margaret his wife, of Baltimore county, ch. 177, 1821 Md. Laws (Feb. 19, 1822).

37. *See* Table 13 in Appendix 1.

38. *See* Tables 3 and 5 in Appendix 1, showing that women petitioners obtained relief more often than men, and that partial divorce acts were more likely to follow wives' petitions than husbands'. *See also* Table 4 in Appendix 1, showing that property issues surfaced after 1815.

39. Roll call votes occurred in 16 percent (31 of 197) of all petition situations from 1805 to 1815, and in 7 percent (15 of 226) from 1816 to 1825. *See* Tables 10 and 11 in Appendix 1.

40. *See* Table 13 in Appendix 1.

41. *See* Table 3 in Appendix 1.

42. 1824 HOUSE JOURNAL at 117. In another case in the same session, the House refused to adopt even a partial divorce when Richard and Frances Hopkins had already agreed to live apart and signed a separation agreement. *Id.* at 43.

43. 1822 HOUSE JOURNAL at 47.

44. 1823 HOUSE JOURNAL at 41.

45. The House of Delegates also adopted a general divorce bill of unknown content in the 1824 session, though the delegates must have known the Senate would block it. This and later general divorce debates are discussed in Chapter 7.

46. Wallingsford v. Wallingsford, 10 Md. (6 H. & J.) 398 (1825).

47. 1824 HOUSE JOURNAL at 78.

48. *See* A. DOUGLAS, THE FEMINIZATION OF AMERICAN CULTURE (1977); M. RYAN, CRADLE OF THE MIDDLE CLASS: THE FAMILY IN ONEIDA COUNTY, NEW YORK, 1790–1865, at 83–98 (1981); N. COTT, THE BONDS OF WOMANHOOD: "WOMAN'S SPHERE" IN NEW ENGLAND, 1780–1835, at 126–159 (1977).

49. I have not found any literature on the family law beliefs of early nineteenth-century evangelicals. This is clearly an area needing further research.

50. *See* Table 3 in Appendix 1.

51. An antenuptial contract might have protected it. Otherwise, with the exception of a few personal items, the husband became the owner of any property brought to the marriage by the wife if he reduced it to his possession before the divorce. For more on these rules, *see* R. Chused, *Married Women's Property Law: 1800–1850*, 71 GEO. L. J. 1359 (1983).

52. *See* Tables 4 and 15 in Appendix 1. Table 15 reports that 69 percent of the acts resulting from petitions sought by wives in some way limited the rights of husbands in property of their wives, but not the rights of wives in property of their husbands. Only 20 percent of the acts sought by husbands contained analogous provisions. Remember that all divorces adopted in this decade were bed and board acts.

53. Between 1826 and 1836, 89 percent (81 of 91) of the partial divorces contained economic terms, while only 24 percent (24 of 102) of the complete divorces did.

54. This was true only if the private act preserved the obligation of husbands to pay for wives' debts. After 1826 it was routine for the legislature to excuse men of that obligation in partial divorces.

55. For a summary of these and other changes, *see* Chused, *supra* note 51, at 1404–1409. Maryland followed the same general patterns. *Id.* at 1368–1381.

56. This was the language used in the first bed and board divorces adopted in 1816. It continued to appear in basically the same form in many acts passed through the following decade.

57. An act for the relief of Elizabeth Harding, of the city of Baltimore, ch. 104, 1823 Md. Laws (Feb. 3, 1824).

58. An act to divorce Amelia Maddox and Samuel H. Maddox, her husband of the City of Baltimore, ch. 207, 1823 Md. Laws (Feb. 26, 1824).

59. *See* Table 15 in Appendix 1.

60. *Id.*

61. There is nothing firm in the extant legislative journals to confirm that marital fault motivated some of the legislative decisions about the economic terms of private acts. One possible example arose from Ann Merryman's 1821 petition for a divorce. It was met with a counter petition from her husband. 1821 HOUSE JOURNAL at 84, 118. This was a bit unusual; the vast bulk of cases did not involve petitions from both spouses. *See* Table 5 in Appendix 1. The bill divorcing Ann from William was reported to the House with a *feme sole* provision, but it was removed by amendment on the floor. 1821 HOUSE JOURNAL at 151. The act eventually adopted was a simple one-line statute divorcing the parties from bed and board. An Act for the relief of Ann Merryman of Baltimore, ch. 170, 1821 Md. Laws (Feb. 19, 1822). No reasons for this action are reported in the legislative journal, though the merits of William's opposition may have caused it.

62. *See* Table 15 in Appendix 1.

63. The story of Sarah and Charles Warfield, described in detail in the next chapter, exemplifies this possibility.

64. BILHARTZ, *supra* note 5, at 105–107. *See also* COTT, *supra* note 48, at 126–159, for materials on the religious and educational roles of women in the New England family.

65. Between 1816 and 1836, 22 percent of the legislative divorces contained a custody award. *See* Table 4 in Appendix 1. For material on the general development of child custody case law in the early nineteenth century, *see* Zainaldin, *supra* note 13.

66. Section 2 of An act to divorce Samuel Keplinger, of the city of Baltimore, from his wife Mary Keplinger, ch. 2, 1837 Md. Laws (Jan. 5, 1838), grants custody to Samuel. The journal reports on this act confirm that its passage was completely uneventful.

67. Two awards arose after husbands filed petitions, and two others when both spouses filed. In one custody case, the petitioner is not known; this case is not included in the figures in the text.

68. Virginia Polk v. William Williams, Chancery Court Chancery Papers, MdHR 17, 898-10309-1/4, S 512 (Baltimore City, 1837). The act divorcing Virginia Williams, nee Polk, from her husband Isaac Williams was silent on child custody. An act to divorce Virginia Williams, from her husband, Isaac Williams, ch. 239, 1834 Md. Laws (Mar. 18, 1835). Isaac, however, actually took care of their daughter. The child was born in 1824, the year before the Williamses separated. Isaac died shortly after the divorce was passed, and the child went to live with her paternal grandfather. In 1837, Virginia filed an action to obtain custody of her daughter, then 13 years old. The case was hotly disputed, with the grandfather alleging that his ex-daughter-in-law was plotting to kidnap her child. Virginia's daughter, the evidence suggested, did not wish to live with her mother, and the court refused to force her to do so. The daughter died shortly after the case was concluded.

69. *See* Zainaldin, *supra* note 13.

70. An act for the relief of Adelaide V. Lowe, of Frederick County, ch. 100, 1822 Md. Laws (Feb. 4, 1823). The first custody award was made only one year after an indirect Senate election was held.

71. Dielman-Hayward File, Md. Hist. Soc'y. Bradley attended the United States Military Academy and in 1814 began a military career as a third lieutenant. He resigned his military commission two days after marrying Adelaide Vincendi.

72. Another act passed during the 1824 session also precluded support claims against the husband by the custodial wife. An act for the relief of Benjamin Cromwell of Baltimore County, ch. 114, 1824 Md. Laws (Feb. 17, 1825). Overall, this was an unusual provision.

73. An act for the relief of Catharine Fridley, of Washington County, ch. 88, 1823 Md. Laws (Feb. 3, 1824); An act to divorce Amelia Maddox and Samuel H. Maddox, her husband of the City of Baltimore, ch. 207, 1823 Md. Laws (Feb. 26, 1824).

74. Twenty-five percent of the acts adopted between 1826 and 1836 had custody provisions. *See* Table 4 in Appendix 1. Only one of these custody awards went to a man. This high level of activity was not reflected in the debates on the floor of the General Assembly, at least as reported in the legislative journals. There were a number of amendments and votes on other questions, but only three custody amendments were reported. They all occurred between 1837 and 1841. Each amended a bill to award custody to a wife.

5. The State of Divorce Law in 1825: The Import of Sarah and Charles Warfield's Saga

Abundant details are known about the discord of only a few of the couples whose marriages came before the Maryland General Assembly. Comparing the tribulations of one unfortunate pair—Sarah and Charles Warfield—to the disharmony of other separated couples of the time adds detail and nuance to the contours of family law in 1825.[1] The stories of the Warfields and their peers verify that family law was a bit different in 1825 than in 1790. Charles Warfield's desire to rule his household like a small fiefdom was slightly out of phase with the historical moment. The scope of change, however, must be cautiously stated. Though wives were supposed to influence the domestic scene, patriarchy was still widely accepted. Divorce, while available in some cases, was unusual. For most couples marriage, for good or ill, was still a lifelong arrangement.

Sarah Goddard married Charles Warfield in Baltimore on January 29, 1811. Just over thirteen years later, Sarah's attorney filed a bill of alimony, with her brother John Goddard serving as her next friend. Shortly before the alimony bill was filed, Charles Warfield wrote Goddard a long, somewhat mysterious letter.[2] It is hard to know if it was the product of a sane or delusional mind. But whatever the exact state of Warfield's disposition, he was clearly a man who had absorbed some of his culture's traditional icons. Sprinkled through his letter were reverence for a nonevangelical Christ, justice for property owners, love through obedience to a patriarch, reluctance to divorce, hesitancy to hang dirty linen in public, and quiet compassion. In addition, divorce had become enough of a public issue that he felt a need to justify his actions to his friends and business associates.

At one level, the text was a simple plea for help by a despairing man wishing to rid himself of an unwanted, disobedient spouse. It exemplified the disappointed expectations for a marriage that fulfilled neither the developing romantic ideal of the early nineteenth century nor the traditional paternal model of earlier times. When read as the confused reflections of a husband disappointed in matters of both power and romance, the missive began innocently enough:

> It must be known, that at the time I married your sister, I was actuated by sentiments of compassion. Previous to our marriage, I observed to an acquaintance, I did not wish to be the means of rendering any person miserable; and, as I had rashly, as things turned out, entered into an engagement, and your sister insisted on a compliance, I would marry her. Since, there has been a succession of circumstances, calculated to render a mans life uncomfortable.
>
> My views in relation to this life—provide the means for a decent support, and live in an unassuming manner, in the discharge of the respective duties, looking for the hope, revealed in Christ.
>
> Some short time since, I thought it best for Mrs. W. and myself to divide our habitation, to lodge and eat separate; we seldom eat our meals in peace, and beside, there is other circumstances, in my judgment, that makes such a course an act of prudence. I did not contemplate extending the breach further; and hoped these means would be a corrective, that in a short time they might be dispensed with.

But, Warfield wrote, "[C]ircumstances that occurred . . . last evening, makes it necessary I should take another step." After laying out a detailed account of his prior day, he described a "distress," in terms making it clear he thought his wife had poisoned his food. He was "relieved by a discharge of my *supper* from my stomach, on the stair steps; otherwise, in a few minutes, I would have been in another world." And so, Warfield continued,

> I believe the proper course for me to pursue, for the present, is to eat at the Fountain Inn Tavern, where I am now just going to get my dinner. . . . Although Mrs. W. and myself, have never lived in that harmony that should mark a matrimonial relation; hitherto, I have not consented to the propriety of a separation, for example sake: now, I am decidely of the opinion, that an entire separation ought to take place. . . .
>
> You will perceive I write, as to a friend; you need not calculate on any modification of the above. Under these circumstances, it would be best for yourself and me to come to some amicable terms of settlement. I would be willing to give something, but not much; for me and my estate to be entirely freed from your sister. . . . It is far from my wish to injure your sister or your family; I purchased for her a great variety of flower pots and every thing else that ought to make any reasonable person contented.

.... Genuine love, never degenerates into servile obedience—Justice and Love, is the two great points, in matters moral and divine; those that believe this, have no grounds to persecute me. What is to be done, let it be done immediately, that things may be quiet. Unless we come to some terms immediately, I expect my dwelling will be closed, and I will take lodgings for your sister, for it is impossible for us to live together, and maintain the christian character.

But, as the last paragraph suggests, the letter was also filled with musings not easily attributable to the mind of a typical star-crossed husband living with a disobedient wife. It was published, along with a number of other documents, in a pamphlet Charles prepared just before he filed his answer.[3] Statements of persecution and paranoia were sprinkled through the pamphlet, including these in the letter to Goddard:

For a length of time, say about two years, I have been so teazed and tormented, that it has, literally, been the means of almost destroying my life. When I arise in the morning, it has been my first calculation to meet, during the day, those that are either seeking my Property, or subjugation to some religious party. Sometimes . . . linen sheets, old green carpets, etc. are hung out in full length at the windows of Mrs. C. and Mr. B.—dwelling houses; Hugh B—is exceedingly officious, as all weak men are, when there is a prospect of their being noticed; the black boy opposite, I have no doubt was employed to treat me with ridicule: the black man next door, shook a carpet in my *face*, apparently with design; when I have been walking the street, I have been insulted; I am watched and have been for a length of time on every side, and almost at all hours, as well when I go to the privy as when I go to my dwelling house. This is a mere hint at the afflictions I am called in the providence of God to sustain. . . .

I do not know that I have in my possession a single paper, that has not been examined; neither do I know of a place in my house, where I can with confidence place a single paper for twenty four hours, without having it examined. . . . In the neighbourhood, where I was born, every negro was allowed a box to himself; to have concerned therewith, it was regarded disgraceful. *My rights ought to be respected as much as a Negroes.*

The pamphlet contains other allusions to overblown paranoia and imprudent behavior. A memo of "SOME HINTS" printed in the pamphlet was a veritable catalog of people Warfield maintained knew something about his endless persecution. In its midst are the likes of:

Has not C. W. [Charles Warfield] been accused of insanity, and great exertions made to establish this point? Has not opportunities been looked after, to that end? Has C. Ws opposers, in any instance, been able to prove it? Is C. W. to be subjected to this sort of persecution?

A notation at the end of the letter to Goddard, written by Warfield later as commentary for the pamphlet, describes some of the consequences of his strange and imprudent behavior:

> Being frequently in custody, by the Sheriff, I deem it prudent to have these documents printed: for it seems to me, my opposers are disposed to lay hold of an opportunity, when my strength is exhausted by labours that devolve, to vex me. Therefore, they are printed, that I may be prepared to afford my friends some information, if need be; otherwise, I am not desirous to circulate any impressions that I may hold.

Warfield's jail time resulted from his failure to respond to Sarah's alimony bill. He did not file an answer (along with the newly printed pamphlet) until February 2, 1825, about a year after the case began. The court file contains notations that on November 19, 1824, and January 11, 1825, the sheriff was ordered to bring him in. His pamphlet is full of suggestions that he did not get along with his attorney. He claimed in his answer that he provided materials for the answer immediately after seeing his wife's alimony bill.[4] He also published in his pamphlet two letters to his lawyer complaining about the lack of service.[5] And his answer did not contain an attorney's signature; it may have been filed *pro se*.

In any case, it must have been a strange sight watching someone of Warfield's high economic status be dragged off to jail. At the time of their marriage, Sarah alleged in her bill, Charles was "a merchant and in comparatively humble circumstances, to his present condition." His "present condition" must have been quite comfortable, given the admission in Charles's answer that he was worth $10,000 at the time of his marriage. Though denied by Charles, Sarah alleged he was worth $150,000 when she filed for alimony. Charles said he was worth less than half that amount. In any event, this was a story of family disarray in the upper brackets of Baltimore society.

Sarah Warfield, of course, claimed in her bill of alimony that she was blameless. The conduct of Charles, she argued, was "wholly without cause or justification," since "she has in all things faithfully discharged her duty as a wife, and her reputation is without blemish or reproach." Charles, according to Sarah, was base and morose, forcing her to endure "abuse and violence, almost without the intermission of a day." She could ask for nothing for dinner save what was laid before her. Water was poured over her head at the table. After a time Charles sent her to the kitchen to eat her meals and frequently locked her up. Sometimes she escaped and managed to get food from her mother.

> [S]he has borne with these indignities and sufferings for a long while, from a faint hope that some change in his conduct would take place; and from that reluctance which every delicate mind must feel at the exposition of such circumstances to the world.

On December 30, 1823, about three weeks after he wrote to John Goddard seeking a settlement of his marital affairs, Charles sent Sarah a letter saying,

> [A] separation between yourself and me must take place. This note may be understood in the same *lites* and points of interest as though I had expelled you from my dwelling and board. You will have until the close of to morrow to remove from my dwelling house, after which time you will not be accommodated by me in my dwelling house with boarding.

After returning from church the following Sunday, Sarah found herself locked out of the house. She then moved in with relatives and lived without any support from her husband.

Charles, in the answer he filed on February 2, 1825, painted only a marginally different picture of his marriage. He admitted striking his wife shortly after their marriage when she called him a liar:

> C. W. does not justify his conduct in this, it was the effect of abhorrence, suddenly excited: otherwise, after much forbearance, he knows of no acts of violence by him, on his wife, unjustifiable.—In many instances, he has laid his hand on Mrs. W's mouth to stop her insulting language, and took her by the hand and led her out of the room; having no object in view, other than peace.

But he denied encouraging the servants to disobey and abuse his wife, claimed that Sarah unjustifiably accused him of having intercourse with the cook on the way to church, and repeated his allegation that she poisoned his dinner shortly before they separated. As a result, Charles admitted, he locked the doors between the back apartment and the main house during the last few days she was in the house, though she was always free to go out the front door.

Finally, religion played a part in Warfield's self-image as a persecuted man. Along with references to those seeking his property, Warfield complained in his answer that the "conspiracy, contemplating his ruin," joined by Mrs. Warfield, may have originated "about Religion." Later, in a letter to his attorney, he opined that "the advocates for Religion have been the principle cause of the difficulties." It is quite possible that Sarah Warfield, like many of her peers, was attracted to an evangelical movement. Warfield clearly did not like the newer, fervent forms of worship, writing in his letter to John Goddard that he preferred the Friends, and found an Episcopal church "too gay."

Despite all of this, Charles claimed in his answer that,

> [n]o intentions to separate were entertained until December 7, 1823. He threw several tumblers of water and cups of coffee in her face; and for a short time before their separation, did supply himself with a pitcher of water, when at his meals; he found it to be necessary; without, there was much bad feeling displayed.

On March 26, 1825, the court found the pamphlet Charles filed with his answer irrelevant and declined to pay it heed. The chancellor also required Charles to file another answer with more details about his financial condition. In the second answer, filed on July 12, Charles claimed that he did not know the value of his property, lived in a retired situation, and was willing, if required, to sell his effects for $50,000. Though interrogatories were filed late in 1825 by Charles, seeking additional information from Sarah, the case then languished.

The reason for the judicial inactivity is apparent in the legislative record. On January 31, 1826, Sarah and Charles jointly filed a petition for a divorce in the Senate.[6] That body passed it only four days later.[7] The bill then went to the House of Delegates, where it was defeated, reconsidered, and, on February 16, 1826, passed.[8] About a month later, the court ordered the alimony action dismissed, with costs assigned to Sarah.[9]

In spite of all the accusations of villainy by both sides and the paranoid ramblings of Charles, the parties managed to settle their dispute. The preamble to the Warfield divorce act noted that the parties "lived apart for nearly two years previous," and that they did on

> the twenty-fifth day of January, eighteen hundred and twenty-six, enter into articles of separation, whereby the said Charles did agree to settle a sufficient maintenance upon the said Sarah Warfield, during her life, and in consid-

eration thereof, she hath agreed to relinquish all her right and interest in his present or any future estate he may acquire, and the said Charles Warfield having in execution of the said articles, conveyed to John Goddard, in trust for the said Sarah, during her natural life, a certain house and lot on the south side of Baltimore street, in the city of Baltimore.

The rest of the act annulled the rights of each spouse in the property of the other, designated Sarah a *feme sole*, excused Charles from paying the future debts of Sarah, and divorced the parties from bed and board.

The settlement adds to the puzzling qualities of the case. Though much of Charles's behavior seemed bizarre or even crazy, he was obviously able to deal well enough with reality to end his marital travail. Indeed, he (or perhaps his attorney) was not above planning for the smooth handling of the divorce. In addition to the early attempts by Charles to settle the matter with John Goddard's intervention before the Alimony Bill was filed, he took other steps to ease the path to marital dissolution. The letter Charles wrote to Sarah on December 30, 1823, was artfully crafted. He took special care to notify Sarah that his actions could be understood "in the same lites and points of interest as though I had expelled you from my dwelling place and board," thereby establishing a ground for Sarah to use in claiming alimony and laying the foundation for a later divorce petition. Charles also admitted cruel behavior in his answer, all the while protesting his innocence to the larger public through his pamphlet. The settling of the case, therefore, was hardly startling. Rather it suggests the sort of allegations people thought it necessary to make in court and legislature in order to rid themselves of unwanted spouses and confirms that settlement of economic issues eased the path to passage of a private act. Even at this early date, divorce by "consent" of both parties was at times attainable.

Despite all the adroit admissions and concessions in the alimony pleadings, however, it is difficult to believe that the Warfield marriage was other than hellish. While law or lawyers surely had their impact on the contours of the case, the multitude and variety of spiteful behaviors recited by the Warfields must have had at least some basis in reality. The passing of thirteen years from the wedding until Sarah was locked out of the house suggests that the Warfields, and many of their peers, were loath to run the divorce gauntlet in even the grimmest of settings. Charles, in his peculiar fashion, said as much in his pamphlet. In addition, the reluctance of the House of Delegates to pass the Warfield divorce bill—passage coming only after a negative decision was reconsidered—symbolizes the depth of marital disaffection and cruelty required to obtain even a bed and board divorce jointly sought by both parties.

Many others in only marginally different circumstances failed in their quests for relief from marital discord. Susannah and John Orr married in the late 1700s and separated in 1796 because of John's allegedly cruel and inhuman treatment.[10] In an 1816 bill of alimony, Susannah claimed that shortly after separating from John while he was in prison, she inherited a farm from her brother. When John was released, he entered the farm and took possession of it by force, leaving her destitute. She tried to obtain a legislative divorce in 1802, but given the history of that era, there was not a chance of obtaining relief.

Rather than try again for a divorce, Susannah filed an alimony petition in 1816 seeking a portion of the rents and profits from the farm and an injunction against John's wasting the asset. John answered the alimony petition, charging that Susannah was living as the wife of his brother George Orr. He also said that he, rather than Susannah, owned the farm, but that papers supporting his position had been lost. The exact outcome of the case is not known, although an injunction against waste was in effect for at least the time it took the court to resolve the title dispute.

Susannah's failure to file another divorce petition in 1816, even though she was represented by counsel, conveys some feeling for the legislative divorce milieu. It is unlikely she could have obtained a divorce from the General Assembly. Even assuming that her once-imprisoned husband actually took possession of Susannah's farm, she may have been in an adulterous relationship with her husband's brother. That was hardly a situation likely to elicit sympathy from the likes of Roger Brooke Taney. Nor had the Orrs come to an agreement about how to resolve their economic disputes. Sarah Warfield may not have been an angel, but she was not an adulteress and had managed to come to an agreement with her estranged husband. Better to keep Susannah Orr chained to her felonious husband as a deterrent to aberrant sexual behavior than release her from her marital vows. And if John Orr's allegations of adultery were unfounded, legislative refusal to grant a divorce simply emphasizes the depth of marital discord required to alter marital obligations.

In sum, the idea that divorce was undergoing some reform in the early decades of the nineteenth century must be stated with great caution. Even disregarding the thousands of cases of marital unhappiness that must have littered the early nineteenth-century landscape, we see that many cases of *serious* marital discontent were unlikely to lead to a divorce of any sort. Only a tiny portion of couples divorced in that era. While a case like the Orrs' might have supported an alimony petition, that was likely to be the full extent of intervention by the legal system. Women in the "standard" situation—attempting to survive after a husband deserted or after separating from a husband who then took control of all family assets—could rarely hope to obtain legislative relief.

Alimony, of course, often was not a very helpful remedy. Even without a complete search of court files, many were found with "standard" allegations. Some contained allegations of behavior the legislature sometimes acted upon, such as adultery. Most of the time no evidence of a final result appears in the alimony files. When allegations suggested the husband had left the area, proof that the bill was served is almost always absent, suggesting that the process did little good. Even when service was accomplished, the best result available was typically the filing of a security bond, which presumably would be paid upon if the husband failed to produce some support for his wife. Even after a bond was secured, a husband could evade continuing economic obligations, other than loss of the cost of the bond, by simply leaving the jursidiction.

Some women did obtain alimony relief, either in the form of monetary payments or the posting of a bond providing funds when a husband failed to pay ordered alimony. Thus Alice Jones managed to get a very small *ne exeat* bond of $75.00 out of her seaman husband, but the only note about the status of the defendant was that he was in custody.[11] And Eleanor Harland, who charged her husband Thomas with converting all of the property she brought to the marriage into $2,000 in cash shortly after the wedding, going off to the West Indies, and kicking her out of the house upon his return, managed to get a court to order a *ne exeat* bond in the amount of only $666.66, exactly one-third of the value of her property. The traditional dower-thirds for women was apparently at work.[12]

In this environment, Penelope Butman, who filed both alimony and divorce petitions in 1818,[13] had virtually no chance of obtaining a divorce. She married Joseph in 1814 in Providence, Rhode Island. They came to Baltimore, where "through the idleness and worthlessness of the said Joseph [she] has been obliged to support both herself and him." Joseph, Penelope alleged, left her at Christmastime in 1817, returned later, and sold off their household goods to pay his debts even though he was working in Philadelphia. The court noted in the file that security in a writ of *ne exeat*[14] would be set at five hundred dollars if the defendant could be served. The legislature did not give her the time of day. Her petition was filed, but nothing more occurred.[15] Penelope Butman may have confronted a world in which the horrors of the Warfield marriage expressed the minimum amount of cruelty, barbarity, and ill usage typically required to obtain a divorce when proof of adultery was lacking. Though by 1825 the scope of dominion and control a typical husband was expected to exercise over his wife may have been ameliorated by conceptions of romance, partnership, and domesticity, divorce was still saved for unusual cases. Pamela Sampson's early nineteenth-century life with her drunken husband George was probably not very different from Sarah Warfield's water torture by Charles. Despite large ebbs and flows in Maryland's divorce policies between 1800 and 1825, marriage was a lifelong, but not always romantic, adventure.

Notes

1. The details described in this chapter come from Sarah Warfield v. Charles Warfield, Ch. Ct. Chancery Papers, MdHR 17, 898–12108, S 512–11926, 1/39/5/5 (Baltimore City, 1824), and An act to divorce Charles Warfield and Sarah his wife, of the City of Baltimore, ch. 186, Md. Laws (Feb. 16, 1826). Their history is particularly rich because Charles assembled a pamphlet with "Some general remarks, etc. for the perusal of Charles Warfields friends." The twenty-page booklet, which he filed in court, reprinted legal papers and letters. An edited transcription of the pamphlet may be found in Appendix 3.

2. The letter, dated Dec. 7, 1823, was the first item in the pamphlet, described in the prior note, put together by Charles Warfield.

3. *See supra* note 1.

4. This notation is in the answer near the end of p. 15 in the pamphlet.

5. These letters were dated July 5, 1824, and Oct. 13, 1824.

6. 1825 SENATE JOURNAL at 76. Filing in the Senate was very unusual. The vast bulk of petitions moved from the House of Delegates to the Senate.

7. *Id.* at 81.

8. 1825 HOUSE JOURNAL at 249, 253, 325.

9. The matter of costs is interesting. Their allocation was probably part of the settlement. But the major expenses of the litigation were not court fees but payments to attorneys. In a letter Charles wrote to his attorney on July 5, 1824, he enclosed $200, bringing his total expenditures up to that point to $460, "which is as much as I feel myself authorized to expend; except I obtain a divorce, then I would be willing to expend eight hundred dollars more, in the way of compensation and for expenses that might accrue." These numbers compare fairly closely with the fees paid in the Barnum case (discussed in Chapter 6) a few years later. There is no way to tell how many family law litigants and petitioners used lawyers. Although many alimony case files contained no indications that a lawyer was used, that does not definitively resolve the issue. Furthermore, the ability of members of the House of Delegates to file divorce petitions for their constituents may have reduced the need for formal legal representation.

10. The use of language like "cruel and inhuman" or "cruel and barbarous" was commonplace in alimony petitions.

11. Alice Jones v. Kinsey Jones, Baltimore County Court Chancery Papers, MdHR 40, 200–539, 2/15/11/55 (1824).

12. Eleanor Harland v. Thomas H. Harland, Baltimore County Ct. Chancery Papers, MdHR 40, 200–532, 2/15/11/55 (1824). At common law, a wife surviving her husband was entitled to dower—a one-third interest for life in all real estate owned by her husband at any time during the marriage. In the early nineteenth-century some states adopted statutes giving wives a right to one-third of all the property of their deceased husbands. This tradition of thirds was apparently followed in the *Harland* case.

13. Since I do not have a complete collection of alimony cases, I do not know how common it was to file simultaneously in both a judicial and legislative venue. Even from my incomplete search, however, I found a number of cases where women had at one time, though not necessarily at the same time, filed in both places.

14. A writ of *ne exeat* was originally used in the ecclesiastical courts to force husbands about to depart the jurisdiction to post bonds. Wives had to file an affidavit that their husbands were about to leave.

15. 1818 HOUSE JOURNAL at 61.

6. The Revival of *A Vinculo* Divorce and a Child Custody Twist, 1826–1836

Introduction

As in 1816, some noteworthy transitions in Maryland legislative divorce practice occurred in 1826 when a new Senate took office.[1] A reformist mood percolated through the Maryland General Assembly. *A vinculo* divorces reappeared and accounted for about half of the divorces passed in the following decade.[2] At the same time, the level of dispute in the legislature declined. The Senate blocked passage of House bills only half as often as in the prior decade.[3] The rate at which petitioners obtained divorces rose to its peak level of 47 percent, with more than half of both the female and Baltimore petitioners gaining relief.[4] Roll call votes and amendment proposals during debates on enacted bills materialized at about the same rate as during the 1816–1825 period.[5] But reformers dominated the polling,[6] approving acts and resolving amendment proposals in ways that tended to favor *a vinculo* divorces rather than inhibit their adoption.[7]

The revival of *a vinculo* divorce was received with particular pleasure by some who previously had obtained bed and board divorces. Ten persons partially divorced in earlier legislative sessions petitioned for and obtained complete divorces in this era. And before the history of private bill divorce was concluded, six other "double" divorces passed.[8] Mary Snowden managed to turn her 1824 bed and board divorce into a complete one at the 1826 session; she obtained custody of her children and the return of her maiden name to boot.[9] And John Yeamans, who in 1822 had obtained a bed and board divorce from his wife Sarah and annulled her ability to claim any interest in property he acquired after passage of the private act, procured a complete divorce.

Although the exact reasons for granting Mary Snowden a complete divorce are not known, the passage of this bill only two years after her bed and board act was a distinct signal of shifting family law preferences. Reappearance of *a vinculo* divorces represented a new look at old legislative standards. The message was heard by others. Thomas Knock, who during the Taney era had obtained only a bed and board divorce after his wife gave birth to a mulatto child,[10] returned during the 1829 session and gained passage of a simple one-line *a vinculo* act.[11] Thomas Ward, who unsuccessfully petitioned the legislature in 1817 before obtaining a partial divorce during the 1819 session,[12] returned three more times seeking a complete divorce. His first revisit to the legislature, in 1821, met with success in the House of Delegates, but like many other bills of that period, it failed in the Senate. Ward must have sensed the futility of further action for a time, for he did not return to the General Assembly again until 1830. His request for a complete divorce again passed only in the House of Delegates. Adoption of a simple one-line *a vinculo* act during the following session finally ended Ward's twelve-year quest for release from his marital vows.[13]

Shifts in treatment of property owned by divorcing couples also emerged after 1826. Typical property provisions in partial divorces changed so that the property rights of both spouses in the property of the other, rather than just the rights of husbands in the property of wives, were limited.[14] In addition, provisions plainly intended to have retroactive effect appeared in some acts. The former provisions may have reflected a growing reliance upon settlement agreements between divorcing men and women. As the Warfield divorce saga suggests, the General Assembly sometimes passed divorce acts shortly after the parties settled their familial differences. The appearance of retroactive provisions suggests a continuing use of property regimes to penalize particularly unsavory parties or gain control over assets left behind by deserting spouses.

Finally, child custody awards took on an interesting twist. As in the prior decade, a number of women obtained custody of their children. But, despite the reappearance of complete divorce, women in general, and women with children in particular, were much less likely than men to obtain passage of *a vinculo* acts. Among successful male petitioners, almost two-thirds obtained *a vinculo* divorces. Successful women petitioners obtained complete relief less than half of the time.[15] Though women were more likely than men to file divorce petitions,[16] and the General Assembly was more likely to grant a woman's petition,[17] acts with custody provisions for women usually bestowed only partial divorces.[18] Legislative reluctance to allow women with children to remarry might explain these data, but it is also possible that many women hesitated to seek complete divorces. A substantial proportion of all the bed and board acts were the result of petitions filed by women.[19] Absent special provisions in a private act, economically dependent women with children seeking *a vinculo* divorce lost the economic support of their ex-husbands and risked impoverishment if they could not find a new husband willing to marry into an instant family. It is also possible that settlement agreements provided for termination of maintenance payments upon creation of a new family. In either case, bed and board divorce might have been the only practical alternative. Though the exact cause of the divorce pattern is speculative, there is no doubt that quite decisive gender distinctions operated in the distribution of complete and partial divorces after 1826.

For the first time Maryland family law assumed the basic structure it was to retain for the rest of the nineteenth and much of the twentieth century. Though still operating as a legislative system, complete divorces were available for adultery and certain forms of cruelty. Property division took on new importance, and women became the presumed custodial parent. Settlement agreements and other "behind the scenes" tactics began to regularize the process, opening more space for consensual decrees and "polite" resolution of family disarray.

The Politics of Divorce

The reforms were not without political causes. Constituent pressures and cultural changes certainly explain some of the shifts in legislative activity. The number and proportion of petitioners from Baltimore, for example, continued to grow at a healthy pace.[20] In addition, the new policies were consistent with a range of changes beginning to occur in most areas of the country in the economic status and legal constraints imposed upon women. Married women were regarded not only as the producers and molders of future citizens of the republic, but also as victims of male desertion, intemperance, and violence. Widespread sympathy for westward expansion from all parts of the political spectrum may have made it easy for men to disappear into the frontier,[21] but it also produced sympathy for women widowed by harsh conditions in the West or left behind in settled territory. As a result, widows gained benefits from new statutes obliging their spouses to leave them a certain share of their estates; abandoned and deserted women got some relief through divorce reforms, statutes granting them *feme sole* status, and welfare reforms; poor women obtained a small degree of freedom by the repeal of statutes permitting their imprisonment for debt;[22] equitable separate estates became more widely used and recognized;[23] and women heading households secured the right to file claims for federal land grants.[24] Easier access to divorce, particularly for abandoned women, and greater attention to economic needs of wives and children were in harmony with such changes in the status of women. While the number of families in disarray may not have increased during the opening decades of the nineteenth century, divorce was emerging as an acceptable method for resolving some of the travail.

At the same time gender reforms were making dents in the array of marital property and family law rules, commercial development was encouraging removal of limitations on the alienability of property. The final demise of primogeniture after the Revolutionary War, conveyance reforms, the early nineteenth-century diminution in dower rights adopted in many areas,[25] and even the widespread use of *feme sole* status in private acts were all consistent with an increased desire for free alienability of property by many segments of the body politic. The General Assembly's greater use of complete divorce and property provisions in partial divorces undoing marital property constraints on *both* husbands and wives was also consistent with a wish for easy transfer of property. So was increased reliance on settlement agreements to resolve the economic difficulties of divorce. Passage of married women's property laws in the 1840s depended on their ability to attract support from both traditional commercial interests wedded to property transfer and reformers concerned with unfair constraints on the legal status of wives. That private divorce acts adopted in Maryland just before the married women's property act era contained similarly diverse attractions to delegates from quite different areas of the state should not be a surprise.[26]

The 1820s and 1830s also witnessed the demise of oligarchic forms of political control in many areas of the country. Election reforms, expansion of suffrage, disintegration of both the Federalist and Republican parties, and the rise of Jackson Democrats, anti-Jacksonians, and, by 1832, Whigs ushered in a new political era. Though Maryland's political parties and institutions did not neatly mirror all national trends, the sparks of change were certainly present. On a national level, James McPherson described the general contours of political debates between 1832 and 1849 as follows:

> Whigs [or anti-Jacksonians] were the party of modernization, Democrats the party of tradition. Whigs wanted to use the federal and state governments to promote economic growth through aid to internal improvements and the chartering of banks; Democrats tended to oppose such institutions of economic growth as banks and corporations, especially after 1840, because they feared that state-legislated economic privilege would threaten equal rights. Most advocates of temperance and public schools and black rights and prison

reform were Whigs; most opponents were Democrats. Most Whigs sub-
scribed to an entrepreneurial ethic that favored industrialization and urban
growth; many Democrats retained the Jeffersonian agrarian heritage of hostility or at least unease toward these things. Most Whigs welcomed the future; many Democrats feared it.[27]

At least through the early 1830s Maryland only partially fit this description. The political pattern of family law reform was particularly out
of sync with the idea that Whigs looked to the future and Democrats did
not. The state at large was dominated by anti-Jacksonians; Jackson Democrats dominated Baltimore.[28] Segments of both parties were interested in
reforms, at least electoral ones, in the late 1830s.[29] Jacksonians easily took
on the rhetoric of opposition to established aristocracy and old-line control of politics, even though aristocratic families continued to dominate
rural politics in the Eastern Shore and southern areas of Maryland.[30] Anti-
Jacksonians, particularly in Baltimore, strongly desired greater representation in the Maryland legislature.[31] While the rise of reform currents
around the country may have changed the contours of the debate in Maryland on temperance, prison reform, and women's rights, the underlying
coalitions in divorce votes did not change very much in this era. Divorce,
more than other areas of reform, led to the formation of alliances across
both demographic and political boundaries. Delegates from the rural
south, with its played out tobacco lands and large population of Catholics[32] and slaves, remained mostly opposed to divorces. Delegates from
other regions continued to vote for them.[33] At least on family law issues,
regional differences were more important than political divisions.[34] Divorce was an issue that could, in McPherson's language, appeal to those
from parties of tradition as well as modernization.

The explanation for the lack of distinct political allegiances on
questions about women and divorce may be based on three special features
of the political landscape in the 1830s and early 1840s. First, there were the
previously noted ways in which reform proposals about women and marriage attracted adherents from quite different backgrounds.[35] Arguments
about free transfer of property, fair treatment, male aristocracy, or deserted
women elicited empathy from a wide assortment of people. Aristocrats
may have had little sympathy for a poor woman left behind when her
husband disappeared to unknown areas of the frontier, but, in this new
era of unarranged marriages, they understood the plight of daughters who
married scoundrels and empathized with sons whose wives strayed from
the fold. The cross-cultural attractions of divorce had particular relevance

to a state like Maryland, where Eastern Shore aristocrats, still in control of the political reins in their counties as late as 1840,[36] could join forces with urban commercial interests and western frontiersmen in approving both married women's property reforms and private divorce bills.[37]

Second, although Jackson Democrats may have been the conservative anti-reform party by the late 1830s and 1840s, Andrew Jackson himself was twice caught in major disputes about women. During the 1828 election, he was pilloried by some for marrying his second wife before the divorce from his first wife was final.[38] If Democrats were politicians of tradition, then divorce, at least on the national level, was neither novel nor politically suicidal. And after he entered the White House, Jackson took great offense at anyone who challenged—and many did—the virtue of Peggy Eaton, the wife of one of his cabinet members. Indeed, the refusal of John C. Calhoun to include her on his guest lists contributed to his eventual split from Jackson, a man who demanded the utmost loyalty.[39] Calhoun's radical vision of state sovereignty riled Jackson, but his treatment of Eaton sorely tested Jackson's need to publicly respect contemporary visions of feminine virtue.

Both incidents made it easier for politicians to approve divorce. Jackson's "life style" justified the use of divorce for many. In addition, his second wife died shortly after he was elected. Even though Jackson was technically an adulterer and a bigamist, her death made it more difficult for those appalled by Jackson's behavior to publicly vilify the couple. His unstinting defense of Peggy Eaton's virtue also made it easier for one claiming to be unjustly accused of adultery to garner public sympathy. Both episodes suggest that divorce and sexual controversy did not automatically create great political risk during this era. If divorce carried stigma with it, Jackson probably reduced its impact by his own behavior. At a minimum, his conservative stance on other issues of the day reduced the electoral importance of his private life. And if a notion common to the mid-twentieth century—that divorced men were mildly flawed and divorced women were scandalous—was absent or politically unimportant, then Jackson's experience may have eased the pathway to divorce for many less well-known citizens.

Thus Maryland's legislators voted on divorce bills across party lines.[40] Although anti-Jacksonians and Whigs voted for general divorce bills at a slightly higher rate than Jacksonians and Democrats, that overall result mirrored only long-standing regional variations in Maryland.[41] Furthermore, Whigs voting in favor of quite narrow general divorce legislation tended to oppose many private divorce bills. Southern Whigs, for example, voted in favor of narrowly drawn general bills but opposed private divorce legislation. This inverted behavior further emphasizes the traditional, non-political contours of much of the family law debate in Maryland.

Finally, Maryland politicians were frequently of a different sort than those running the state at the turn of the nineteenth century. Though southern areas were still governed by the old oligarchy, other areas selected a much more diverse group of legislative representatives.[42] Those occupying higher positions of authority—governors and United States senators and representatives—were also from different social settings than those of their predecessors at the turn of the nineteenth century. Governors and congressmen were twice as likely to be lawyers. Fewer slaveholders served in high office, and they disappeared after 1836. The number of officials with relatives in public offices was lower, falling dramatically after 1836. Office-holders during this period were less likely to be from rural areas and more likely to be well educated.[43]

The Contours of Divorce

One special case of "double" divorce—the adoption of an *a vinculo* act benefiting a couple previously divorced from bed and board—entertained during the 1829 and 1832 sessions, reveals how the contours of divorce were enlarged after 1825. A divorce petition from David Barnum of the city of Baltimore was presented on February 1, 1830. Its consideration "created a great excitement in Baltimore."[44] This was a clash of titans.[45] David Barnum was an Episcopalian, anti-Jacksonian hotel proprietor who was one of the wealthiest men in Baltimore around 1830.[46] Sarah Barnum, the niece of Robert Gilmor, Jr., a wealthy merchant,[47] hired Roger Brooke Taney, Jonathan Meredith, and John Latrobe to represent her.[48] Latrobe alone received a fee of $900 for his work, a tidy sum for the time.[49] In his diary Latrobe reported:

> For motives that I never could understand the gentleman applied for the divorce on the grounds of the adultery of his wife, and the application was resisted with all the vehemence proper to a conviction of the utter falsity of the charge. . . . The lady was handsome; she had suffered grievous wrong; more than one beautiful woman appeared as a witness and there was a "concatenation" of circumstances that afforded a wide field for ingenious discussion on both sides.[50]

The lawyers pulled levers never used before in the General Assembly. The Barnum divorce progressed in a unique way. On the day David Barnum's petition was filed, the House debated and approved a rarely made motion authorizing the Committee on Divorces to "examine such witnesses as may be produced by either of the parties."[51] Adoption of this motion not only confirmed the unusual quality of the Barnum episode, but also emphasized the informality of the standard legislative divorce process. The next day each party was ordered to bear the expense of the witnesses whose attendance they required.[52]

About three weeks after the divorce petition was read in the House, an attempt to force the Committee on Divorces to file its report failed.[53] A few days later, on February 25, a report was filed recommending against the passage of a divorce.[54] Almost immediately two attempts were made to withdraw the report and return the case to the Committee.[55] When those attempts failed, a minority report was filed.[56] This was unheard of in divorce cases. On February 26, the House read and approved a report replacing the Committee's report. This new version read:

> The Committee on Divorces to which was referred the petition of David S. Barnum, praying a divorce from his wife Sarah Barnum, have had the same under consideration, and beg leave to report, that after a long and tedious consideration of the subject, they do not find the allegations of the petition supported by the facts, and therefore ask that the petitioner have leave to withdraw his petition.[57]

An attempt to amend this report so that nothing appeared in the record "to impeach the character or credibility of any of the witnesses who have testified in the case" failed. Apparently the House, or at least a large portion of it, believed that David Barnum or some of his witnesses had lied.[58] The General Assembly came to the defense of Sarah Barnum, much as Andrew Jackson was then defending Peggy Eaton from similar allegations of marital misbehavior.

The same day that the substitute report denying David a divorce was approved, Sarah Barnum filed a petition of her own for a bed and board divorce.[59] Perhaps the form of her request—for a partial divorce—was controlled by the preferences of one of her attorneys, Roger Taney. A select committee was appointed to report a bill, which was done the same day. Things must have been moving too quickly for David. His lawyers, Charles T. Flusser, James W. McCulloh, and John V. L. McMahon, filed an application the next day asking for "the grant of those rights and privileges to which every party charged is of right entitled, and desiring to be furnished with a copy of her petition against him; and to be allowed a reasonable time to procure the testimony, which he could procure, to repel the allegations of the petition."[60] The application was tabled. Later the same day, the rules were suspended in a 51 to 16 roll call vote, and the bill filed on Sarah's behalf was taken up for consideration.[61]

During the debate leading to passage of the bill, the preamble was amended with the addition of the following language:

> Whereas, it is manifest, from the charges made against Sarah Barnum by her husband David S. Barnum, in his late petition for a divorce; and, from the facts proved by the witnesses examined in relation to the said charges, that the said parties can never live together in harmony and peace; and that the said Sarah Barnum, by being placed under the farther control of her said husband, might be exposed to the continual apprehension of ill usage: Therefore, [rest of bill]. . . .[62]

This highly unusual language confirmed that the House relieved Sarah from any further obligation to live with David because he concocted false charges of adultery against her. The Senate passed the bill the same day as the House after refusing on a voice vote to remove the preamble from the bill.[63] The act also contained provisions retroactively limiting the rights of both spouses in the property of the other, a fitting end to a marriage in which both probably brought significant assets to the relationship.

The denouement came three years later when Sarah Gilmor, lately Sarah Barnum, petitioned for and obtained passage of a "double" *a vinculo* divorce from David Barnum.[64] Passage of this act was blessedly uneventful.[65] It is not known if Taney had anything to do with this second legislative effort. But assuming that nothing major happened between the 1829 and 1832 sessions, the second divorce was granted for the "ill usage" occasioned by the untruthful allegations of David Barnum. This family of titans, or at least Sarah's side of it, may have been treated more generously than average divorce petitioners. Nonetheless, the Barnum case discloses that some of the harsh limits on divorce of the Warfield era[66] were dissipating or changing. Cruelty or ill usage was enlarged to include damage to a woman's virtue and reputation as a ground for divorce, at least among the upper class. As Sarah Gilmor's uncle, Robert Gilmor, Jr., noted in a letter accompanying payment of John Latrobe's legal fee,

> I send you enclosed a check for 800 D. designed to compensate you in some degree for professional services on the late occasion at Annapolis.
> But there still remains a debt due from her and all the members of our

family for the friendly interest you took in her case, and the real zeal and exertion used to vindicate her fair name, and release her from the unhappy thraldom in which she was bound.[67]

The Contours of Marital Property Rules

Two other "double" divorces reveal that the General Assembly altered more than divorce grounds after 1826. In 1828 Leah Hubbell gained passage of a complete divorce, though she had been partially divorced in an earlier session.[68] In the act, the General Assembly provided that

> Leah Hubbell, or her legal representative had the right to ask, claim and receive, from the said Josiah Hubbell all of the property which she possessed before her intermarriage with him, and that came to his hands, which he may not have returned, or the value thereof, if the same cannot be specifically delivered.[69]

Adelaide Lowe, divorced from bed and board in 1822, obtained similar relief in the *a vinculo* act she obtained in the 1830 session.[70] Since marital property rules typically gave a husband total ownership of the personal property and, immediately upon its acquisition, management rights over the real property of his wife, such provisions effectively annulled prior wealth transfers.

Retroactive provisions like those in the Hubbell and Lowe acts were not unusual for this time period. Between 1826 and 1832, the standard *a vinculo* act contained no property provisions, but the typical bed and board legislation contained provisions restricting the rights of both spouses in the property of the other[71] and annulling the obligation of husbands to pay the debts of wives. About half of the mutually restrictive property provisions contained language precluding the rights of either spouse in the property of the other, "whether acquired in any manner whatever, before or after the passage of this act."[72]

Since most of the property restrictions affected both spouses, the legislature probably was trying to clear away some or all of the economic underbrush of failed marriages. But the retroactive provisions, if effective, had the result of obliterating dower—the right of a wife to receive upon the death of her husband a life estate in one-third of all real property held by the husband at any time during the marriage—while nonretroactive provisions left such rights intact for property acquired before the divorce.[73]

The shift to retroactive provisions therefore had mixed effects on women. In cases in which women brought property to their marriages, retroactivity benefited them by releasing the assets from marital property rules.[74] In cases in which a major asset was land owned by the husband, retroactivity destroyed all dower rights and thereby limited the wealth of women after divorce.

Retroactive property provisions also gave the legislature a new weapon to use if they wished to punish a spouse for particularly egregious behavior. Since divorce itself was fault-based, there was often no need to use property incentives to control behavior. George Carey discovered that during the 1832 session, when his petition was met with a counter-petition from "many responsible persons residing" in his neighborhood. The Senate divorce committee reported that

> [t]he conduct of the said George towards his wife . . . has been highly flagitious, and is stated to have been the original cause of the disturbance of their connubial harmony. However abandoned and profligate his wife appears to be, your committee are of opinion that the conduct of the said George attributed to him in the counter petition, ought to prevent him from obtaining the relief sought for, and therefore recommend the rejection of said bill.[75]

Carey's petition, granted by the House,[76] failed in the Senate. Despite the easy use of fault to screen the divorce petitions, the Hubbell and Lowe "double" divorces may have been cases in which property provisions took on deterrent roles. As in the period 1816–1825, behavior norms may also have played a part in the passage of some partial acts that limited only the rights of husbands in property of their wives, and other acts that contained no property provisions.[77] Thus, these provisions may have precluded husbands who deserted their wives from returning later and claiming their marital rights in property brought to the marriage by the abandoned wife.

The stimulants causing the appearance of expressly retroactive terms in divorce acts are obscure. The provisions certainly echoed Jacksonian antipathy toward aristocracy. The General Assembly, with fewer rural landowners and slaveholders in its ranks,[78] apparently found it easier to completely disentangle the economic lives of divorcing spouses. The last of the old Federalist and Republican guard were cleared out of the Senate by 1826. It is also possible that not much thought was given to the issue, since retroactive provisions did not disappear until after the publication of a couple of judicial opinions paying lavish attention to the scope of marital property rights.

Expressly retroactive language disappeared from the acts after 1832. In that session, the Senate committee, reporting on a House-passed bill granting the petition of Sarah Block for a divorce from her husband Arthur, observed that "soon after [the marriage] the husband disposed of all the personal property acquired by the wife, and immediately left her." In addition, Sarah was living in a house provided by her parents. She, like Leah Hubbell and Adelaide Lowe, wanted protection from Arthur's disposal of this asset.[79] The House bill contained a provision retroactively abolishing the rights of Arthur in the property of Sarah. The Senate committee reported:

> The object of such legislation is to deprive Arthur M. Block of all title to property, that the laws may have vested in him by marriage. It is believed that the title which Arthur M. Block prior to the passage of the proposed act, may have acquired in the wife's property by marriage is vested, and the right thereto is as clearly defined, as property which he may have obtained by his own industry; security to such sort of property it is to be presumed would be conceded to him in common with other citizens of the state, and which he could not be deprived of but by the judgment of his peers, or the law of the land. On the other hand, if the rights of Arthur M. Block, now proposed to be transferred to his wife, is designed as alimony or maintenance apportioned for the injury done by the husband, neglecting or refusing to make an allowance for the wife's support, it is believed that such a measure would be deemed an exertion of judicial authority, and if so, the act would necessarily be void as the bill of rights declares, "That the legislative, executive and judicial powers of the government ought to be forever separate and distinct from each other."[80]

The committee recommended, and the Senate adopted, an amendment so the bill mutually restricted the property of both spouses in a nonretroactive fashion. In the circumstances of the case, that did Sarah precious little good. And express retroactivity then disappeared from the legislative agenda.

The 1832 debate in the Block case may have been stimulated by several court decisions. The first, rendered in 1829, was the only reported opinion on the scope of legislative authority to adopt private legislative divorces. The second case was an unreported trial level dispute over the validity of a retroactive property clause in an 1830 private bill. And the last, decided in 1830, produced an exhaustive judicial exposition of marital property rules.

An unusual bed and board divorce enacted during the 1823 session provided that during the joint lives of Casparus and Mary Meginnis, Casparus was to pay to John Crane, as trustee for Mary, three hundred dollars per year for her use and benefit. The trustee was given authority to sue for the funds. In addition, the legislature stated, "it shall be the duty of the court before which the suit is brought to try the same at the term to which the bill is made returnable."[81]

When Casparus Meginnis failed to make payment, Crane filed suit. The case wound its way to the Maryland Court of Appeals, which in 1829 invalidated the payment provision of the private act.[82] The court decided that the legislature had actually enacted an alimony provision, and that this enactment unconstitutionally intruded on the exercise of judicial power previously granted the courts by the 1777 alimony statute. That part of the Senate report in the Block case reminding legislators of their limited role in the alimony arena strongly echoed the language of the *Meginnis* court.[83]

The second case, *Reeder v. Reeder*,[84] was an 1831 alimony case in Saint Marys County. Susannah and James Reeder married in 1809. Susannah petitioned for and obtained a bed and board divorce from the General Assembly at its 1830 session.[85] The act contained a "standard" retroactive property clause severing the ties each spouse held to the property of the other, "whether acquired in any manner whatever before or after the passage of this act." Shortly after obtaining the divorce, Susannah filed a court action seeking alimony and an injunction barring James from interfering in her right to inherit from her father's estate. The Reeders apparently separated in 1812. Before the separation, James Reeder agreed to give up any interest he had in the estate of Susannah's father. When the father died some years later, however, James obtained a judgment against the estate for $5,000, presumably the value of James's marital rights in the property willed to Susannah. Confessing that it was unusual to grant an injunction against the enforcement of a judgment, the court still gave Susannah the relief she sought. During the following legislative session, the General Assembly, perhaps responding to *Reeder* by insuring that like results did not recur, declined to adopt any retroactive property provisions.

Finally, *Helms v. Franciscus* [86] arose in an enormously complex setting. Suffice it to say that when Anna Wandelohr married Lewis Helms in 1819, she was said to have attached herself to a scoundrel interested only in her wealth. After much ado, including the jailing of Lewis for failure to pay debts owed to relatives of Anna, they signed a separation agreement. This agreement was the subject of the case. In his opinion, Judge Bland detailed an array of common law and equitable rules of marital property, noting that the separation agreement was unenforceable because married partners could not contract between themselves, and that equity ameliorated the harsh common law marital property rules by enforcing the married woman's separate estate, requiring husbands to provide an equitable settlement if wives used their dower or separate property to pay marital debts and enforcing agreements of husbands to provide a separate maintenance in the event the parties separated. Unfortunately, Bland noted, the Helms contract was not enforceable as a separate maintenance agreement, because it took the form of a detailed property settlement and Lewis had no property of his own out of which such a maintenance could be paid. Finally, treating the case as one for alimony, Bland found no basis for its payment since there was no evidence of adultery or physical cruelty.[87]

The court, obviously looking for a way to assist a reputable woman against a nefarious moneygrubber, decided that it should protect a woman "under some peculiar circumstances" from the "sinister views and objects of the husband in marrying his wife."[88] Even though a separate maintenance award was not possible, the court did find it appropriate to protect a woman's property in such circumstances. In addition, a wife's inability to sign a contract with her husband did not bar the husband from waiving or releasing any rights he had in property of the wife. As a practical matter, therefore, the court enforced the separation agreement by treating it as an express waiver by Lewis Helms.

The important part of this opinion for our purposes is its exhaustive rehearsal of the rights of husbands in the property of wives and the stated reluctance to diminish those rights absent the strongest of equitable concerns. We cannot be sure the opinion was read widely, but it is likely that some legislators at the 1832 session were both aware of *Helms* and willing to insist upon adherence to traditional common law and equitable practice. The proportion of lawyers in the legislature began to rise after 1830.[89] And the slow development of an American family law treatise tradition was having an impact on the contours of the legal world.[90] Like Kent, in his traditionalist *Commentaries on American Law*, Maryland's judges were issuing opinions more conservative than the reformist predilections of the General Assembly. The courts placed limits on the legislature's ability to modify vested property interests in private divorce acts.

Reluctance to allow tinkering with "vested" property rights was much more likely to injure women than men. An estate by the curtesy, the common law right of a husband to manage and take the profits from the real property of his wife, was deemed to be a vested, possessory estate. While it could be altered or abolished prospectively, estates in force prior to adoption of any new legislation could not be changed. The right of a wife surviving a husband to take a one-third interest for her life in any real property owned by her husband during their marriage was given the more ephemeral name of the inchoate right of dower. Dower, which gave wives no day-to-day management authority over the property of their living husbands, was not thought to be a vested, possessory estate until after a husband died. It was therefore subject to legislative modification without fear of judicial oversight. These rules meant that a wife's marital property rights were secure from legislative modification only after her husband died, while a husband obtained immunity from legislative change of his marital property rights immediately upon marrying a woman owning property or upon receipt by his wife of any property by way of purchase, gift or inheritance.[91]

Judge Bland's opinion in *Helms* is also a forceful reminder of the ability of both courts and legislators to construct flexible remedies when they found it necessary. Indeed, Bland may have been well known for such behavior. Despite his statements in *Helms* that, absent adultery, alimony required proof of physical cruelty, it is likely that he did not always impose such limits on judicial relief.

Hewitt v. Hewitt was a fairly standard alimony case in its reported version.[92] On October 7, 1825, Martha Hewitt sought an allowance from Eli Hewitt on the grounds that he treated her with great cruelty and violence, refused to let her live with him, and declined to provide any adequate maintenance for her even though he had a large real and personal estate as specified in a schedule attached to the bill. The defendant, it was said, admitted the facts alleged. On October 10, the court ordered Eli Hewitt to pay Martha Hewitt $350 per year in two equal payments per year, one on April 10 and the other on October 10. The following year, Martha Hewitt filed a new petition alleging nonpayment. On May 15, 1826, the court ordered service on the defendant and enforced payment when it was not voluntarily forthcoming. "The payment of other installments of the alimony was enforced in like manner; after which the case was terminated by the death of the defendant."[93]

The Chancery Court Records at the Maryland Hall of Records tell a somewhat different story.[94] It turns out that Eli Hewitt had been declared a lunatic. His trustee was given the authority to admit the facts of Martha Hewitt's petition and pay her a just and equitable maintenance from the lunatic's estate. The records confirm that a petition and answer with admissions were filed, along with a list of his property. They also indicate that difficulties in the marriage were present only in the last few years, and that the parties were both in their sixties. The property was valued at $4,175, and included houses, lots, a farm of 350 acres, 25 slaves, and other property. There then follow a series of enforcement orders, the last one dated in May 1827. The file also contains a rambling, incoherent six-page statement from Eli Hewitt filed in November 1826.

The *Hewitt* case is fascinating. It verifies that the alimony process was used to provide for the wife of a lunatic who was so uncontrollable that all admitted she should not be forced to live with and care for him. This is not exactly the sort of cruelty one would expect as a basis for an alimony petition. The courts, like the General Assembly, were moving to broaden the realms in which spouses could obtain relief against their mates. The admission of the allegations by a trustee and the speed with which the entire process was initially handled also show that it was a cooperative venture by Martha Hewitt, the trustee, and the court to get her support from a fairly well-to-do man gone bonkers. Even in the 1820s the domestic relations process was subject to manipulation to serve purposes not thought of when the rules were established.

Children and Divorce

Shifts in the handling of divorce and property arguably were minor compared to changes in the treatment of children. The frequency of custody provisions reached its peak between 1826 and 1836.[95] A quarter of all acts and more than two-fifths of the partial divorces adopted in that decade contained provisions about children. Compared to the late eighteenth century, when legislatures adopting divorces paid attention to children only if they were mulattoes eligible for sale into servitude, when husbands had the right to the labor and wages of their offspring, and when women seeking divorce faced the prospect of separation from their progeny, this was a sea change of major proportions. Within only a few decades, legal institutions changed presumptions so that children of divorcing parents should live with mothers rather than fathers. Indeed, the structure of legislative divorce policy between 1826 and 1836 linked mothers and children together in remarkably strong ways. The general use of bed and board divorce for women petitioners prevented the introduction of stepfathers into many of the divorcée-headed households. The custody arrangements were firm reminders that mid-nineteenth-century mothers were becoming inextricably bound to their children.

That same notion may also have caused the appearance of another curious phenomenon. In 1826 name-change clauses suddenly appeared in many divorce acts. About 20 percent of the acts adopted between 1826 and 1836 in response to wives' legislative petitions allowed women to use their maiden names after divorcing.[96] It is possible that the name changes simply codified a long-standing tradition. Cornelia Dayton found indications of informal name changes after eighteenth-century divorces in Connecticut.[97] The practice also may reflect something as noncontroversial as insuring that wives could no longer rely on the credit of their ex-husbands. But amid a culture increasingly devoted to images of family, romance, and virtue, the name-change provisions might represent quite complex cultural instincts. They may have denoted both the vitality of a newly independent family unit and the failure of wives to mold their prior families into cohesive, emotionally secure social units; acknowledged both the social status of women emotionally or physically deserted by men and the legitimacy of male unions with different women; affirmed the connections of children to mothers and freed fathers from social responsibility for their offspring; and confirmed both the right of divorced women to obtain credit and hold property in their own names[98] and the ability of divorced men to repudiate their prior support obligations. For some divorcing women, use of their original names may have placed a stamp of legitimacy on new social roles; for others it may only have emphasized their failures and loss of marital security. It is interesting to note that the name-change provisions appeared in the same era in which women who made radical statements, such as Fanny Wright and the Grimké sisters, declared their freedom and public status by speaking publicly in mixed audiences about slavery, and women, particularly Quakers, began using the podium in religious settings.[99] While those in the General Assembly were certainly not making radical statements by including name-change provisions in divorce acts, there is a peculiar consistency between radical claims for recognition and the use of name-change provisions to relabel the status of "new" families sanctioned by the adoption of legislative divorces.

Notes

1. This Senate had three holdover members.
2. *See* Table 1 in Appendix 1.
3. *See* Tables 11 and 14 in Appendix 1. Table 11 shows that the House of Delegates and the Senate disagreed 25 percent of the time between 1816 and 1825, but only 13 percent of the time in the following decade. Table 14 shows that 15 percent of all divorce petitions led to the passage of bills by the House but not the Senate during the 1816–1825 period, while only 7 percent met the same fate in the following 10 years.
4. *See* Tables 2 and 3 in Appendix 1.
5. *See* Table 10 in Appendix 1.
6. *See* Table 13 in Appendix 1, for general voting patterns. Votes in favor of divorces continued at almost as high a rate as in the prior decade, despite the reappearance of *a vinculo* divorce.
7. In the House of Delegates, there were seven amendment proposals. Four amended partial bills to complete divorces. Two others were failed attempts to amend complete divorces to partial ones. Only one try to amend a bill to *a vinculo* failed. Thus, six of the seven amendment debates favored complete divorces. In the Senate, seven of the nine outcomes of amendment efforts favored total divorces. Two amendments to bed and board passed, but six failed. And one amendment to a complete divorce was adopted. *Contrast* the outcomes in the prior decade described in Chapter 4. *Contrast also* the enormous number of amendments proposed between 1837 and 1841, when debates over the use of partial divorces peaked. *See* Tables 10 and 11 in Appendix 1.
8. About 6 percent (16 of 289) of all complete divorces passed in Maryland after 1826 were "doubles."
9. An Act for the relief of Mary Snowden, of Cecil County, ch. LXXXIII, 1826 Md. Laws (Feb. 13, 1827) supplanted An act to divorce Mary Snowden, and her husband, John Snowden, of Cecil County, ch. 106, 1824 Md. Laws (Feb. 14, 1825).
10. This act is discussed in Chapter 4.
11. A supplement to the act entitled, an act to divorce Thomas Knock and Margaret his wife, of Baltimore county; passed at December session, eighteen hundred and twenty-one; chapter one hundred and seventy-seven, ch. 175, 1829 Md. Laws (Feb. 22, 1830).
12. Act to Divorce Thomas F. Ward and Ann Ward from Bed and Board, ch. LXXIX, 1819 Md. Laws (Jan. 29, 1820).
13. An act for the relief of Thomas F. Ward, of Saint Mary's County, ch. 278, 1831 Md. Laws (Mar. 13, 1832). Several couples who were divorced from bed and

board after 1826 also returned to the legislature and obtained additional relief. It is possible they did not expect to be able to get complete divorces when they first filed. But it seems more likely, given the divorces granted to Mary Snowden and others, that their personal circumstances changed. Perhaps a desire to remarry stimulated their return to the General Assembly.

14. *See* Table 15 in Appendix 1.

15. *See* Table 5 in Appendix 1. Of the enacted divorces petitioned for by men, 88 percent (35 of 40) were complete divorces, but only 40 percent (51 of 128) of those generated by women were *a vinculo*. These numbers are derived by taking the number of successful petitioners gaining complete divorces from the top half of Table 5 and dividing those numbers by the total of successful petitioners for both kinds of divorces. Thus, for example, the women's number for complete divorce, 51, is divided by the women's total for complete *and* partial divorces (51 + 61 = 128) to arrive at approximately 40 percent.

The data in Table 5 also show that the tendency for women to dominate partial divorces continued through 1841, when the last partial divorce was adopted by the General Assembly. For the entire study period more than three-quarters of the bed and board divorces were requested by women, but just more then half of the complete divorces had women as petitioners.

16. *See* Tables 5 and 8 in Appendix 1. It is important to remember that women could only sue for alimony if they divorced from bed and board. Once a complete divorce was passed, the alimony jurisdiction in the courts disappeared.

17. *See* Table 3 in Appendix 1.

18. In 43 percent (33 of 77) of the bed and board divorces granted to women between 1826 and 1836, the mothers obtained custody of their children. But only 24 percent (12 of 51) of the complete divorces obtained by women in the same decade contained custody awards to wives.

19. *See* Table 5. It is possible that these women sought *a vinculo* acts, but obtained only bed and board relief from the General Assembly. But the enormous gender differences in the petition source for enacted partial bills strongly suggest that some women preferred bed and board acts.

20. *See* Tables 6 and 7 in Appendix 1. Table 7 shows that the proportion of petitioners from Baltimore rose to 38 percent during the 1826–1836 time period.

21. R. H. WIEBE, THE OPENING OF AMERICAN SOCIETY 140–141 (1984).

22. Maryland banned the imprisonment of women for debt in the 1824 session. An act to abolish imprisonment of Females for Debt, ch. 206, 1824 Md. Laws (Feb. 26, 1825).

23. R. Chused, *Married Women's Property Law: 1800–1850,* 71 GEO. L. J. 1359, 1365–1381 (1983).

24. *Id.* at 1404–1409; R. Chused, *The Oregon Donation Act of 1850 and Nineteenth Century Federal Married Women's Property Law,* 2 LAW & HIST. REV. 44, 47–53 (1984).

25. Chused, *supra* note 23, at 1389–1397. On dower issues, see M. SALMON, WOMEN AND THE LAWS OF PROPERTY IN EARLY AMERICA 141–184 (1988).

26. A similarly diverse attraction to marital property reform was present in

the handling of both federal land grants in the far Northwest and the Oregon married women's property acts. Chused, *The Oregon Donation Act, supra* note 24, at 44, 55–56, 69–78.

27. J. M. MCPHERSON, ORDEAL BY FIRE: THE CIVIL WAR AND RECONSTRUCTION 21 (1982).

28. W. H. RIDGWAY, COMMUNITY LEADERSHIP IN MARYLAND, 1790–1840: A COMPARATIVE ANALYSIS OF POWER IN SOCIETY 104 (1979). In the 1824, 1828, and 1832 presidential elections, Maryland electoral votes were split between Jackson and the anti-Jacksonians. The Whigs carried the state in the next four elections. CONGRESSIONAL QUARTERLY, GUIDE TO ELECTIONS 225–229 (1975). Elections for members of the United States House of Representatives led to split delegations through much of the period. The Whigs got a clean sweep in the 1843 elections, but a split delegation reappeared at the next election in 1845. *Id.* at 553–581.

29. W. W. SMITH, THE WHIG PARTY IN MARYLAND, 1826–1856, at 132–143 (Thesis U. Md. 1967).

30. Ridgway, *supra* note 28, at 134–158.

31. *Id.* at 113–114.

32. McPherson pictures Catholics as generally anti-reform in this era. MCPHERSON, *supra* note 27, at 19–20.

33. *See* Table 13 in Appendix 1.

34. *See* Table 16 in Appendix 1. For those cells in Table 16 with large enough sample sizes, party affiliation made virtually no difference in the roll call votes on divorce bills. Regional variations subsumed party groupings. Thus the Whigs, who fared well electorally in both the Eastern Shore and the South, split dramatically along regional lines on divorce bill votes, with those from the Eastern Shore voting in favor of divorce bills 63 percent of the time, while those from the South were in favor only 38 percent of the time.

35. *See supra* text accompanying note 26.

36. RIDGWAY, *supra* note 28, at 134–135. W. H. WILLIAMS, THE GARDEN OF AMERICAN METHODISM: THE DELMARVA PENINSULA, 1769–1820, at 170–180 (1984), also noted the continuing conservative and isolated political traditions of the Eastern Shore through the nineteenth century.

37. *See* Table 15 in Appendix 1.

38. J. MAYFIELD, THE NEW NATION 1800–1845, at 104–105 (1961).

39. *Id.* Peggy Eaton, the much younger wife of John Eaton, Jackson's Secretary of War, was the notorious daughter of a tavernkeeper. Jackson viewed her as the victim of slanders from the upper class. *See* L. F. KOHL, THE POLITICS OF INDIVIDUALISM: PARTIES AND THE AMERICAN CHARACTER IN THE JACKSONIAN ERA 42–43 (1989).

40. Divorce was not the only issue upon which opinion crossed party lines in this era. Electoral and governmental reform proposals, generally designed to reduce the power of the counties with small populations, also caused disagreement along regional lines. Between 1833 and 1836, representatives from the South and Eastern Shore, whether Democrat or Whig, tended to vote against proposals to

redistrict the House of Delegates or to elect the Senate directly. W. W. SMITH, ANTI-JACKSONIAN POLITICS ALONG THE CHESAPEAKE 118–119 (1989).

41. *See* Table 16 in Appendix 1.

42. RIDGWAY, *supra* note 28, at 134–158.

43. R. E. LEIPHEIMER, MARYLAND POLITICAL LEADERSHIP, 1789–1860, at 18, 36, 62, 84, 103, 104 (1969) (Thesis U. Md.).

44. J. E. SEMMES, JOHN H. B. LATROBE AND HIS TIME 1803–1891, at 208 (1917).

45. This phrase is borrowed from Paula Petrik, who used it in oral presentations to describe settings in which the routines of divorce in Montana departed from typical ritual passage through the courts. For details, see P. PETRIK, NO STEP BACKWARD: WOMEN AND FAMILY ON THE ROCKY MOUNTAIN MINING FRONTIER, HELENA, MONTANA, 1865–1900, at 97–114 (1987).

46. RIDGWAY, *supra* note 28, at 270. Ridgway placed Barnum as the seventh wealthiest man in the 1824–1834 era. A David Barnum of Baltimore was reported in the 1830 census to be living in a household with 39 adult men, 10 adult women, 4 children under 10 years of age, 13 slaves, and 8 freed African-Americans. His hotel was therefore a fairly large establishment.

47. The Gilmor family was also quite wealthy. Robert Gilmor was a successful Presbyterian merchant. *Id.* at 227. His son, Robert Gilmor, Jr., was only slightly less well off than David Barnum, and was ranked as the nineteenth wealthiest man in Baltimore in the 1824–1834 era. *Id.* at 272.

48. SEMMES, *supra* note 44, at 208.

49. *Id.* at 209.

50. *Id.* at 208.

51. 1829 HOUSE JOURNAL at 272.

52. *Id.* at 278. On Feb. 5, Dr. John Bukler and George Howard were ordered "attached" when they failed to appear after being served with subpoenas to testify before the Committee on Divorces. *Id.* at 322.

53. *Id.* at 433.

54. *Id.* at 535.

55. *Id.* at 537–539.

56. *Id.* at 540–541.

57. *Id.* at 549–550.

58. A motion was also made to place a copy of all the evidence taken in the David Barnum case in the archives of the House of Delegates. This was a unique motion, again revealing the special nature of this case. 1829 HOUSE JOURNAL at 550.

59. *Id.* at 551.

60. *Id.* at 554–555. The fact this motion went nowhere implies that routine procedures were not as claimed by David Barnum's attorneys.

61. *Id.* at 566–567.

62. *Id.* at 568.

63. 1829 SENATE JOURNAL at 234–235. An act for the relief of Sarah Barnum, of the city of Baltimore, ch. 193, 1829 Md. Laws (Feb. 27, 1830).

64. An act to divorce Sarah Gilmore, of the city of Baltimore, from her husband, David S. Barnum, ch. 75, 1832 Md. Laws (Feb. 18, 1833).

65. 1832 HOUSE JOURNAL at 197, 239, 244–245, 251; 1832 SENATE JOURNAL at 103, 140, 149.

66. *See* Chapter 5.

67. SEMMES, *supra* note 44, at 210.

68. Hubbell was first divorced in the 1818 session. An act for the relief of Leah W. Hubbell, of Dorchester county, ch. 68, 1818 Md. Laws (Jan. 27, 1819).

69. A Supplement to an act, entitled, An act for the relief of Leah W. Hubbell, of Dorchester county, passed at December Session eighteen hundred and eighteen, chapter sixty-eight, ch. CLVII, 1829 Md. Laws (Mar. 12, 1830).

70. A Supplement to an act, entitled, An act for the relief of Adelaide V. Lowe, of Frederick County, passed at December session eighteen hundred and twenty-two, chapter one hundred, ch. 52, 1830 Md. Laws (Feb. 7, 1831).

71. *See* Table 15 in Appendix 1. Of the partial divorce acts passed between 1826 and 1836, 62 percent contained provisions about the property of both husbands and wives.

72. *See, e.g.*, An Act for the relief of Susanna Holmes, of Baltimore County, ch. 107, 1830 Md. Laws (Feb. 17, 1831).

73. If the parties were only divorced from bed and board, property acquired after divorce might also be encumbered by dower absent statutory provisions to the contrary.

74. It may be that this impact occurred only with regard to real property, in which wives retained an ownership interest. Personal property, on the other hand, became the husband's, suggesting that there were no rights of a wife in the property of a husband to terminate.

75. 1832 SENATE JOURNAL at 57.

76. 1832 HOUSE JOURNAL at 90.

77. *See* Table 15 in Appendix 1.

78. LEIPHEIMER, *supra* note 43, at 104, reports the decline in rural and slaveholding politicians serving as governors or members of the United States Congress from Maryland. Ridgway notes a similar trend for areas other than the South. RIDGWAY, *supra* note 28, at 160–185.

79. 1832 SENATE JOURNAL at 75. Arthur probably could not have sold the property outright, even if he held title, because of dower rights. But he could have used it as security for a loan.

80. *Id.*

81. An act for the relief of Mary Meginnis, ch. 95, 1823 Md. Laws (Feb. 5, 1824).

82. Crane v. Meginnis, 1 G. & J. 463 (Md. 1829).

83. The General Assembly definitely understood the *Meginnis* message. During the 1833 session, in the year following the Block debate, the General Assembly approved an act partially divorcing Emeline and John Hall. Section 2 of the act provided "[t]hat the County Court of Somerset, as a court of equity, or the High Court of Chancery, be authorised to grant such alimony in this case as may appear just and proper." An Act to divorce Emeline R. Hall of Somerset County from her

husband John M. Hall, ch. 161, 1833 Md. Laws (Mar. 6, 1834). This highly unusual provision recognized that alimony decisions were judicial rather than legislative functions.

84. Susannah Reeder v. James Reeder, St. Marys County Ct. Equity Papers, MdHR 17, 898–10630, S 512–10479, 1/39/3/17 (1831).

85. An Act for the relief of Susanna Reeder, of Saint Mary's County, ch. 47, 1830 Md. Laws (Feb. 7, 1831).

86. 2 Bland Ch. 519 (1830).

87. Bland restricted the alimony right to physical cruelty, although court files indicate that not all judges construed the right so narrowly.

88. Helms v. Franciscus, 2 Bland Ch. 519, 550 (1830).

89. LEIPHEIMER, *supra* note 43, at 104.

90. Two major treatises with traditional attitudes toward family law appeared between 1816 and 1830. T. REEVE, LAW OF BARON AND FEMME (1816); J. KENT, COMMENTARIES ON AMERICAN LAW (4 vol. 1826–1830). Volume 2 of Kent's COMMENTARIES, at 31–108, contained the first American summary of divorce law. He reported on the policy of New York to permit complete divorce only in the case adultery and criticized easy divorce:

> We meet with a great variety of practice and opinion on this subject, in this country and in Europe, and among ancient and modern nations; but the stronger authority, and the better policy, is in favour of the stability of the marriage union.

Id. at 35. He also disliked broad marital property rules which,

> unfortunately, [withdraw] from the wife those checks that were intended to preserve her more entirely from that secret and insensible, but powerful marital influence, which might be exerted unduly, and yet in a manner to baffle all inquiry and detection.

Id. at 139. Despite Kent's traditional views, his treatise could be read by Maryland legislators as endorsement for the passage of some complete divorces and the careful allocation of marital property.

Kent, of course, did not speak for everyone. Though he was enormously influential in the growth of chancery courts in the Northeast, his traditional views were under review during the same epoch in which *Helms* was decided. 2 J. STORY, COMMENTARIES ON EQUITY JURISPRUDENCE AS ADMINISTERED IN ENGLAND AND AMERICA 596–655 (1836), contains a long chapter on marital property. Story's views on married women were somewhat more modern than Kent's.

91. Later in the nineteenth century, some courts began to allow legislatures to modify the marital property rights of husbands. *See, e.g.*, Rugh v. Ottenheimer, 6 Or. 231 (1877). By that time, however, many of these rights had been prospectively altered or abolished for so long that the change in rules about vesting had only marginal significance.

92. 1 Bland Ch. 101 (1825).

93. *Id.* at 103.

94. Martha Hewitt v. Eli Hewitt, Ch. Ct. Chancery Papers, MdHR 17, 898-8833, S 512-8776, 1/38/4/76 (Anne Arundel, 1825).

95. *See* Table 4 in Appendix 1.

96. *Id.* Of the 128 divorces petitioned for by women in this time period 26, or about 20 percent, had name-change clauses. They appeared at only a slightly higher rate in complete divorces than in partial divorces. Maiden name clauses were in 17 percent (13 of 77) of the bed and board acts and 25 percent (13 of 51) of the *a vinculo* acts sought by wives. There were also 3 name-change provisions among the 13 acts passed after both spouses filed petitions for a divorce.

97. C. Dayton, Women Before the Bar: Gender, Law and Society in Connecticut, 1710–1790, at 326–327 (1986) (Thesis, Princeton).

98. Name changes did not appear only in complete divorce acts. Of the 29 name changes between 1826 and 1836, 14 were in partial bills. This suggests that clearing up credit understandings may have played a role in the sudden appearance of these provisions.

99. Fanny Wright, a reformer who lectured on the topics of abolition and female sexuality, broke American gender taboos by addressing audiences of both men and women in 1828. Angelina and Sarah Grimké, sisters in a prominent slave-owning family in South Carolina, began an abolitionist speaking tour in the Northeast in 1836. S. M. Evans, Born for Liberty: A History of Women in America 78–81 (1989). More recent history holds an interesting mirror up to the name-change provisions of 1826 and later years in Maryland. The refusal of many women in the 1960s and 1970s to adopt their husbands' names was surely a declaration of individual worth and status apart from a marital relationship. Whether the same may be said for the nineteenth-century events is obviously open to question.

7. The Arrival of Judicial Divorce, 1837–1841

The Politics of General Divorce Legislation

We tend to think of the legislative process as hopelessly cumbersome. The arcane quality of representative bodies creates an image of inaccessibility and procedural irregularity. These notions have been given some legitimacy in the family law context by studies finding that divorce courts were easier to use than the private bill process in the North-central United States.[1] Access to the legislatures was difficult, since they sat in one location rather than many. The idea that nineteenth-century citizens might find it easier and more convenient to obtain a legislative divorce than a judicial one is therefore somewhat strange. By the middle of the nineteenth century, however, the Maryland General Assembly was passing divorces as fast as courts in some other states.[2] This is no small matter. For if the legislature was routinely passing divorces on liberal grounds, a narrowly drawn general divorce bill that legislators assumed would remove them from future divorce debates was unlikely to draw support from reformist quarters. That is the outline of the Maryland story. The inverted voting pattern on private and general divorce bills in Maryland's House of Delegates[3]—with those voting for private bills voting against general ones and those voting for general bills voting against private ones—is a dramatic signal that the shift of divorce to the courts was not a far-reaching reform of family law norms.[4]

The state's divorce rate lagged behind many areas of the country through the early decades of the nineteenth century, but the difference grew significantly smaller by 1840. Baltimore City residents severed marital ties at a rapidly increasing pace between 1820 and 1840, reaching a level as high as or higher than some areas in the Midwest.[5] Although the number of legislative petitioners fell, especially in Baltimore, after the adoption of general divorce legislation at the 1841 session of the General Assembly,[6] the arrival of judicial divorce did not lead to a sharp increase in the rate at which people sought to divorce. Available data on both legislative and judicial petition rates show there was a temporary drop in the divorce application rate during a four-year period of confusion following adoption of the general divorce bill. But the combined court and legislative petition rate then rebounded, rising to a level above the pre-1841 pace.[7] The legislature apparently absorbed most if not all of the demand for divorce before 1841.

There are a number of signs in the legislative record that the legislative divorce process was fairly routinized by 1840. Access was not a major problem. Except for counties in the western panhandle, Annapolis was not far off. Between legislative sessions, elected delegates almost surely were sought out in their home districts by parties seeking a divorce. Those representatives wishing to pursue such matters for their constituents probably brought relevant materials with them to each session. Virtually all divorce petitions were filed by delegates from the districts in which the petitioners resided.[8] Travel and communication problems did not confine the legislative divorce process to the rich and famous. In addition, lawyers traveled to Annapolis each legislative season. With a chancery court having statewide jurisdiction sitting in Annapolis, both judicial and legislative claims could be conveniently handled at the same time. Baltimore residents certainly did not have any trouble filing divorce petitions. Between 1837 and the passage of the general divorce act at the 1841 session, about half of the divorce petitioners were from Baltimore City.[9]

The divorce acts had also become quite simple and uniform. Virtually all of the divorces passed after 1837 were *a vinculo*.[10] They were usually barren of complicating property, custody, and name-change provisions.[11] The virtual disappearance of property provisions from the acts[12] suggests that a *de facto* requirement arose forcing most petitioners to resolve their economic differences before seeking legislative assistance. Complicated economic arrangements by some divorcing couples were probably worked out in settlements not visible in the legislative record. Given the increasing resistance to the work load imposed by the private bill process that surfaced after 1836, such a requirement made some sense. Further credence is given to the notion that the private bill process was in part becoming a consensual divorce system by data showing that passage rates for men and women petitioners evened out for the first time.[13] The proportion of acts with custody provisions fell dramatically, either because the presumption granting women custody of children had become so strong that legislative intervention was no longer necessary to insure "appropriate" behavior by fathers or because it became common for such issues to be settled prior to the filing of a petition for divorce.[14] Most of the acts were brief one-liners that simply announced a divorce. In short, the divorce acts became standardized, with about half of the petitioners obtaining relief from a legislature attuned to accepting marital rifts as part of the cultural landscape of the General Assembly.

The adoption of many simple divorces does not mean, however, that marital acrimony was nonexistent or that the General Assembly always acted without contentious debates. It merely indicates that the outer contours of the divorce process were standardized, that conflict about the core meaning of divorce was less intense than forty years before. When disputes did surface, they only confirmed that divorces were being passed on increasingly liberal grounds.

Controversial *a vinculo* divorces like that granted to Virginia and Isaac Williams, for example, must have been particularly distressing to traditional delegates.[15] Virginia's divorce petition provoked a counter-petition from her husband.[16] Both sides were given authority to summon witnesses.[17] An attempt to defer the bill to the next General Assembly failed, the final version of the act was substituted for the committee version in a 53 to 20 roll call vote, and the bill passed only after a second roll call vote produced a 42 to 30 majority.[18] Just a decade earlier, the preamble to the Williams's divorce act would have been unthinkable:

> Whereas, it appears to this General Assembly that Virginia Williams and Isaac Williams, have been living separate and apart for seven years last past; And whereas, it also appears that although no imputation can properly rest upon the moral character or conduct of either party, the affections of the parties are so entirely alienated as to preclude all hope of their living together in harmony and peace;—Therefore, . . . [they are] divorced, a vinculo matrimonii.

The Williams divorce was part of a continuing debate on whether divorces should be complete or partial. More amendments on this subject were proposed between 1837 and 1841 than during any other period. About a fifth of all enacted bills ran the amendment gauntlet.[19] But, in contrast to the Taney era, those favoring *a vinculo* divorces generally prevailed. Four-fifths of the bills subjected to an amendment controversy provided for complete divorces at the conclusion of the floor debate.[20] Amendments came up in the House of Delegates and the Senate at about the same rate with about the same outcomes. In short, it is likely that traditional members of the General Assembly opposed to divorce were having less and less success in maintaining stringent limits on the use of *a vinculo* divorces. Eighty percent of all divorces passed between 1837 and 1841 were complete.[21] Just as demands for roll call votes were used by legislators frustrated by the liberalization of divorce at the turn of the nineteenth century,[22] so traditionalists used amendment proposals as their parliamentary device after 1836.

In such a setting, ridding the legislature of the private bill process became more attractive to those with traditional rather than reformist views of the family. Delegates like John Lewis Millard,[23] who clung to traditional family values while inveighing against the procedural irregularities of the legislative process, were natural supporters of narrowly drawn bills shifting divorce to the courts. All such delegates needed were the votes of a few centrist delegates for a limited bill. It was reasonable for them to expect that alliance to materialize. It is often much easier for public officials to empathize with the troubles of individuals personally pleading their cases than to publicly favor broad, meaningful reforms in matters rife with moral, ethical, and religious conflicts. For some delegates without strong personal beliefs in family law reform, it eventually became easier to vote for a narrow, politically "safe" general divorce bill than to continue casting potentially risky votes for individual private bills. Not even the prospect of retaining power over the divorce process in the legislature could indefinitely forestall the ceding of family disputes to the courts.

The case of Jane and James Rock is a nice example of how the political process worked.[24] An alimony complaint was filed in the Saint Marys County Court in 1842.[25] The Rocks married on April 9, 1839. James, Jane alleged, was repeatedly cruel to her, forcing her at times to leave the house for fear of his violence. Ultimately, she said, he deserted her. At the time they were married, she owned "considerable property, real and personal." Jane's petition argued that James married her for money and eventually deserted her. The year before the alimony filing, she lodged a divorce petition with the General Assembly. A private bill passed the House despite a negative committee report,[26] but it failed when the Senate declined to debate more divorce bills after the passage of general legislation.[27] Despite the House of Delegates' willingness to divorce the Rocks, the general divorce bill they approved at the same session would not have provided the couple with any relief. Abandonment, under the terms of the general bill, required absence from the state for five years, but the facts as found in the alimony file confirmed that the parties married only three years before litigation began and that James departed just before Jane went to court. Jane Rock evoked sympathy in the House for herself, but the facts of her case, and hundreds of others that had come before the General Assembly, failed to create the political empathy and support needed for a broad general divorce bill.[28]

The act that finally emerged from the General Assembly's 1841 session was indeed quite modest. *A vinculo* grounds included only adultery, impotence, marriages unlawful *ab initio*,[29] or abandonment with absence *from the state* for five years. "Cruelty of treatment" supported only a bed and board divorce.[30] The statutory grounds were narrower than those adopted in Pennsylvania and other Northern states five decades earlier.[31] Most states did not require proof of departure from the state in order to obtain a divorce on desertion grounds. Some Northern states also made cruelty a ground for complete divorce.[32] Iowa's statute, adopted at about the same time as Maryland's, permitted divorce for cruelty or "indignities."[33]

History of Early General Divorce Bills

Passage of this narrow general divorce bill culminated a thirty-three-year struggle.[34] Even as hundreds of private divorce petitions were filed and debated, a steady stream of proposals to alter the private bill process or grant courts jurisdiction to entertain divorce cases appeared in the General Assembly.[35] Process proposals were made in eighteen of the thirty legislative years from 1811 to 1840, and general bills were filed in twenty-five of the thirty-three years from 1809 to 1841. Divorce bills passed one house and failed in the other four times before an act was finally adopted.[36]

Although the Whigs took over the Maryland General Assembly at the 1836 elections, and gained a huge 60 to 19 majority in the 1840 House of Delegates election, divorce was not a strongly partisan issue in Maryland in this time period.[37] The reforming tendencies of the Whigs did eventually affect the shape of electoral, redistricting, and legislative changes.[38] But the close votes on general divorce legislation continued to reflect regional variations more than party affiliations.[39] Adoption of further divorce reforms after the Democrats regained control of the House of Delegates in 1842 confirms that divorce was not a partisan issue.[40]

Like the private bill story, this lengthy series of debates had its hills, valleys, and strange detours. Until the 1820s general divorce bill proposals were dispatched with little fanfare. Committees given leave to introduce bills often did not bother to produce them. Bills reported to the floor were tabled or killed by referring them to the next General Assembly.[41] Controversy was kindled by even the simplest process proposals. It took more than a decade, for example, to insure the regular formation of a standing committee to entertain divorce petitions. The first proposal for a committee, submitted to the 1811 session of the House of Delegates, was quickly defeated.[42] A committee was formed in the 1817 session,[43] but it did not become an institutional fixture until the General Assembly convened in 1822. Two attempts to form a divorce committee failed that year before a motion to reconsider finally carried the day.[44]

The committee ado was intimately involved with disputes over the imposition of procedural requirements on divorce petitioners. The member of the House of Delegates most active in making divorce proposals in the early 1820s was John Lewis Millard, a wealthy, anti-Jacksonian plantation owner who represented Saint Marys County from 1819 to 1826.[45] Though from the southern region of the state, he must have been a sometime ally of the Eastern Shore patricians on divorce questions. In two roll call votes taken in 1822 and 1823, he voted in favor of divorces.[46] One of these votes was for a complete divorce, since the bill passed by the House was amended by the Senate to a partial bill before its final passage.[47] Millard was therefore a modest family law reformer somewhat outside of the typical mold of Southerners who served in the House of Delegates during the first half of the nineteenth century.

Millard dove into the divorce question when the General Assembly gathered in 1822. He was the first to move for the creation of a standing committee during that session.[48] His effort failed, but when the House later reconsidered the issue and created a committee, Millard was named one of its members.[49] One of his actions as a committee member was to move

> [t]hat the committee on divorces report favorably on no petition until they shall be satisfied that the parties concerned have had sufficient time to file any vouchers with said committee, in order to counteract the allegations of the party applying for such divorce; and that in future no favorable report be made by the said committee, on such applications, unless the party applying shall have given public notice, for the space of three weeks, in some one or more newspapers published in this state, nearest to the residence of the party so applying, of their intention to make such application to this legislature.

Though the motion failed,[50] confirming both the informal qualities of the legislative divorce process and its roots in serving local constitutent needs, it was part of a more general conception Millard had about the nature of judicial and legislative roles. In fact, we have an unusually complete picture of Millard's views on divorce. The process concerns evident in his notice proposal, which was also submitted with minor variations at the 1823 and 1825 sessions,[51] must have been a motivation for his introduction of a general divorce bill during the 1822 session, and in each of the following three meetings of the General Assembly.[52] He also participated in framing a report issued by the 1822 divorce committee stating its willingness to recommend complete divorces only upon strong proof of adultery.[53] What emerges is a picture of a delegate concerned with the airing of potentially scandalous adultery allegations under procedures lacking the accountability of traditional equity courts. Reform, at least for Millard, was a complex mixture of aristocratic concerns about process, reputation, and family honor. In the preamble to one of his procedural proposals, he merged the three realms, stating that

> bills of divorce are reported upon partial representations, and the party . . . hath given no notice thereof to the other party . . . , whereby the general assembly may not only be oftentimes imposed on and deceived, but injustice be committed, and the peace and happiness of families be jeoparded.[54]

Whatever reformist tendencies existed in the House of Delegates during the Taney and post-Taney eras reached their high point in the 1824 session, when a general bill was proposed and passed. Disarray in Maryland's political parties reached a peak that year. Neither the Republican nor Federalist parties controlled the House. Independents had a majority. Election turnover was extremely high, with 70 percent of the House of Delegates seats occupied by members not present in 1823.[55] Andrew Jackson, though a serious presidential contender, had not yet become the central figure of a well-constructed political organization.

The demise of the old political parties brought new opinions about divorce to the House of Delegates. Two bills were filed in the 1824 session, one by Millard and the other by Joseph Merrick of Washington County. Although the provisions of these bills are not known, the contents of other reports issued by divorce committees the prior two sessions make it likely that they permitted complete divorce for adultery and partial divorce for cruelty or ill usage.[56] In any case, Millard and Merrick were both appointed to the committees responsible for writing the bills. Merrick's bill was reported to the House floor on January 24, 1825, and passed without a roll call vote on February 23.[57] The bill was sent over to the Senate the next day. Within hours, the Senate read the bill three times on special order, rejected it, and returned it to the House of Delegates.[58] There is no better signal of the differences between the two houses of the General Assembly. The Taney and post-Taney Senates rejected not only complete private divorce bills,[59] but general reform measures as well. It is difficult to believe that Millard and Merrick really thought their bill had a chance of passage. Given the history of the Taney era, passage of the bill by the House of Delegates has the flavor of a protest.

The easing of divorce standards, particularly for *a vinculo* acts, after 1826 was accompanied by fairly constant, but unsuccessful, pressure to adopt general legislation. Concerns over procedure still generated some pressure for change. One private bill failed because there was "no proof of the respectability of witnesses."[60] And another attempt to require news-paper notice failed.[61] But in this era more attention was paid to general divorce bills than to procedural issues. Three bills were introduced in the 1826 session, two in 1827, and one in each of the following two sessions. The last two failed on close votes in the House.[62] Very little is known about the contents of these bills, though it is likely that they bore little resemblance to the act finally passed in the 1841 session. What floor debate tidbits exist confirm that some of the bills were much longer and contained sections wholly different from the later legislation.[63]

Debate on divorce reached a second crescendo in the 1829 session. The Barnum divorce saga—the *cause célèbre* of that General Assembly—may have convinced some legislators there was a need for general divorce legislation.[64] The prior year, the House of Delegates had a jolly good time passing nine different amendments to a general divorce bill—each change removing a county from the bill's coverage—before referring the bill to the next General Assembly in a 37 to 30 vote.[65] The same gambit did not work in 1829.[66] Indeed, divorce opponents must have been afraid that passage of a general bill was imminent after a motion to strike the enacting clause failed.[67] Two days later a rare quorum call brought more delegates than usual to the House floor for debate on the bill. A motion to insert the phrase "a mensa et thoro" in the first section of the bill, probably with the intention of precluding complete divorces, failed. Another amendment prohibiting remarriage after all divorces was first passed and then rejected, leaving a marriage prohibition in effect only for those guilty of adultery. And a third amendment barring divorce if a grand jury refused to indict an offender failed.[68] But in a vote of 38 to 35, the bill was defeated.[69]

The winds of reform were strong enough, however, to generate one minor piece of legislation at the 1829 session. The day after defeat of the general divorce bill, the House agreed to "enquire into the expediency of providing by law for the finding of fact, by the county court or some other . . . authority, preparatory to applications for divorces, to the General Assembly."[70] About two weeks later, the Senate, which had a similar proposal under consideration, approved a bill which was quickly agreed to by the House.[71] After twenty-one years of discussion, Maryland finally let courts into the divorce process, but only to report on the facts when one of the parties to a divorce sought judicial assistance. Given the expense of a full-blown judicial process and the inconvenience of having to pursue remedies before two different bodies to complete a divorce proceeding, the legislature remained the primary fact-finding forum in divorce disputes.[72] Indeed, after 1829, the General Assembly continued to discuss changes in its own procedural rules rather than compel divorce petitioners to lay out their proofs to a judge. The House meeting in 1833 gave its divorce committee authority to examine witnesses, but there is no indication they regularly heard direct testimony.[73] And, during the same session, an attempt in the Senate to require compliance with the 1829 statute failed.[74] Rather than force petitioners to court, the Senate ordered the divorce committee to hear those disputes on which it had reported unfavorably for failing to use the court commission procedure.[75] The impact on the use of the court process was obvious. Only four fact-finding divorce case files are extant in chancery records of the Baltimore County Court. All were filed between 1830 and 1835. Whatever temptation existed to use the court process before filing a petition with the legislature then disappeared.[76]

After the 1829 session, there was a three-year hiatus in proposals for general divorce bills.[77] When the issue resurfaced in 1833, it arrived with a new sense of urgency to rid the General Assembly of the time-consuming flood of divorce petitions. Members of the Senate were particularly concerned. That was quite understandable. The Senate was a much smaller body than the House.[78] The deluge of divorce petitions must have had an impact on the senators' work load, even though private bills usually were considered first, and often rejected, by the House. During the 1833 session, for example, forty-one divorce petitions were filed, of which twenty were considered by the Senate. That year's Senate divorce committee submitted a report begging for help by forcing all petitioners to use the 1829 court commission process:

> The committee would require a compliance with that act not merely because it is a law in full force and operation, and therefore entitled to weight

and respect, but because they are decidedly of opinion that it contains most salutary provisions, by an observation of which on the part of the petitioners, the legislature would be enabled to decide with more correctness and propriety, as that act requires a petition to be filed in the county court, setting forth the grounds of complaint and a *subpoena* to be issued for the party complained of, and the appearance and answer of that party, it not only guards that party against all secrecy and surprise but it supplies the alleged causes of complaint, to the disproof of which, testimony can be directed, and affords an opportunity of presenting the defence in a manner best suited to the case. The committee also conceive that it is highly proper and desirable to have the testimony to be used in the investigation of such subjects taken under a commission as provided by that act, inasmuch as the proceedings will be public, the witnesses confronted by and subjected to the cross examination of the opposing parties, and being known may be impeached and discredited. Moreover, the proceedings being before a tribunal vested by law with full power to take the testimony, will be better secured against the falsehoods and misrepresentations of witnesses by adding to the moral obligation to speak the truth, the penalty of legal paying for false swearing. In conclusion the committee would recommend to the senate for the reasons above mentioned to adopt a rule to require compliance with the said act of assembly, and to adhere to that rule in all cases except such as are not embraced or provided for by said act, and perhaps in such as from the violent and brutal conduct of one of the parties, or other not less urgent circumstance, the immediate action of the legislature shall be demanded.[79]

Neither the proposal to require compliance with the 1829 legislation nor other proposals for general divorce legislation garnered much support between 1833 and 1835. Private acts were then being adopted with increasing frequency and the grounds were liberalizing. Reformists in the House of Delegates were becoming less and less interested in ridding themselves of the divorce "nuisance." Nonetheless, the senatorial plea for help set the tone for the divorce debates in these and later sessions. During the 1835 session, for example, Mr. Jones of Somerset County on the Eastern Shore proposed to amend the state constitution to "require the assent of two thirds of each branch of the Legislature to annul a marriage contract."[80] The proposition, which required the approval of two successive General Assemblies, passed both houses that session.[81] At the next meeting of the General Assembly the proposal was pressed by the Senate. Only five days after Mr. Hambleton raised the issue, the Senate confirmed its wish to require a supermajority for divorces and sent the bill to the House.[82] This time, the House—less concerned than the Senate about work loads and procedural deficiencies—defeated the measure, 38 to 24.[83]

After the Whigs took over the Senate in the controversial 1836 election,[84] that body took the lead in pressing for general divorce reform. Though members of the House of Delegates made several divorce-related proposals after 1836,[85] all of the major proposals for general legislation were initiated in the Senate.[86] On the surface, these events conform to the notion that the Whigs were the party of reform. But the actual debates delineate a much more complex picture of traditionalists pushing for general "reform." Reports on the debates in the 1839, 1840, and 1841 sessions are particularly revealing.

The 1839 Senate passed a general divorce bill without controversy in a 12 to 4 roll call vote.[87] When the bill got to the House, John T. Mason, a Democrat from Washington County in the Maryland panhandle, tried unsuccessfully to have the bill assigned to the Committee on Grievances and Courts of Justice rather than the Committee on Divorces.[88] The latter was chaired by another Democrat, Thomas C. Risteau of Baltimore County, who routinely opposed consideration of general divorce bills during this period. As Mason must have expected, the Committee on Divorces filed an unfavorable report on the Senate bill immediately after it was assigned the task of reviewing it.[89] Risteau's later motion to strike the enacting clause from the bill passed in a 31 to 27 vote.[90] Democrats held a 46 to 32 majority in the House of Delegates in this session. Those participating in the divorce roll call voted 25 to 15 in favor of striking the enacting clause. Whigs voted the other way, 11 to 4.[91] The apparent party differences, however, were regionally based. Democrats from the north central region around Baltimore, who generally voted in favor of private bills, voted 12 to 4 against the general bill. Whigs from the south, who generally opposed private bills, voted for the general one 9 to 0. Democrats and Whigs from other areas split evenly in the voting, the former 13 to 11 against and the latter 4 to 3 against. The roll call vote was a perfect example of a legislature willing to hear the plaintive cries of individual, miserable spouses in debates on private bills while declining to take a public stand in favor of any general statutory relief.[92]

The next day, the Senate, still complaining about the informality of the legislative divorce process, sent the House a message asking its members to reconsider the divorce bill:

> The subject intended to be conferred upon the courts of equity in the State, is one which now occupies a great portion of the time and attention of the General Assembly; which could be more profitably employed in matters more interesting to the public and State at large—and from the mode in which the statements of these private grievances are presented to our consideration,

being based frequently and indeed in almost every instance upon ex parte testimony, and without notice to the adverse party, great injustice must often be the consequence.[93]

The House responded that it "cannot concur therein."[94]

Risteau, seizing upon the Senate's concern about the "great injustice" occurring in the divorce process, then revived a bill he had previously offered to define methods for the receipt of evidence by legislative divorce committees. The House took the bill off the table and passed it, but the Senate, unwilling to expand its legislative duties with more cumbersome procedures, rejected it.[95] The outcome also confirms that the private bill divorce process was procedurally informal in comparison with standard court routines.

A similar story unfolded the following session. The Senate passed a bill, 12 to 5, after sending it back to committee for some redrafting work.[96] On the House floor, the bill was effectively gutted of most of its important provisions. The run of amendments offered strongly implies that the bill was framed almost exactly like the one passed the following session. Assuming that was so, amendments first were passed which deleted the most important grounds for both complete and partial divorces. Then adultery was added as the primary ground for both sorts of divorce. The amended bill was then defeated in a 33 to 26 vote.[97] Both Democrats and Whigs voted against it, the former 25 to 21 and the latter 8 to 5.[98] Even southern Whigs, anxious to rid the General Assembly of the private divorce process, voted against it 8 to 7. After all the amendments passed, it must have been too conservative, even for some traditional southern delegates. Reform-minded legislators surely opposed its passage.

Revisions of the 1829 court commission legislation were proposed two days after the House defeated the general divorce bill, and eventually were passed by both houses.[99] The changes made the process somewhat more accessible by holding the hearings before a justice of the peace rather than a chancery court.[100] The Senate attempted to put some teeth into the new legislation by adopting a standing rule requiring its use:

> Ordered, that after this session the senate will not entertain any bill or petition for a divorce, unless the proof in support of such bill or petition shall have been taken in conformity with the acts of Assembly on the subject, and presented with such bill or petition; and that the committee on divorces, in every case, report if said laws have been complied with.[101]

Despite the rule, more private divorces were passed during the opening two months of the 1841 legislative session. The Senate again passed a general bill, this time in a matter of only four days.[102] Risteau tried, but this time failed, to steer the bill to the divorce committee. After three weeks of deliberation the Committee on Grievances and Courts of Justice reported favorably on the bill. It took more than a month of efforts to bring it up for consideration on the floor. Debate finally went forward only after a quorum call to gather up wayward members. A motion to reject the bill failed on a 36 to 36 tie vote, and it squeaked to passage 37 to 35.[103] As in the 1839 vote, regional variations dominated party preferences.[104] After more than three decades of debate, frustration with the constant consideration of divorce petitions finally overcame the reluctance of centrist delegates to vote publicly for a general divorce bill.[105]

Links Between Divorce Reform and Married Women's Property Acts

As we know from the debates generated by radical reform proposals in the second half of the nineteenth century,[106] divorce tended to generate much greater public controversy than reforms in other areas of law affecting women. That was certainly true of Maryland in the early 1840s. Property law, lacking the sometimes strident moral and religious overtones of divorce, was an easier mark for reformers. The General Assembly, without anything like the contention surrounding the divorce issue, passed a series of bills on married women's property during the same era divorce reform was in the air.

Despite the different levels of contention surrounding divorce and property law, the causes for reform of both areas were quite similar. The strong links between divorce and property rules have already been noted. The ongoing debates over the propriety of complete versus partial divorce constantly reminded legislators of the ways marriage defined the economic rules of family life. Just as liberal divorce rules could attract adherents across political lines, so too could reform of marital property rules. Impetus for both property and divorce reform came from concerns about daughters losing assets to dissolute husbands, commercial concern about free alienability of property, and empathy for the plight of impoverished women left legally entangled in the economic lives of deserting men. These were problems that crossed economic and political divisions. Upper-class women trapped in bad marriages could generate as much sympathy in their male peers as impoverished mothers struggling to survive without their departed husbands could induce in theirs.

The onset of serious, national economic problems in 1837 was the catalyst for reform. It created strains in attitudes toward both marriage and property.[107] Desertion left some women with property subject to the claims of their departed husbands' creditors. Wealthy women found themselves in economic straits when assets they brought to their marriages disappeared under the weight of their husbands' debts. In such harsh economic times, "innocent" wives from many cultural settings, encumbered by husbands' debts and culturally obligated to care for the educational, moral, and physical needs of children, became sympathetic subjects for corrective legislation. Precluding access to a married woman's property by the creditors of her husband was one way to approach the problem. Another was to regularize the ability of women to escape from the economic ties of marriage. In a state like Maryland, which had long hesitated to adopt general divorce legislation, it is not surprising that property reforms would be debated in the same era in which private divorce grounds were expanding. Nor is it surprising that a few legislators sitting on the fence on divorce questions would finally agree to vote in favor of a narrowly drawn general bill.

Three property acts were adopted between 1840 and 1842. The first, passed during the 1840 session, allowed a married woman to enter into contracts insuring the life of her husband, with benefits payable to her as separate property for her own use if she survived her husband or to her children if she died first.[108] The following year the General Assembly, on the same day it approved the general divorce bill, exempted a married woman's real estate from debts owed by her husband.[109] This was a standard married women's property act, much like those adopted in most states in response to the economic depression of 1837 and later years.[110] Its passage was remarkably uncontroversial, passing on a lopsided roll call vote of 56 to 5.[111] General divorce proposals, always dispensed with on close ballots, were obviously much more controversial.

Finally, a third, much more detailed married women's property act emerged during the 1842 session.[112] It was sponsored by John Causin, a Whig delegate from Saint Marys County who was a major supporter of a federal plan to support states in serious economic trouble by selling off public lands.[113] Causin also voted in favor of the general divorce bill passed at the prior session.[114] The property act confirmed the right of married women to own real property and slaves "together with their natural increase" in their own names without the need for a trustee. The right to manage and control slaves, however, was left with husbands.[115] Married women also gained the ability to write wills, provided their husbands gave consent, and the right to invest, control, and retain the profits from up to $1,000 obtained by their "skill, industry or personal labour."[116] The focus on real property, management of slaves, and the consent limitation on will writing were quite traditional and Southern. The earnings provision, however, was remarkably modern for its time. Like much of the history of Maryland divorce law, its married women's property legislation displayed a remarkable "contrast between slavery and steam power, past and future, convention and change."[117]

Conclusion: "Liberalism" and Legislative Reform

The divorce debates in the Maryland General Assembly were full of historical surprises. Political party affiliation was less important to voting patterns than the cultural mandates of regional affiliations. Family law debates led to different alliances than those of many other issues of the day. But the most intriguing conclusion must surely be the "liberalism" of the private act process and the "conservatism" of the general act passed by the Assembly. Legislative activity, it turns out, was full of complexity, irony, and, perhaps, perversity. On the surface of things, one might assume that people voting in favor of private bills would favor general legislation embodying like principles. That this did not occur is a resounding warning to historians of all stripes that single institutions may speak with many, variously nuanced voices.

The voices discovered here teach some important lessons. People hear individual stories differently than they hear open-ended debates. The former may create empathy or distance, sympathy or hatred, concern or indifference, pity or distaste. People react to stories and see them as structures with people inside. Broad debates allow easier discussion of morality, religion, and virtue. They invite calls to fear and hatred less easily made in the presence of a fellow citizen's chronicle of specific events.

The notion that people's stories and culture's debates are different had its impact on judges as well as legislators. Judges must listen to at least two kinds of voices—those of legislators enacting legal norms and those of parties appearing before them. After the legislature adopted a narrow divorce act, the courts were confronted with pitiable tales outside the apparent scope of the general legislative norms. Such dissonance, as the last chapters of this volume attest, created stress for both the courts and the

General Assembly. When the courts insisted on following the narrow confines of the new divorce act, and even further confining its reach, during the years immediately after its adoption, the legislature reinvigorated the private act process. After a new state constitution finally ended the private act process in 1851, the courts, again faced with stories of misery not reached by a strict reading of the general legislative norms, gradually opened up the divorce process. Methods emerged that allowed some parties to obtain consensual divorces. And, in eras after the period of this study, abandonment and cruelty definitions were gradually liberalized. In short, it is difficult for legal institutions, whether legislative or judicial, to forever resist tales of misfortune presented to them on a regular basis.

Notes

1. The data show that divorce rates in the North-central United States rose after adoption of general divorce statutes. M. Schultz, *Divorce in Early America: Origins and Patterns in Three North Central States,* 25 Soc. Q. 511, 518–519 (1984).

2. Maryland's court system was organized in a very unusual way. In addition to the county courts, a chancery court with statewide jurisdiction sat in Annapolis. This made it very easy for the early bar to file matters in one place, be it court or legislature, during each legislative session. Although there was a large drop in legislative divorce petitions filed for Baltimore residents after the adoption of general divorce legislation at the 1841 session of the General Assembly, this does not mean that the trek to Annapolis was a significant barrier to divorce. The 1841 drop occurred because everyone thought—mistakenly, as it turned out—that adoption of general divorce legislation ended the private bill process. Maryland was also a reasonably small state with decent transportation systems compared to the expansive and more primitive areas of the newer states to the west.

3. *See* Tables 13 and 16 in Appendix 1. In general the data in Table 13 show that delegates from areas likely to vote for private bills voted against general bills, and that other delegates likely to vote against private bills voted for general bills. These general patterns held regardless of political party affiliation. For example, delegates from the Eastern Shore voted in favor of private bills 67 percent of the time between 1837 and 1850. But they voted in favor of general bills only 38 percent of the time. The southern delegates cast yes votes only 38 percent of the time in private bill debates, but voted favorably 62 percent of the time on general bills.

4. This, of course, does not mean that the courts will automatically keep divorce within the narrow confines envisioned by the legislature. Divorce litigation is notorious for differences between legislative mandate and day-to-day practice. The Hewitt alimony petition, described in the last chapter, surely reminds us of that history.

5. Schultz, *supra* note 1, at 518, found that the overall divorce rate in the Missouri, Illinois, and Ohio counties he studied was 14 per 100,000 population in 1840. Ohio's rate was only 8 per 100,000. Table 9 in Appendix 1 shows that Maryland's legislative divorce rate was just less than 7 per 100,000 in 1840, and Baltimore City's had climbed to more than 18.

6. *See* Table 2 in Appendix 1.

7. Not counting legislative petitions in which the residence of the parties is unknown, there were 164 petitions filed in the legislature by residents of Baltimore City and County between 1837 and 1841. From 1842 to 1845, the four-year period following adoption of general divorce legislation, only four legislative petitions were filed from the Baltimore area. But, according to Maryland Historical Society computer records, 75 petitions were filed in Baltimore County Court and 6 in Maryland Chancery Court, for a total of 85 in both judicial and legislative forums. From 1846 to 1850, 193 Baltimore area petitions were filed, 61 in the legislature, 118 in Baltimore County Court, and 14 in Maryland Chancery Court. In sum, an average of 33 divorces were sought yearly between 1837 and 1841 from residents of the Baltimore area, 21 between 1842 and 1845, and 39 between 1846 and 1850. While there was some disruption by the transition to concurrent judicial control of divorces, the overall divorce petition rate rose gradually in accordance with general trends established in the legislature before 1841.

8. For the petitions filed in 1841, for example, in which the residence of both the petitioner and the delegate are known, 50 were from the same and 7 were from adjacent counties.

9. *See* Table 7 in Appendix 1.

10. *See* Table 1 in Appendix 1.

11. *See* Table 4 in Appendix 1.

12. *Id.*

13. *See* Table 3 in Appendix 1. Women petitioners gained divorces more frequently than did men for more than thirty years after 1805. Between 1805 and 1836, 45 percent of the petitions submitted by women led to the adoption of divorce acts. Only 29 percent of the men's petitions led to legislation. Between 1837 and 1841, just under half of the petitions of both women and men were granted. The evening up of the rates was therefore a significant policy adjustment.

14. *See* Table 4 in Appendix 1.

15. An act to divorce Virginia Williams, from her husband, Isaac Williams, ch. 239, 1834 Md. Laws (Mar. 18, 1835).

16. 1834 HOUSE JOURNAL at 54, 172. She, in turn, filed a response to the response, the only triple filing discovered in the journals. *Id.* at 475.

17. *Id.* at 168, 179–180.

18. *Id.* at 474, 479–480.

19. *See* Table 10 in Appendix 1, which gives a figure of 17 percent for the 1837–1841 period. If the 1836 session is also included, 22 percent (35 of 162) of all enacted bills went through some sort of amendment discussion.

20. Between 1836 and 1841 there were 35 amendments proposed. Twelve attempts to reduce complete bills to partial ones failed, and sixteen attempts to make partial divorces complete prevailed. In the other 20 percent of the amendment

debates, six bills were amended to partial divorces, and one attempt to alter a partial divorce to a complete one failed.

21. *See* Table 1 in Appendix 1.

22. *See* discussion in Chapter 3.

23. Further discussion of Millard may be found in the text accompanying notes 45–57.

24. Other good examples are *Nes v. Nes*, discussed in note 72 *infra*, an 1832 divorce completely lacking in proof of adultery, and the Williams divorce, discussed just above in the text. The Nes legislative divorce was *a vinculo*, but the 1841 legislation would have permitted a bed and board divorce at best. And the Williamses were probably not eligible for any sort of divorce under the 1841 act.

25. Rock v. Rock, St. Marys County Ct. Equity Papers, MdHR 19, 731–312, 1/57/9/56 (1842).

26. 1841 HOUSE JOURNAL at 167, 187.

27. 1841 SENATE JOURNAL at 197.

28. Hannah J. Ely v. Judah Ely, Baltimore County Ct. Chancery Papers, MdHR 40, 200-1878, 2/15/12/74 (1837), was similar to the *Rock* case. Hannah Ely obtained a complete legislative divorce at the 1836 session. An act to divorce Hannah J. D. Ely, of Baltimore City, from her husband, Juda Ely, ch. 107, 1836 Md. Laws (Mar. 2, 1837). The act allowed Hannah to resume use of her maiden name, Fearson, granted her custody of her children, and provided her with the right to contract. Her contemporaneously filed alimony petition, brought by her relative and next friend Jesse Fearson, alleged that her husband Judah abandoned her and left her without any means of support. The court eventually required one James Carter, who held $290.05 of Judah's money, to disgorge the funds to Hannah. Judah had apparently left the state and never responded to notices published in the *Baltimore Gazette*. The file does not reveal when Judah left, but it is likely that he had not been gone long enough to support a divorce under the 1841 legislation.

29. This would include, for example, marriage by relatives.

30. An act to give to the Chancellor and the County Courts as Courts of Equity, jurisdiction in cases of Divorce, ch. 262, 1841 Md. Laws (Mar. 1, 1847). The full text of the statute is reproduced in Appendix 2.

31. G. RILEY, DIVORCE: AN AMERICAN TRADITION 44–45 (1991).

32. *Id.* at 45–46.

33. *Id.* at 46.

34. The first general divorce bill was filed in the 1809 session of the General Assembly. *See* Table of General Bill Proposals in Appendix 2.

35. *See* Tables of Process Proposals and General Bill Proposals in Appendix 2.

36. These events occurred in the 1824, 1838, 1839, and 1840 sessions. The earliest involved a bill that passed the House of Delegates; the others passed only the Senate.

37. W. W. SMITH, ANTI-JACKSONIAN POLITICS ALONG THE CHESAPEAKE 151–152 (1989).

38. Although in 1836 the Whigs were badly outpolled by Democrats in the selection of electors to indirectly choose senators, the districting system favoring

small counties gave them a bare 21 to 19 majority of the electors. This led to a major controversy and, eventually, helped generate the electoral reforms of 1838. *See* C. N. EVERSTINE, THE GENERAL ASSEMBLY OF MARYLAND 1776–1850 at 462–498 (1982).

39. The 1841 divorce bill, for example, got through the House on a 37 to 35 vote. Whigs from the south voted for it 11 to 2, but those from the Eastern Shore split 7 to 7. Democrats from the north central region voted against it 15 to 2, but those from other areas voted for it 15 to 11.

40. The Whigs approved tax increases during the 1841 session which turned out to be a major political liability. The Democrats regained control of the House of Delegates, 43 to 35, in the 1842 elections. SMITH, *supra* note 37, at 171–173.

41. *See* entries in the Table of General Bill Proposals from 1809 to 1823 in Appendix 2.

42. 1811 HOUSE JOURNAL, at 45.

43. 1817 HOUSE JOURNAL at 17.

44. 1822 HOUSE JOURNAL at 5, 7, 30.

45. Around 1830, he owned 1,000 acres and 35 slaves. Millard was among the wealthiest men in the county. W. H. RIDGWAY, COMMUNITY LEADERSHIP IN MARYLAND, 1790–1840: A COMPARATIVE ANALYSIS OF POWER IN SOCIETY 315, 319 (1979).

46. In 1822 he voted to grant Francis B. Mitchell a divorce, 1822 HOUSE JOURNAL at 111, and in 1823 he did the same for Catherine Fridley, 1823 HOUSE JOURNAL at 20.

47. 1822 SENATE JOURNAL at 63.

48. 1822 HOUSE JOURNAL at 5.

49. *Id.* at 30.

50. *Id.* at 38.

51. A motion to require the divorce committee to provide adequate time for filing responses and for placing a notice in a newspaper for three weeks before a divorce petition was filed failed to be adopted in the 1823 session. 1823 HOUSE JOURNAL at 9. At the 1825 session, Millard tried again to mandate three weeks' notice in a newspaper, but failed. 1825 HOUSE JOURNAL at 30.

52. 1832 HOUSE JOURNAL at 96. *See also* 1823 HOUSE JOURNAL at 42; 1824 HOUSE JOURNAL at 38; 1825 HOUSE JOURNAL at 29, 99.

53. 1822 HOUSE JOURNAL at 47.

54. 1825 HOUSE JOURNAL at 30.

55. L. S. DEMAREE, MARYLAND DURING THE FIRST PARTY SYSTEM: A ROLL-CALL ANALYSIS OF THE HOUSE OF DELEGATES, 1789–1824, at 147–148, 172 (1984) (Thesis U. Mo. Columbia).

56. The 1822 report approved divorce only for adultery. The 1823 report suggested that ill usage was an appropriate ground. Bed and board divorce was the context for both reports, which are discussed in Chapter 4 on the Taney era.

57. 1824 HOUSE JOURNAL at 38, 74, 150.

58. 1824 SENATE JOURNAL at 60; 1824 HOUSE JOURNAL at 150.

59. *See* discussion in Chapter 4.

60. 1826 HOUSE JOURNAL at 344–345.

61. The proposed Senate rule was engrossed for a third reading, but then apparently died. 1828 SENATE JOURNAL at 141. It would have required notice before applications for all private bills, not just divorces.

62. *See* the Table of General Bill Proposals in Appendix 2.

63. For example, debates on one of the 1826 bills contained amendments to a section 19 with multiple subsections, proposals on various annulment grounds such as duress and idiocy at the time of marriage. 1826 HOUSE JOURNAL at 299–300. Another divorce bill would have applied only to Baltimore City. *Id.* at 219, 382.

64. The Barnum story is told in Chapter 6.

65. 1828 HOUSE JOURNAL at 223–224. Queene Annes, Saint Marys, Frederick, Caroline, Baltimore, Prince Georges, Harford, Cecil, and Allegany Counties were removed.

66. A motion to exclude Prince Georges County from the bill's coverage did not pass. 1829 HOUSE JOURNAL at 377.

67. *Id.* at 355.

68. This proposal echoed the English tradition, discussed in Chapter 2, that influenced the legislature before 1805.

69. *Id.* at 375–377. The number of votes cast in the roll call vote was the largest of any on divorce in the nineteenth century. The next largest was the 37 to 35 vote approving the general bill at the 1841 session.

70. 1829 HOUSE JOURNAL at 382.

71. *Id.* at 561, 562, 584.

72. Although commissions were used by some couples, the legislative journals rarely reported receiving reports from judicial commissions. The first reported in the journals was in the debate on the Alderson divorce, adopted during the 1830 session. 1830 HOUSE JOURNAL at 209. Other examples of court commission proceedings are extant, such as the petition filed by Elizabeth Nes against her husband Samuel in 1831. Nes v. Nes, Baltimore County Ct. Chancery Papers, MdHR 40, 200-IIII, 2/15/12/25 (1831). Elizabeth alleged that they married in 1818, but that Samuel used abusive language, repeatedly threatened her, and drank. She "sustained so great injury in mind and health as to render her separation from her said husband by legislative enactment (that being the most effective mode) requisite to the preservation of her health and to the restoration of her mental peace and quiet." There are no allegations of adultery in the record. Despite Samuel's wish for a reconciliation, the next legislative session divorced them *a vinculo* and gave Elizabeth custody of the children. An act to divorce Elizabeth Ness, of the city of Baltimore, from her husband Samuel Ness, ch. 242, 1832 Md. Laws (Mar. 18, 1833). Even relatively poor people apparently used the court commission process. James Hammer, for example, was accused of once pledging his and his wife's bed to a broker to get money for his own amusements. He was also accused of drinking, having "indiscriminate intercourse with lewd women," and beating his wife Mary. Mary Hammer v. James J. Hammer, Baltimore County Ct. Chancery Papers, MdHR 40, 200-1619, 2/15/12/57 (1835). The legislature completely divorced the Hammers during the 1835 session. An act to divorce Mary Hammer, of the City of Baltimore, from her husband James J. Hammer, ch. 190, 1835 Md. Laws (Mar. 25, 1836). The last

note in the file is a farewell "love" letter from James in which he calls himself "forsaken," promises to drown his sorrows in drink, and repents of his conduct toward Mary.

73. 1833 HOUSE JOURNAL at 126–127. A larger proposal to permit examination of persons and papers at the expense of the party applying for a divorce failed.

74. 1833 SENATE JOURNAL at 263–264, 288–289.

75. *Id.* at 319.

76. There are no divorce cases in the Maryland Hall of Records database of Baltimore County Court records for the years 1836 through 1841. Divorces start to reappear in 1842, when the General Assembly gave the courts authority to grant divorces. Five were filed in 1842; 188 more were filed between 1843 and 1850, or about 24 per year.

77. A proposal to adopt general *feme sole* provisions to avoid the need for partial divorces was made during the 1832 session, but went nowhere. 1832 HOUSE JOURNAL at 430, 526, 619.

78. Until the electoral reforms took effect in the 1838 session, the House of Delegates had 80 members, the Senate 15. From 1838 on the Senate had 21 members, one for each county plus one for Baltimore City, serving six-year, staggered terms. The House of Delegates dropped to 79 for the 1838–1840 sessions, after which the number changed slightly from time to time depending on population shifts. *See* EVERSTINE, *supra* note 38, at 491–493.

79. 1833 SENATE JOURNAL at 263–264.

80. 1835 HOUSE JOURNAL at 122–123.

81. *Id.* at 169; 1835 SENATE JOURNAL at 227.

82. 1836 SENATE JOURNAL at 25, 26, 32, 40. These entries run from Dec. 29, 1836, to Jan. 3, 1837.

83. The House Committee on Divorce filed an unfavorable report on the supermajority proposal. 1836 HOUSE JOURNAL at 88. Unfortunately, the contents of that report are not known. The roll call vote is reported *id.* at 123–124.

84. *See* discussion in *supra* note 38.

85. A general bill proposal was defeated at the 1836 session after garnering an unfavorable committee recommendation. 1836 HOUSE JOURNAL at 294, 475. Another proposal to require use of the 1829 court commission procedure failed the following year, 1837 HOUSE JOURNAL at 50, 55, 70, as did a general bill, *id.* at 255, 516, 653. Another general bill got nowhere in the 1838 session. 1838 HOUSE JOURNAL at 75. Finally, an unusual idea to impose a tax on divorce did not get out of committee. 1839 HOUSE JOURNAL at 67.

86. *See* table of General Bill Proposals in Appendix 2.

87. 1839 SENATE JOURNAL at 7, 60.

88. 1839 HOUSE JOURNAL at 186, 252–253.

89. *Id.* at 253.

90. *Id.* at 397, 400–401.

91. The political preferences of a few delegates could not be traced. The information in the text paragraph on the party affiliations of Mason and Risteau, the size of the Democratic majority in the House of Delegates, and the tabulation

of party voting preferences are all taken from NILES NATIONAL REGISTER 101 (Oct. 12, 1839).

92. *See* the discussion of this phenomenon at the end of Chapter 1.

93. 1839 HOUSE JOURNAL at 431.

94. *Id.* at 436.

95. *Id.* at 191, 219, 322, 567. 1839 SENATE JOURNAL at 249, 294.

96. 1840 SENATE JOURNAL at 12, 30, 31, 32, 33.

97. 1840 HOUSE JOURNAL at 143, 175–176, 178–179.

98. The party votes were tabulated using the party affiliations listed in NILES NATIONAL REGISTER 99 (Oct. 17, 1840).

99. A bill supplementary to an act passed December session, eighteen hundred and twenty-nine, chapter two hundred and two, relative to the taking of Testimony in all applications for Divorce, ch. 238, 1840 Md. Laws (Mar. 9, 1841). The court commission revision bill was first proposed on February 5, 1841. Its history is reported at 1840 HOUSE JOURNAL at 189, 301, 337, 340, 394; 1840 SENATE JOURNAL at 150–151, 187.

100. The text of the act may be found in Appendix 2.

101. 1840 SENATE JOURNAL at 196–197.

102. Leave was obtained to report a bill on Jan. 3, 1842, and it was passed on Jan. 6. 1841 SENATE JOURNAL at 10, 11, 14.

103. 1841 HOUSE JOURNAL at 70–71, 168, 185, 237, 437, 438.

104. Southern Whigs voted for the bill 11 to 2. Other Whigs split 8 to 7 in favor. Democrats from the north central region voted against the bill 15 to 2. Other Democrats split 15 to 11 in favor. These data were prepared by comparing the roll call votes to the party affiliations listed in the NILES NATIONAL REGISTER 104 (Oct. 16, 1841).

105. 1841 SENATE JOURNAL at 226–227. The Senate's refusal to consider adopting more private divorces created the final major burst of disagreement between the House and the Senate. The high rate at which the House or Senate blocked bills passed by the other between 1837 and 1841 (*see* Table 11 in Appendix 1) is fully explained by the long-delayed passage of general legislation. If the 21 bills passed by the House but blocked by the Senate during the 1841 session are excluded, the controversy level was nearly the same as in the eras before and after the adoption of the general bill. Table 11 shows that the two legislative bodies disagreed on bills 13 percent of the time in both the 1826–1836 and the 1842–1849 eras. Removing the 1841 session blockages by the Senate from the 1837–1841 era produces a 12 percent (20 of 167) dispute rate.

106. *See* E. Clark, *Matrimonial Bonds: Slavery and Divorce in Nineteenth Century America,* 8 LAW & HIST. REV. 26 (1990).

107. The relationships between harsh economic realities and married women's property legislation in Maryland is well told in E. WARBASSE, THE CHANGING LEGAL RIGHTS OF MARRIED WOMEN, 1800–1861, at 155–159 (1960) (Thesis Harvard U.).

108. An act in respect to Insurances for Lives for the benefit of Married Women, ch. 212, 1840 Md. Laws (Feb. 23, 1841).

109. An act regulating Executions against Life Estates in Lands or Tenements, ch. 161, 1841 Md. Laws (March 1, 1842). The title of this act may be a bit mysterious to those uninitiated in the rituals of marital property law. Upon marriage, a husband obtained management and control rights over the real property of his wife. Absent surviving encumbrances, a woman regained her property upon the death of her husband. He therefore had the equivalent of a life estate in her lands. Though mysterious, the statute's title is an accurate description of the style of rights limited by the act's simple terms:

> *Be it enacted by the General Assembly of Maryland,* That no real estate hereafter acquired by marriage, shall be liable to execution during the life of the wife, for debts due from the husband.

110. *See* the discussion of the relationship between the early married women's property acts and economic difficulties in R. Chused, *Married Women's Property Law: 1800–1850,* 71 GEO. L. J. 1359, 1400–1404 (1983).

111. 1841 HOUSE JOURNAL at 269–270. It is interesting that Thomas C. Risteau, who routinely opposed general divorce bills (*see supra* text accompanying notes 89–90), was one of the five opponents.

112. An act to regulate conjugal rights as they regard property, ch. 293, 1842 Md. Laws (March 10, 1843).

113. WARBASSE, *supra* note 107.

114. 1841 HOUSE JOURNAL at 442.

115. The act was silent as to management of real estate. The debt protection measure adopted the previous year placed some limit on husbandly control rights. And standard equity law allowed separate estate deeds to define each spouse's management rights in the property during the life of the husband. Presumably those rules governed.

116. For a comparison of this act with the terms of married women's property legislation adopted elsewhere, *see* Chused, *supra* note 110, at 1397–1404.

117. R. J. BRUGGER, MARYLAND: A MIDDLE TEMPERAMENT, 1634–1980, at 187 (1988).

8. The Demise of Legislative Divorce

Introduction

During the three years following adoption of general divorce legislation, only eleven divorce petitions were filed with the General Assembly and no private bills were passed. It was generally understood that divorce was no longer a legislative matter. The General Assembly's respite from family law debates, however, was brief—interrupted both by squabbles over the meaning of the recently passed general divorce act and, in the 1845 session, the sudden reappearance of private acts. In six of the seven sessions of the General Assembly following adoption of the first general divorce act, amendments were made to the statute.[1] Pressure to rejuvenate the private divorce process came from two powerful sources. The lack of judicial authority to grant *a vinculo* divorces for cruelty led some women to seek legislative aid. That pressure, together with the political exigencies generated by a legislative divorce petition from the governor of Maryland, led to the rebirth of the private bill system. Twelve divorce petitions were filed with the General Assembly during the 1845 session, and six divorces were passed. By 1849, divorce petitions were rolling in at the 1840 rate.[2]

Adoption of a new state constitution in 1851 marked the end of legislative divorce in Maryland. Section 21 of the new charter provided simply that "[n]o divorce shall be granted by the General Assembly."[3] Like the General Assembly's initial refusal to pass private acts after the passage of a general divorce bill in 1841, the banning of legislative divorces effectively narrowed the scope of remedies for the unhappily married.[4] The resulting shape of Maryland family law enlarged incentives for "creative" legal strategies, if not for falsified testimony, in divorce litigation. Not until the modernization of Maryland's divorce statutes in the twentieth century were wives in violent marriages able to sue for complete divorces without a waiting period.[5]

The Hiatus in Adoption of Private Bills

Members of Maryland's General Assembly assumed that adoption of general legislation at the 1841 session would end the private divorce system. No other conclusion can be drawn from either the Senate's refusal, immediately after passage of the divorce bill, to debate any private bills[6] or the General Assembly's rejection of all private bills for the following three sessions. In addition, bizarre judicial constructions of the general divorce act between 1842 and 1845 were countered by the General Assembly with further general legislation rather than private divorce acts.

Some judges clearly felt constrained to exercise care in resolving cases under the new divorce statute. Thus, Judges Purviance and Magruder, when granting Susan Houx a divorce from her husband, David, shortly after the general act was adopted, prudently wrote of both David's infamous temperament and the substantial evidentiary support for finding him guilty of adultery:

> The testimony furnished by all the witnesses go to establish the abandoned character of the defendant, proving him to be a drunkard, a gambler, a man of cruel treatment to his wife, utterly depraved in all his habits, frequently in company with women of ill fame, but strict proof is furnished of his infidelity to the marriage vow by the testimony of Dr. Kolb and Davis.[7]

The judges hearing her case in Baltimore had good reason to be careful. Susan Houx had unsuccessfully petitioned for a divorce at each of the two legislative sessions held just before her court filing.[8] Her second attempt generated some controversy. The House of Delegates passed a bill even though it received an unfavorable committee recommendation and survived an attempt to amend it to a partial divorce.[9] The *Houx* case is also a reminder that filing for a judicial divorce invoked a more elaborate procedural system than did seeking a private act. The need for witnesses and hearings provided a role for lawyers as advocates, a role played in the legislative process by members of the House of Delegates serving their constituents.

Other courts were not as careful as Judges Purviance and Magruder. The first amendments to the divorce act were surely generated by *Stewart v. Stewart*, a divorce case filed by Elizabeth Stewart in Baltimore on February 6, 1843.[10] The Stewarts were involved in marital controversy over a sixteen-year period. Joseph Stewart applied to the legislature for a divorce at the 1827, 1828, 1830, and 1831 sessions.[11] He was joined by his wife in 1831, and she obtained passage of a partial divorce that year.[12] In addition to the standard bed and board provision, the act granted Elizabeth *feme sole* status and specifically precluded her from remarrying during the life of Joseph.[13] The Stewarts had no children. Her divorce complaint alleged that she had "demeaned herself . . . in a manner which has acquired for her the favorable opinions of all with whom she is acquainted" since the legislative divorce. Elizabeth also believed the private act she obtained at the 1831 session was an *a vinculo* divorce since her ex-husband was remarried and raising a new child. She claimed she was ignorant of the terms of the act and did not learn of its contents until shortly before filing her court bill. Officials in the General Assembly, she alleged, told her to go to court under the new divorce legislation rather than file another legislative petition. She therefore sought a divorce to meet her "peculiar circumstances." Her husband, apparently anxious to normalize his own family status, filed an answer the same day his ex-wife went to court, agreeing with the allegations in Elizabeth's complaint and asking that a divorce be granted. This was plainly a cooperative judicial adventure by the Stewarts. The court, however, was not amused. It dismissed the case without opinion the day after the bill and answer were filed.

The allegations found in the *Stewart* complaint confirm that the General Assembly thought it was out of the divorce business after 1841. But they also suggest that some of the parties who obtained legislative divorces either were blissfully unaware of the terms of their private acts or were ignoring them when so inclined. The former conclusion is perfectly compatible with the legislature's writing and adopting private acts without requiring the parties' presence. The latter assumption suggests the lack of uniform understandings about the moral connotations of family formation, marriage, and divorce. There is certainly evidence that some people "remarried" prior to obtaining a divorce or formed new families without regard to the niceties of legal norms. Recall that President Jackson was scandalized by some for remarrying before his divorce was final.[14] Mary Gwinn and Susannah Alexander sought legislative relief after charging their husbands with bigamy.[15] And surely those departing for the frontiers without their spouses formed new families without regard to their marital status. It is also possible that women like Elizabeth Stewart, wishing to remarry, were more reluctant than men in general, and her prior spouse in particular, to start a new family without the sanction of the state.

In any case, the Stewarts must have returned to the legislature for assistance after the court dismissed their case. Rather than get back into the private bill business, however, the General Assembly responded with a general bill warning against consensual divorce while simultaneously affirming the duty of a court to entertain divorce petitions from partially divorced plaintiffs.[16] Consensual answers to a divorce petition, the act states, "shall not be taken of itself as conclusive proof of the facts charged." This provision was an obvious manifestation of legislative fear of consensual divorce. It was perfectly consistent with a number of earlier, and arguably ineffective, pronouncements in the legislative journals that divorces could be obtained only upon adequate proofs[17] and with an amendment to the general divorce act, adopted the following year, which imposed a two-year residency requirement on divorce plaintiffs if the events giving rise to the divorce claim occurred outside of Maryland.[18] Though the legislature had rarely imposed stringent evidentiary requirements on the parties seeking adoption of private acts, it feared that loose judicial proof practices would turn a narrow general divorce act into a broad one. Traditional Maryland was not about to take the place of Pennsylvania or Indiana as the divorce mill of the mid-nineteenth century.[19]

The other section confirmed that the courts had jurisdiction over a request for a complete divorce even if the parties had previously dissolved their bed and board obligations and required any court that had dismissed a divorce petition because the plaintiff was previously divorced to reinstate the case. This was surely written as a directive to the *Stewart* court, which reinstated Elizabeth's complaint on April 17, 1843, and commissioned Joshua Dryden to take testimony in the case. Dryden reported back to the court on the testimony of three witnesses called by Elizabeth. Joseph, maintaining his consensual posture in the matter, did not produce any witnesses. All the witnesses said they had known the Stewarts for more than twenty years, that the couple had lived apart since at least 1831, that Joseph had remarried, and that Elizabeth should be divorced. In language standard for the time, each witness was asked: "What is the general character of the complainant for chastity, industry and upright deportment, and in what estimation is she held by those who are acquainted with her?" And, of course, they all praised Elizabeth's virtue.[20]

The *Stewart* case is a good illustration of how the traditional underpinnings of narrow divorce statutes were eventually undermined by the emotional content of family tribulations and careful preparation by lawyers handling family law matters. Despite the legislative admonitions against consensual divorce, the court could only take the testimony presented to it. If Joseph declined to produce a case, Elizabeth was still entitled to a divorce if she produced evidence to support her complaint. Legislative efforts to prohibit divorce by consent added evidentiary hearings and costs to the divorce process, but did not always preclude the granting of divorces when only marginal testimony supporting a divorce ground existed and the parties wished to end their relationship. And in settings where either a husband or a wife was not around, one-sided evidentiary hearings made the entry of a divorce decree much more likely. It was hardly surprising that the *Stewart* court finally entered an *a vinculo* divorce decree on May 16, 1843. Joseph Stewart's divorce saga, completed almost sixteen years after he first applied to the General Assembly for relief, exemplified many of the changes in Maryland family law during the middle of the nineteenth century.

The General Assembly continued to retreat from some of the strictest terms of the divorce statute, both by general legislation and eventually by reopening the private bill process. Though never enacting divorce grounds as broad as those in many states to the north and west, a few notable changes were made in the original divorce act passed at the 1841 session. The most important modification, passed during the 1844 session, loosened the abandonment ground for a complete divorce. The requirement of absence from the state for five years was replaced by a provision that "abandonment has continued uninterruptedly for at least three years, and is deliberate and final, and the separation of the parties beyond any reasonable expectation of reconciliation."[21] It is apparent that objections to adoption of divorce reforms eased a bit after adoption and use of the 1841 act occurred without any further outpouring of opposition from family law traditionalists.

This revised abandonment ground was the subject of another lengthy divorce saga involving Jehu and Elizabeth Brown. The Browns married in 1824, and, according to Jehu's 1846 complaint seeking a judicial divorce, they slept apart from each other beginning in 1830 and separated in 1836.[22] Jehu petitioned the General Assembly for a divorce in 1834, after obtaining and filing a report under the terms of the 1829 court commission legislation. The House of Delegates declined to pursue the matter, filed near the end of the session, for lack of time.[23] Elizabeth returned to the legislature in 1837, and her husband returned the following year, but neither effort progressed very far.[24] Their experience certainly undermined any suggestion that use of the 1829 legislation permitting judicial fact-finding prior to submission of a legislative petition for divorce was wise.

The 1844 amendment to the divorce act prompted Jehu to try again.

Before filing his court petition, he worked out a property settlement call-ing for the bestowal upon Stephen Boyd as trustee for the "use and benefit of the said Elizabeth" of all property "coming to her from her deceased father . . . which was the only property she ever possessed" along with a "sum much more than commensurate with any claim she could have had on his very limited property if he [Jehu] had died." Jehu then filed his complaint seeking a divorce on the ground of Elizabeth's abandonment.

Despite the settlement, the case became a contest. Elizabeth chal-lenged Jehu's account of their relationship, arguing that she left the house-hold because of his "cruel and unnatural treatment," and seeking alimony despite the provision in the separation agreement by which she consented to accept the property bestowed upon her trustee "in full satisfaction and discharge of all claim of dower and of every other claim" against Jehu "whether in the nature of alimony or otherwise." The divorce and prop-erty disputes between the parties were central to only a part of the court's resolution of the matter. First, in a highly cramped reading of the 1844 revision of the abandonment ground,[25] the High Court of Chancery[26] opined:

> This latter law, it is supposed by the complainant's solicitor, not only changes so much of the act of 1841 . . . as makes it necessary that the party complained against, should have remained absent from the state for five years, but renders absence from the state, for a *period*, unnecessary. It is not clear, however, that this is the true construction of the act of 1844. Its language . . . does not say that absence from the state for *any period*, shall not be necessary to entitle a party to an absolute divorce, but that absence *for five years*, shall not be required.

The court, taking the traditionalist impulses of the legislature quite seriously, then refused to grant even a partial divorce. Although Section 3 of the 1841 act allowed the decree of a bed and board divorce without regard to the duration or location of an abandonment, the court still found that "the facts alleged, and proved, do not bring this case within the pro-visions" of the divorce acts:

> Having selected their own remedy by the execution of this deed, after the actual separation had lasted nearly or quite ten years, no sufficient reason has been assigned, why within less than three months from the date of the deed, this court should be called upon absolutely to dissolve the marriage. It is not alleged or proved, that any circumstances have transpired since the execution of the deed, which render it necessary or proper, that the relations of the parties as established by that instrument, should be changed, and the court

would be most reluctant to do so, especially in the manner, and to the extent proposed by this bill, unless a case of strong urgency was made out, as the effect of such a change upon the rights secured by the deed might occasion embarrassing, if not injurious consequences. . . . [A] decree of . . . [partial divorce] is rendered unnecessary, and would, perhaps, be improper in this case, in consequence of the deed of separation, by which the parties have placed themselves, very much in the condition with respect to each other, which the law would have empowered the court to do, by decreeing a limited divorce.[27]

The opinion left a mixed legacy. It made a shambles of the abandonment ground and left the bed and board provisions seriously weakened. On the other hand, it reaffirmed the legitimacy of separation agreements reposing property in a separate estate for the benefit of a married woman.[28] The legislature stepped in to "correct" some aspects of the *Brown* result, adopting a private bill divorcing the Browns *a vinculo* during the 1847 session,[29] and, at the next session, passing general legislation permitting the use of the three-year abandonment ground even when both parties stayed in Maryland for the entire period of their separation.[30]

Concurrent Jurisdiction: Family Law Complexities After Renewal of the Private Bill Process

The *Brown* case illustrates the growing complexity of divorce law in Maryland in the mid-1840s. In addition to the apparently unqualified ability of private individuals to *de facto* divorce themselves from bed and board by using separation agreements,[31] the legislature reappeared as a forum for resolving marital disputes. Figuring out which remedial path to take must have been a nightmare for some and a financial boon for lawyers willing to handle divorces.

It is not possible to draw a complete picture of the strategic options available to divorce petitioners. Several of the more important parameters, however, are apparent. First, by 1850, judicial practice made the cruelty ground more difficult to prove than the abandonment ground. While women in need of immediate protection from violent husbands could use the bed and board cruelty ground to advantage, the typical divorce case probably proceeded more quickly and smoothly if abandonment was its legal support. The legislature's failure to make cruelty a ground for complete divorce created additional incentives to use adultery or abandonment in divorce pleadings.[32] Second, pressure from a governor wishing to divorce and from women seeking complete and speedy divorces from violent, unsympathetic husbands helped push the General Assembly to re-enter the private act divorce business. Closure of this venue by the 1851 constitution's banning of private divorce bills was a particularly serious matter for women in violent relationships.

Several cases emphasized that successful use of the cruelty ground for bed and board divorce required proof of substantial violence. The courts, imposing traditional norms on the general divorce statute, imported the lore underlying grants of alimony for cruelty from the old 1777 statute into the new divorce statute. Thus, Margaret Snuggrass, who filed an action in Baltimore in 1843, failed in her attempt to obtain either a bed and board divorce or alimony from her husband William.[33] The court concluded that both parties were of excitable temper, but that courts would not interfere in a marriage without "grave and weighty" causes "such as show an absolute impossibility that the duties of the married life can be discharged." Proof of "danger of life, limb or health," or "reasonable apprehension of bodily hurt" was needed. Short of that, the court noted, couples were relegated to seeking help from clergy and friends. Since the grounds for a legal separation under the 1841 statute were not proven, the court was unwilling to create an incentive to separate by requiring the husband to pay either alimony or a separate allowance.

These basic results were confirmed in a series of chancery court opinions in the early 1850s.[34] In each case, the court strongly affirmed the need for proof of physical violence in a "cruelty" case. They gave the same basic meaning to the term as that used by the ecclesiastical courts,[35] amplified by the traditional views of Chancellor Kent in New York.[36] Thus Gertrude Daiger lost her case because the court did "not find proof of a series of acts of personal violence, or danger of life, limb or health, or indeed, any thing approaching to either, which would justify the court in decreeing a separation between the parties."[37] The courts refused to adopt the more open-ended attitude toward cruelty or "ill usage" evident in some private acts adopted earlier in the century—the Sampson divorce during the Jeffersonian era, the Warfield divorce of 1825, or the Barnum act of 1829. As in other parts of the country, "mental cruelty" did not fully blossom until after the period of this study.[38]

Narrow construction of the cruelty ground had important effects on both wives and the judicial process. Many women lacked the economic ability or psychological strength to simply leave their husbands; neither their own assets nor those of family or friends could be relied upon for support.[39] And if they did leave, they risked a husbandly charge of abandonment and loss of any claim to alimony. Nor could they be guaranteed their own economic independence without a complete divorce. While the married women's property acts ameliorated some features of the common law coverture structure, husbands retained significant legal, to say nothing of cultural, controls over their wives' economic lives. Partial divorce decrees could be accompanied by far-reaching property terms, but their issuance was at the discretion of courts quite willing to use their own perceptions of marital fault in framing court orders.

If women had proof of their husbands' adultery, they could sue immediately for a complete divorce. Without such proof, the only legal avenues of exit from a violent marriage were a court order for alimony, a judicial divorce from bed and board because of cruelty, or a legislative divorce. Only the last provided any hope of a total and reasonably speedy release from marital vows. Use of cruelty required proof of violence, and failure to leave the household after cruel behavior could be construed as condonation, a waiver of the husband's marital fault.[40] On the other hand, departure from the household by a wife, who then failed to prove the level of violence necessary to prove cruelty, might allow her husband to divorce her on abandonment grounds. If she was found at fault, economic props, such as alimony, were unavailable. The legal rules created incentives to mislead the courts to obtain complete divorces, increased the importance of legal representation, and raised the costs of obtaining a divorce. If a husband was gone, allegations of adultery or violence could be feigned. And even if he was around, settings could be manufactured. Such strategies, of course, were often expensive to implement. It was probably the arrival of judicial divorce, not the use of legislative private bills, that made resolution of family disputes more difficult for those without significant resources.

Stories were surely "created." In a fascinating vignette, John E. Semmes reported on a case he handled sometime in the mid-nineteenth century in Baltimore:

> She lived on Davis Street, a short street parallel with Calvert Street, entering Lexington Street, nearly opposite the Post Office. The legend is that this part of Baltimore was in olden times called "The Meadows," and a Mrs. Davis, a woman of questionable repute, had an establishment, corresponding with her character, in this locality. In honor of her Davis Street received its name and, as far as I could ascertain, her reputation.

At least, Mrs. Davis (for I shall so name her) was a very worthy resident of such a locality. She told me that her husband had brought a suit against her for divorce; that she would be glad to be shut of him, but that she had a daughter, and she understood that if she made no defense the daughter might be taken from her.

I told her that this was possible. She then said she wished to have the suit resisted. I asked her whether she was guilty of the offenses charged. She said she was, but that her husband was equally bad. I then asked her where her husband was living, and she said with her at the Davis Street house, where they had a saloon. I then explained that her husband continuing to live with her condoned or forgave the offense, and that I would file affidavits, and have the case dismissed. This I did, and the Court directed the husband to pay me a fee of $75.00 which he did not, and I had naught for my work and pigeonholed the case among the cases where the compensation was nil.

Some months afterwards Mrs. Davis reappeared in my office and explained the purport of her visit to be that she wished advice. During her absence her husband would take her clothes out of the bureau or wardrobe and tear them into shreds, and pile them in that condition in the centre of the floor. She would be washing her face, and he would seize the basin, and in other ways make himself "pleasant." She was physically his superior, and goaded to desperation would attack him. The result would be that she would be arrested and locked up for assault.

I told her that there was nothing to do but to treat him in the same way, until he would resist it and strike her, and then to issue a warrant and have him arrested, and to take advantage of his absence to leave the place, taking her daughter and belongings with her.[41]

I heard nothing of her for six months, when she again visited me. She said she had done what I told her, but had not left the place when he was locked up, and that he had behaved so much better for sometime, that she thought it would be alright; but that he was now resuming his old practices, and she wanted to know what she could do.

Then I told her I thought of issuing a writ to seize her husband's property in the saloon to pay my fee of $75 which he had been directed to pay by the Court, but had not paid, and I would write her a letter to that effect, and perhaps if he knew of it, he might leave. I wrote her a letter, and a few days afterwards she came in delighted. She explained that she received the letter and put it in the bosom of her dress, taking care to have a portion of the letter exposed. Her husband, when she was behind the bar, asked what that was, and demanded that she give it up. She declined, and there was a struggle; but he got the letter. He then ordered two furniture wagons, took most of the furniture and departed. I congratulated her upon the success of our efforts and considered the case finally closed.[42]

The interlocking operation of cruelty, condonation of fault, and abandonment meant that "Mrs. Davis" could leave her husband with legal

safety only immediately after violent acts by him. If she left "merely" because of events that made the marriage unpleasant, she risked losing both
a divorce suit and her child. If she stayed, she had to endure. Once she
convinced her husband to leave, she could make an immediate plea for
alimony and, after three years, file for a complete divorce on abandonment
grounds.

There are signs that the entire structure led women trapped in unten-
able marriages to pressure the legislature for private divorces. In 1848, for
example, Rebecca Conway filed for a bed and board divorce from her
husband Thomas so she could live with her parents, and asked for custody of their children.[43] The Conways had married in 1836, and by the
time a divorce was sought they had five sons between the ages of one and
twelve. Rebecca alleged that she was "troubled by the constant dread and
apprehension for the living and safety of herself and her children." She
sought relief from the "intolerable" bonds of marriage. During October
1848 depositions on interrogatories were taken of a number of witnesses.
Mrs. Ann Jane Feinor stated that the habits of Thomas Conway were
"those of a savage and brutal drunkard," and that she saw him "expel his
wife and children from his house, cruelly thrusting and kicking them out
of doors so that they had to seek refuge in the barn from the weather and
from his cruelties." Basil Warfield testified that he heard wild screams,
went outside, and found Thomas Conway, intoxicated, beating his wife
with a stick while she was in labor with their last child. Six others, including the oldest Conway son, confirmed the testimony of physical cruelty.
The court granted Mrs. Conway a bed and board divorce and custody of
the children.

In spite of the brutality of Rebecca Conway's life, the court lacked
authority to divorce her *a vinculo*. There was no proof of adultery. Neither party ever abandoned the marital home. The adoption of married
women's property acts earlier in the decade provided little real help. Rebecca had no resources of her own to place within the acts' protections.
And even if she had assets, Rebecca could never hope to safely manage her
own affairs without an enforceable declaration that her violent relationship
with Thomas was completely over. Nor could she seek a new husband
willing to provide economic support to her and the children. The year
after she obtained court relief, Rebecca applied to the legislature for a complete divorce.[44] A simple one-line act was passed granting her request.[45]

Julia Taylor also obtained legislative relief, although her marriage was
apparently not as base as Rebecca Conway's. Her simple *a vinculo* divorce

act,[46] passed by the General Assembly in the 1849 session, came about a year and a half after judicial proceedings for a divorce were dropped.[47] Julia alleged in her court filing that she married John Taylor "at a very early age" in 1843. "Shortly after her marriage, her husband abandoned himself to low and intemperate habits, to which he continues to this time addicted." The complaint also contained a quite general allegation that John was associating with lewd women. To escape the unpleasantness, Julia went with her two infant children to live with her parents. She sought a complete divorce, custody of the children, and alimony. John answered that the marriage went downhill after a visit from Julia's father in 1844, that his wife's "treatment towards me became entirely changed . . . cold and indifferent," and that her parents were "bent on satisfying their malicious spleen towards me." He also objected to Julia's custody request because she would have to rely on her father, a man of "known profligacy." Whether the child custody claims were made for strategic or emotional reasons is unclear. But the arrival of child custody rules presuming that women were better custodians forced men seeking control over the lives of their children to take judicial action. For reasons not stated in the court file, Julia's lawyer halted the taking of deposition testimony in the case in September 1848. The prospects of a nasty court battle may have convinced the parties to settle their major economic and custody differences.[48] The reasons Julia dropped the case are unknown, but it was unlikely she could have obtained a complete divorce. The charges of adultery in the complaint were only implicit—association with lewd women does not adultery prove. Presumably Julia and her attorney decided that the legislature was either a more hospitable or a cheaper environment in which to resolve her marital woes.

Julia Taylor and Rebecca Conway were only two of a growing stream of people to approach the legislature seeking divorces. Any pretense that such cases were exclusively within the purview of the courts dissolved quickly after 1845 when the General Assembly adopted the first private bills since the adoption of general divorce legislation.[49] Among them was an act divorcing Francis Thomas from his wife Sarah.[50] Francis was the governor of Maryland. Sarah was the young daughter of the governor of Virginia, James McDowell.[51] They met in Washington, D.C., when Francis Thomas served in Congress and wed in 1841, shortly before he won the gubernatorial election. The marriage apparently went badly from the start. Thomas, it is said, was "insanely jealous of his young wife."[52] In 1845, things got so bad that Governor McDowell traveled to Annapolis and brought his daughter home. On February 12, 1846, the Committee on Grievances and Courts of Justice was given leave to bring in a bill divorcing Governor Thomas and his wife.[53] By February 14, the bill was passed.[54]

The uneventful procedural history of the divorce bill hardly tells the tale. Governor Thomas, like Charles Warfield twenty years earlier, caused a pamphlet to be published. The fifty-two page booklet,[55] distributed about the time Governor McDowell carried his daughter back to the Old Dominion,

> amazed the people of two states and the members of the Congress of the United States, for a copy was laid upon the desk of each Senator and Representative. In this astounding publication the Governor gave without any kind of decent reserve, his version of his family troubles and adverted to matters which caused the more charitable of his readers to conclude that he had lost his mind.[56]

Before the controversy ended, Thomas became a defendant in a libel suit over statements made in the pamphlet and, after making wild charges of theft and other improprieties against Judge John Carroll Legrand, attempted to have the judge impeached. Prior to the scandal's eruption, political pundits assumed Thomas was going to be the 1844 Democratic presidential candidate. Governor McDowell took an active role in insuring that Thomas's candidacy floundered.

The Thomas dispute reminds us of the economic and personal trauma that lay beneath the surface of both consensual divorce and magisterial sounding legislative and constitutional reforms of family law. The lofty, romantic sentiments of Senator Richard Carroll, writing to Bishop Kemp early in the nineteenth century of the "grave difficulty and delicacy" of divorce,[57] failed to capture the full day-to-day content of the married lives that came before him. Absconding men, deserted women, adultery, failed public obligations, poverty, and emotional distress were the stuff of contested divorces. Mixture of such matters with politics was sometimes far from delicate. It took a more insightful person than Carroll to understand the potential connections between burgeoning images of virtue and romance and the travails of divorce, economic deprivation, and child custody. Thomas Jefferson, in a poetic note written long before the demise of legislative divorce in Maryland, caught some of the new ironies inherent in mixing politics with the trauma of severing family and parental ties:

> Cruel to continue by violence an union made at first by mutual
> love, but now dissolved by hatred.[58]

The marriages of Sarah and Charles Warfield and of Sarah and Francis Thomas were each dissolved in hatred. Both the Warfield and Thomas pamphlets provide fodder for speculation about paranoia, lunacy, and jealousy. But there are also some remarkable and telling differences between the two cases. Warfield's perhaps delusional icons were those of the late eighteenth century—noncharismatic faith, overreaching patriarchy, and wifely obedience. He raged about perhaps imagined forces that reduced his household power and control. Thomas's jealousy-riven archetypes were "honorable men and virtuous women,"[59] honest, hardworking husbands, and delicate, faithful wives. "No human agency, no persuasion, no covert appeals to my gallantry or generosity," Thomas complained, "could have led me deliberately to court and marry any woman" even charged with a dangerous flirtation, let alone an affair, while a maiden.[60] Sex was "sacred,"[61] and attending to ladies "refines and improves man."[62] The "character . . . unblemished" and honesty of a man is more important than "life itself."[63] In contrast to Warfield, Thomas took pride in never exercising "overruling authority" against his wife.[64]

Thomas speaks with high Victorian sentiments, idealizing images of romance, marital virtue, and gender roles to levels impossible for most to attain. Though Thomas's rhetoric may have soared to extraordinary heights of hyperbole, even for the 1840s, his icons celebrated ideals held by many in the culture. Such sentiments may provide an explanation for the legislature's growing reluctance at mid-century to continue struggling with divorce. The flip side of idealized, sacred sex and overbearing virtue is a studied reluctance to talk publicly about "private" family life. It is therefore easy to see how later nineteenth-century commentators on the episode, perhaps even more reluctant than Thomas's peers to vent such affairs in public, would opine that "the Governor gave without any kind of decent reserve, his version of his family troubles and adverted to matters which caused the more charitable of his readers to conclude that he had lost his mind."[65] Not just the contents of Thomas's pamphlet, but the decision to publicly release it, must have caused many to wonder about his mental stability.

Surely the scandalous qualities of the Francis Thomas affair anguished members of the General Assembly, perhaps enough to make a few of them eager to drop divorce from their day-to-day agenda. In the short run, however, Governor Thomas's plea for a private divorce only helped reinvigorate what was previously thought to be a dead process. The dispute was a public controversy of major proportions. Thomas claimed that he was brought to the point of revealing to the public charges against his wife because she was participating in the airing of calumnies against him by her family and friends. And the stories he told about his wife were quite remarkable. He suggested Sarah committed adultery with at least two men. In addition, Francis alleged she became pregnant by one of her lovers just a month after her wedding and aborted the pregnancy two months later by ingesting a powder. Though Governor Thomas claimed in his pamphlet that procuring an abortion was a "penitentiary offense" in Maryland at the time,[66] his wife probably did not commit a criminal act.[67] Despite stated obeisance to the need for delicacy on the subject, Thomas's description of the abortion was fairly graphic.[68]

> I recoil from setting forth the details of what followed, unless judicially compelled to do it. The written evidence lies now before me of what I must indicate, but I shall do so with as much regard to delicacy as possible. In brief then the embryo was found next morning, under the head of the bed wrapped in her under clothing. And so far was concealment carried, that after washing, and particularly the feet in cold water; when left alone in the room in the morning, she dressed and prepared to descend to the breakfast table as if nothing had happened, and was only prevented by the remonstances [sic] of a lady who learned what had occurred. It is wholly unnecessary to add a comment. Let others decide whether it is not calculated to aggravate the feelings with which I have been harrassed.

Through it all Francis said he hoped that Sarah's family could produce the evidence to disprove his charges. Given the power of Thomas's rage, of course, he cast the burden of proof upon her.

The General Assembly's speedy divorce of Governor Thomas and his wife was important not only for its remarkably scandalous overtones. For it was unlikely that the Governor was entitled to a judicial divorce. Thomas was firmly convinced his wife had committed adultery and had used powder to abort an illegitimate pregnancy, but his lengthy tract contains only weak evidence of the adultery allegations. Furthermore, as he noted in his pamphlet, he could not force his wife, then living in Virginia, to respond in person to a bill or interrogatories.[69] The whole affair surely made it easier for others seeking to legislatively dissolve their marriages without judicial grounds under the 1841 act.

By 1849, the last gasp of legislative hesitancy to pass private divorce acts disappeared.[70] In that session, the House adopted a motion requiring the Committee on Grievances and Courts of Justice to "enquire how far the jurisdiction in cases of divorce, as conferred by law in . . . the

Courts . . . of this State, takes from the legislature, the power of acting on such applicants,"[71] and the committee concluded that the 1841 divorce act gave "full jurisdiction over said cases to the said courts, and makes it obligatory upon parties desiring divorce to seek the same in said courts."[72] The report, however, was laid on the table and never voted on.[73]

In the same session the Senate Committee on Judicial Proceedings, which had been assigned all the pending divorce petitions, complained,

> [t]hat the amount of business of the greatest importance to the general leg-
> islation, and interest of the State, and appropriately belonging to said com-
> mittee, is so great, that they have not the time to investigate the merits of
> divorce bills, and cannot consent to report upon such bills without that thor-
> ough scrutiny, which your committee have ever sought to give to all subjects
> confided to them.

Instead of recommending an end to the private bill process, the Committee "most respectfully ask[ed] to be discharged from the further consideration of all bills for divorce, and recommend[ed] the appointment,
forthwith, by the President of the Senate, of a standing committee upon
divorces."[74] A standing divorce committee was immediately selected.

Alimony After Married Women's Property Reforms

The treatment of alimony and property issues also changed after the adoption of the general divorce act in 1841. The terms of the 1841 legislation
permitting the award of alimony, "property or estate," and payments for
the "support and maintenance" of children substantially broadened the
authority of the courts to deal with the economic aspects of divorce. The
continued existence of the 1777 alimony statute made for additional complexities in cases in which the plaintiff either did not seek a divorce or was
unable to obtain one. The usual problems in alimony cases—locating husbands, finding assets worth pursuing, dealing with court procedures—
were still present,[75] much as they are today. Some other difficulties, at least
in theory, had been solved. The adoption of married women's property
acts[76] theoretically gave wives the right to prevent husbands from running off with all of the household assets, although such events continued
to occur.[77]

The tale of Mary and Otis Harrington exemplifies the changes that
occurred in the economic terms of some divorce cases after the statutory

property reforms. The Harringtons married in 1829 and lived together for only eighteen months. During that time, Mary alleged in her divorce complaint,[78] Otis made repeated efforts to "obtain the control and disposal of [her] . . . separate property." He then abandoned her and lived out of the state for ten or twelve years. The court granted Mary an *a vinculo* divorce on the condition that she file an affidavit as to the nonresidency of the defendant and decreed that the plaintiff was to hold all property she had "at the period of her intermarriage" and the profits from that property, in the same manner as before the marriage.

Even though this case dealt with property set aside in a separate estate before the adoption of a married women's property act, it demonstrated the willingness of the courts to deprive husbands of access to a married woman's separately held property, at least in cases in which her fault did not lead to the divorce, while eschewing the award of alimony. Where wives had no separate property, the courts found it easy to use the traditional thirds of dower law as a basic measure of the amount of alimony or maintenance a wife could obtain at divorce from the income of the husband.[79] Since alimony or other property relief provided for under the divorce statute dealt only with the property of husbands, habit and tradition naturally led to use of thirds.

But changes in married women's property law also made it easier for judges deciding cases involving women with some assets to refuse alimony awards altogether. The need to decree an alimony award as a disguised way of returning property to women after men ran off with it was obviously reduced by the adoption of the property reforms. Amelia Tayman, who proved through the depositions of a large number of witnesses that her husband had assaulted her and her children with firearms, committed adultery, and attempted to sell off her separate property,[80] obtained a bed and board divorce on cruelty grounds. Judge Johnson, noting that the "conduct of the husband here has been, not only such as to furnish well grounded apprehensions of bodily hurt, but has been brutal, and inhuman in the extreme,"[81] ordered that

> the defendant restore and deliver up, to her, the real and personal estate of which she was the owner, or to which she had title at the time of her marriage with the said defendant, and of which the said defendant is now in possession, or which may be under his control, to be held and enjoyed by her, separately, and in the same right, and by the same title as said property was held and enjoyed by her prior to her intermarriage with the said defendant.[82]

The court, however, "in consideration of this restoration to the wife of her own property, and the narrow circumstances of the defendant," refused to make a permanent award of alimony.[83]

The "retroactive" effects of the *Tayman* property decision are interesting. The parties married in 1849, seven years after the passage of the major property act reforms, and separated the following year. The separate estate rights of Amelia were therefore as "vested" as any husbandly rights in wives' property were before the property reforms. In contrast to the concerns about retroactive property awards voiced during the 1832 legislative session,[84] the *Tayman* court's protection of Amelia's property from the depredations of her brutal husband did not recast prior expectations. Retroactivity issues were disappearing from the agenda.

Other aspects of the alimony picture also changed. Although Amelia Tayman did not receive permanent alimony, she did obtain $200 "to enable her to carry on the suit, and . . . [the court reserved] the power to pass such other or further order in the premises, as the exigencies of the case may hereafter, and from time to time, require."[85] This *pendente lite* order was in conformity with a virtually ironclad preference for the award of temporary alimony announced in *Daiger v. Daiger*.[86]

Gertrude married Frederick Daiger in a Catholic rite on February 17, 1848, after she had been courted by him for two years.[87] Her complaint for a bed and board divorce, filed about two and one-half years later, alleged that Frederick began using profane and vulgar language almost immediately after the wedding, frequently threatened to knock her brains out, waved an ax at her on one occasion, threw a knife, book, hammer, and iron stove leg on another occasion, knocked her down three times, and twice withheld food and money for a week. She also charged that Frederick, in a cruel gesture impugning her character and "nuptial rights," petitioned for a legislative divorce during the 1849 session.[88] The petition, Gertrude alleged, was framed with the help of "notorious prostitutes." Notwithstanding his devious actions, "no act of connubial delinquency was or could be elicited or established against her" so the application for a divorce "failed entirely."

Frederick told a different story, alleging in the answer he filed only three days after the complaint that Gertrude was "untruthful, dishonest and grossly intemperate." He learned "with deep mortification" shortly after the wedding that with the help of a priest, Gertrude had "woefully deceived and in fact seduced [him] into marriage with a common prostitute." She was often seen, he charged, passed out drunk in public, lying naked on the street and in houses of ill repute. When he was in Annapolis trying to get a divorce, she took his furniture. He denied most of the allegations of violence, save for one event when he hit her with the handle of a small hammer after she entered his place of business intoxicated and refused to leave.

Several weeks later, Gertrude filed a petition asking the court to order Frederick to devote some of his daily earnings to the case. Otherwise, she argued, she would be financially barred from exercising her right to seek a divorce. The need to gather evidence and take depositions to refute her husband's false allegations required both more time and money than she expected. The court agreed, opining that if a preliminary examination into the merits of the case were made before testimony was gathered and

> a decision made, adverse to the application of the wife, it might have the effect of defeating her suit altogether, before the usual opportunity has been afforded of developing the full merits of the case. . . . There can, therefore, be no doubt, I think, notwithstanding the criminations of the answer, which charges her with adultery, and intoxication, that she is entitled to temporary alimony, and money to carry on the suit, and I feel myself bound to make such allowance, and although the evidence in regard to the circumstances of the defendant is a little contradictory, I consider it better to proceed to make the allowance now, than subject the parties to additional expense of taking proof upon the subject. The allowance will be made with due regard to the modest circumstances of the defendant, and upon the presumption, (warranted by proof), that the wife is capable of making some exertion for her own support.[89]

The court then ordered Frederick to pay Gertrude $40 immediately, and $100 per year thereafter pending resolution of the case. He was also prohibited from disposing of any of his property until further order of the court.[90]

Given the eventual outcome of the case, this temporary alimony result was remarkable.[91] The plaintiff took the depositions of nineteen witnesses, most of whom supported the basic thrust of her story. The defendant called fifteen, who had mostly bad things to say about the plaintiff. The case dragged on for months before the court, on May 27, 1851, dismissed it, without imposing additional costs on either party. Despite the voluminous evidence that the Daigers were utterly incapable of maintaining a scintilla of civility toward each other, the court failed to find proof of that "series of acts of personal violence" needed to support a partial divorce for cruelty.[92]

The depth of hatred and discord evident in the *Daiger* file contrasts dramatically with the simple contours of the journal reports on and text of the last batch of legislative divorces. By 1850 family law and discord had moved into a different mode than that present in 1800. Romance and marriage by agreement sometimes created expectations which, when sundered, produced enormous public rage and antipathy. As virtue became a subject of political as well as family concern, the stakes involved in divorce grew. Governor Thomas's presidential ambitions may have foundered on the shoals of insanity. But his compulsive desire to tell his story in public also provides a clue that family stability was an important part of the national political agenda. The change is also symbolized by the handling of children. The extant historical record of divorce in Maryland reveals no cases in which children of a marriage were the subjects of discord and public controversy before 1800. But by 1850, children were periodically caught up in the brawling. When adults began to see young persons as needing ethical, religious and academic instruction, the design of that guidance became both a matter of general concern and a litigable issue.

By the middle of the nineteenth century, it is difficult to believe that a large proportion of Maryland's politicians wished to grapple with the messy details of such battles. The sheer volume of routine, uncontested divorce petitions was not the only factor driving their resolution into the courts. The political importance and spiteful quality of some divorce and custody disputes grew to levels that made continued legislative attention difficult to support. Memories of the Governor Thomas scandal were still strong and the Daiger saga was ongoing as the Maryland Constitutional Convention met in 1850 to draft a new state charter. Whether the members of that convention knew of the *Daiger* case is a mystery, but it was surely no coincidence that its members adopted provisions barring passage of private divorce acts. Adoption of such acts was "obviously" wrong "because it would occupy too much time, and because it is properly a judicial act."[93] In a forum such as a constitutional convention, disconnected from face-to-face, melancholy pleas of unhappy people, the sheer agony of the divorce and child custody process overcame any lingering sense that the legislature could do a better job than the courts in handling the rough factual and emotional edges of family disputes. The clause banning legislative divorce was inserted in the new constitution without a hint of controversy.[94] From

then on, members of the General Assembly lost contact with the routine
traumas of family life outside their own circle.

Notes

1. Acts were passed at the 1842, 1843, 1844, 1845, 1846, and 1849 sessions.
The 1847 session did not adopt any general divorce legislation. The General Assembly, which switched to a biennial schedule after 1847, did not meet in 1848.

2. Seventy-one petitions were filed during the 1849 session; 75 were filed
in 1841. The passage rate was also similar. In 1849, 37 percent (26 of 71) of the
petitioners obtained relief; in 1841 39 percent (29 of 75) did.

3. THE CONSTITUTION OF THE STATE OF MARYLAND, REPORTED AND
ADOPTED BY THE CONVENTION OF DELEGATES ASSEMBLED AT THE CITY OF
ANNAPOLIS, NOVEMBER 4TH, 1850, AND SUBMITTED TO AND RATIFIED BY THE
PEOPLE ON THE FIRST WEDNESDAY OF JUNE, 1851, at 34 (E. O. Hinkley, ed., 1855).

4. When Maryland adopted a new state constitution in 1851 banning the
passage of private divorce bills, the authority of its courts to sever marriages was
not as broad as in most Northern and Western states. Adultery and abandonment
for three years were the primary *a vinculo* grounds, and cruelty the primary bed
and board ground. But the lack of a cruelty ground for complete divorce placed
women in violent marriages at risk, retarded the development of mental cruelty as
a basis for complete divorce, and increased the incentives to "create" adultery as a
ground for divorce. The basic structure remained intact for the rest of the nineteenth century. *See* AN ACT to repeal sections twenty-five and twenty-six of article
sixteen of the Code of Public General Laws, relating to Chancery, and to reenact
the same with amendments, ch. 272, 1871 Md. Laws (April 1, 1872).

5. *See* Matysek v. Matysek, 128 A.2d 627, 631 (1957).

6. The week after the act was passed, the Senate insisted that it would no
longer entertain divorce petitions. The following message was sent to the House:

> We have declined to reconsider the divorce bills sent to us, and deem it
> inexpedient to do so. The courts now have jurisdiction of these cases, and
> from the greater facility these tribunals have, of hearing both parties, exam-
> ining their witnesses and proofs, and ascertaining the truth of the represen-
> tations on which relief is claimed, the ends of justice will be promoted by
> referring all questions of this sort to the courts. The legislature is necessarily
> obliged to rely on ex parte evidence, and the statements of parties interested
> or their agents; for if the witnesses and parties were to be brought here and
> examined so as to furnish the means of arriving with reasonable accuracy, the
> whole session would be occupied with divorce cases, so much have these,
> much to be regretted applications, increased within the few past years. We
> are therefore constrained to act hastily and upon slight examination when we
> do act, or to consume more of the public time, than could be spared, from

other matters, which no branch of the government but the legislature has power to consider.

It should be remembered too, that our session costs the State over $500 per day, which is equivalent to $100 per hour, for every hour the legislature is actually in session. This will show, if any attention is given to divorce cases, what a large sum it costs the State, in the present depressed condition of our finances. All this is saved by referring them to the courts. We therefore think, that every consideration of justice, policy, and economy requires that the legislature should not entertain applications for divorces, unless under very extraordinary circumstances, and where the courts have no power to grant relief.

7. Susan Houx v. David Houx, Baltimore County Ct. Chancery Papers, MdHR 40, 200-2671, 2/15/13/40 (1842).

8. 1840 HOUSE JOURNAL at 14; 1841 HOUSE JOURNAL at 58.

9. 1841 HOUSE JOURNAL at 280, 509. The bill then failed in the Senate, along with many others trapped in the legislature after the passage of general divorce legislation.

10. Elizabeth Stewart v. Joseph Stewart, Ch. Ct. Chancery Papers, MdHR 17, 898–10973, S 512–10816, 1/39/03/55 (Baltimore City, 1843).

11. 1827 HOUSE JOURNAL at 134; 1828 HOUSE JOURNAL at 264; 1830 HOUSE JOURNAL at 368; 1831 HOUSE JOURNAL at 34.

12. 1831 HOUSE JOURNAL at 34, 470; 1831 SENATE JOURNAL at 303.

13. An act for the relief of Elizabeth Stewart, of the city of Baltimore, ch. 229, 1831 Md. Laws (Mar. 9, 1832).

14. This is discussed in Chapter 6.

15. These disputes are described in Chapter 2.

16. A supplement to an act entitled, An act to give to the Chancellor and the County Courts as Courts of Equity, jurisdiction in cases of Divorce, ch. 198, 1842 Md. Laws (Mar. 6, 1843). The text of this act may be found in Appendix 2.

17. Two references to refresh your recollection are enough to make the point. Recall the discussion in Chapter 2 about the turn-of-the-nineteenth-century requirement that proof of adultery be overwhelming and the much later refusal, discussed in Chapter 7, to pass a bill because of inadequate information about the reputation of witnesses.

18. A supplement to an act entitled an act to give to the Chancellor, and the County Courts as Courts of Equity, jurisdiction in cases of Divorce, ch. 287, 1843 Md. Laws (Mar. 7, 1844).

19. There is general agreement that divorce mills have existed for a long time, slowly moving west with the white population. During the 1840s, Pennsylvania was quite hospitable to divorcing couples, and by the 1850s, Indiana was divorce heaven. G. RILEY, DIVORCE: AN AMERICAN TRADITION 45, 62–67 (1991).

20. Abraham Oliver added that she had "by her industry saved some property." It is unlikely that Elizabeth pursued her divorce so diligently to protect her assets from her husband since the original bed and board private act granted her *feme sole* status.

assets from her husband since the original bed and board private act granted her *feme sole* status.

21. A further supplement to an act entitled, an act to give to the Chancellor, and the County Courts as Courts of Equity, jurisdiction in cases of Divorce, passed at December session, eighteen hundred and forty-one, chapter two hundred and sixty-two, ch. 306, 1844 Md. Laws (Mar. 10, 1845). The text is in Appendix 2. Other legislation was adopted at the 1846 and 1847 sessions allowing a plaintiff to file a divorce bill in his or her home county in addition to the county where the defendant resided and adding a divorce ground for premarital intercourse by a woman that was unknown to her husband at the time of their marriage. *See* Appendix 2. The premarital intercourse provision probably resulted from the petitions of Benjamin Sunderland filed with the legislature in 1845 and 1847. A bill of divorce filed in court simultaneously with his second legislative petition alleged that his wife Mary suffered from "a certain disease or malformation or injury of the genital organs," was "incapable of discharging the duties incumbent upon a woman in the married state," was aware of her condition, and failed to inform Benjamin. Benjamin Sunderland v. Mary Sunderland, Ch. Ct. Chancery Papers, MdHR 17, 898-4596B, S 512-4766, 1/37/1/62 (Baltimore City, 1847). The 1847 General Assembly adopted both a private *a vinculo* act and a general bill on premarital intercourse. An act to divorce Benjamin Sunderland, of the City of Baltimore, from his wife Mary Sunderland, ch. 129, 1847 Md. Laws (Feb. 26, 1848). The court proceeding was then dismissed.

22. Details of the story not found in the reported opinion, Brown v. Brown, 2 Md.Ch. 316 (1846), are in Jehu Brown v. Elizabeth Brown, Ch. Ct. Chancery Papers, MdHR 17, 898-6097, S 512-6181, 1/37/3/40 (Baltimore City, 1846).

23. 1834 HOUSE JOURNAL at 410–411, 600.

24. 1837 HOUSE JOURNAL at 150, 234; 1838 HOUSE JOURNAL at 116, 493. Note that when these petitions were filed the parties had been living in separate locations for less than three years.

25. The *Brown* case may not have been the only one so construing the statute. In John Wolfe v. Jane Wolfe, Ch. Ct. Chancery Papers, MdHR 17, 898–12231, S 512–12043, 1/39/05/21 (Allegany, 1846), the same court refused to grant a complete divorce in a case that appears to have had facts similar to *Brown*. John Wolfe, however, did manage to obtain a partial divorce. Perhaps he and his wife Jane had not signed a separation agreement.

26. This was the chancery court sitting in Annapolis that had statewide jurisdiction, as distinguished from the county courts sitting as equity forums.

27. *Brown*, 2 Md.Ch. at 320–321.

28. The case, however, left unenforceable contracts between husbands and wives not using trusts. Women wishing to obtain property from their husbands upon separation still had to rely upon the use of male trustees. Though confirming the legitimacy of separation agreements, the court refused to undertake any review of the contract to insure that it was not obtained by the husband through duress or fraud. The continued vitality of equitable separation agreements, therefore, may also have been double-edged.

29. An act to divorce Jehu Brown from Elizabeth his wife, ch. 90, 1847 Md. Laws (Feb. 18, 1848).

30. A further supplement to an act entitled, an act passed at December session, eighteen hundred and forty one, chapter two hundred and sixty-two to give to the Chancellor, and the County Courts as Courts of Equity, jurisdiction in cases of Divorce, ch. 245, 1849 Md. Laws (Mar. 4, 1850).

31. The *Brown* case was affirmed by the Maryland Court of Appeals in an unreported opinion. *See* 2 Md.Ch. at 321.

32. A comprehensive study of divorce in Maryland found that this incentive actually had a significant impact on legal practice. L. C. MARSHALL & G. MAY, THE DIVORCE COURT 304 (1932).

33. Margaret Snuggrass v. William Snuggrass, Baltimore County Ct. Chancery Papers, MdHR 40, 200-2929-1/2, 2/15/13/56 (1843). Margaret filed her action through her "next friend" Hiram Snuggrass.

34. Tayman v. Tayman, 2 Md.Ch. 393 (1851); Coles v. Coles, 2 Md.Ch. 341 (1951); Daiger v. Daiger, 2 Md.Ch. 335 (1850); Bowie v. Bowie, 3 Md.Ch. 51 (1850).

35. *Tayman*, 2 Md.Ch. at 399; *Daiger* 2 Md.Ch. at 341.

36. *Daiger*, 2 Md. Ch. at 341; *Bowie*, 3 Md.Ch. at 54.

37. *Daiger*, 2 Md.Ch. at 341.

38. *See* R. GRISWOLD, FAMILY AND DIVORCE IN CALIFORNIA, 1850–1890, at 212–213, n. 89 (1982); B. L. FORD, WOMEN, MARRIAGE AND DIVORCE IN CALIFORNIA, 1849–1872, at 170–190 (1985)(Thesis, U. Cal. Davis).

39. Both GRISWOLD, at 78–87, and FORD, at 120–139, cited just above, found that this occurred in California. Desertion was mostly, though by no means entirely, by men. Women were often left in dire straits in such circumstances. Griswold found that a higher proportion of divorce actions brought by men against women were on desertion grounds than those brought by women against men. But the total number of men faced with desertion allegations was higher. In addition, the most common complaint by women was nonsupport by their husbands. Some of these cases, clustered mostly among the less well-off, involved desertion-like circumstances. GRISWOLD at 92–108.

40. The three-year abandonment ground for complete divorce was clearly useless in such situations.

41. I assume Semmes gave this advice on the theory that she could avoid a charge of desertion or abandonment if she could prove she left out of fear for her and her child's safety. This of course was a risky business given the history of mutual violence in this case. But it does corroborate the important ways in which abandonment and cruelty worked together.

42. J. E. SEMMES, JOHN H. B. LATROBE AND HIS TIME 1803–1891, at 210–212 (1917).

43. Rebecca Conway v. Thomas P. Conway, Ch. Ct. Chancery Papers, MdHR 17, 898-6933, S 512-6974, 1/37/4/57 (Baltimore City, 1848).

44. 1849 HOUSE JOURNAL at 75.

45. An act entitled, an act to divorce Rebecca Conway, of Baltimore City, from her husband, Thomas P. Conway, ch. 138, 1849 Md. Laws (Feb. 22, 1850).

46. An act to divorce Julia Ann Taylor, of the city of Annapolis, from her husband, John T. Taylor, ch. 188, 1849 Md. Laws (Mar. 4, 1850).

47. Taylor v. Taylor, Ch. Ct. Chancery Papers, MdHR 17, 898–11561, S 512–11389, 1/39/04/34 (Anne Arundel, 1848).

48. John Taylor was not the only man who sought custody of his children in the 1840s. Thus John Spence, who in 1849 claimed that his wife Lydia "absented herself from her home and became the associate of persons of dissolute and abandoned character," obtained a divorce and custody of their children. Spence v. Spence, Ch. Ct. Chancery Papers, MdHR 17, 898–10758, S 512–10604, 1/39/03/34 (Baltimore City, 1849). And in another, bitterly contested divorce case, Emily and Richard Jackson, along with Emily's parents, waged a battle over the economic and nurturing rights and obligations of the couple. Emily E. Jackson v. Richard J. Jackson, Ch. Ct. Chancery Papers, MdHR 17 898-8c?5-1/5, S 512-8925, 1/38/4/92 (Dorchester, 1850).

49. One of the first divorces to be passed in the 1845 session granted Townley Loockerman a divorce from his wife Juliana. An act to divorce Townley Chase Lockerman, from his wife Juliana P. Lockerman, ch. 353, 1845 Md. Laws (Mar. 10, 1846). Juliana had filed, but withdrawn, a judicial divorce case in 1842. Juliana P. Loockerman v. Townley Loockerman, Ch. Ct. Chancery Papers, MdHR 17, 898-9397, S 512-9313, 1/38/5/47 (Anne Arundel, 1845). In her bill she alleged that they had lived with her parents, that the defendant failed to provide a promised house, that Townley charged her publicly with "conjugal infidelity . . . yielding himself to some strange mental hallucinations," and that he continued to lurk about her father's house even after he left. As in the *Taylor* case, there were also unspecific allegations of adultery. For unknown reasons her case was dropped, and Townley later filed and won a legislative divorce.

50. An act to divorce Francis Thomas, from his wife Sarah C. P. Thomas, ch. 155, 1845 Md. Laws (Feb. 14, 1846).

51. She was 20 years old when she married Francis, then 42.

52. The details of the Thomas marriage are taken from T. J. C. WILLIAMS, HISTORY OF FREDERICK COUNTY MARYLAND 256–263 (1910). The words quoted in the text above are at p. 259.

53. 1845 HOUSE JOURNAL at 249.

54. *Id.* at 257, 274.

55. Francis Thomas, *A Statement of Francis Thomas Concerning His Domestic Grievances* (1845). Excerpts from the tract are reprinted in Appendix 3.

56. WILLIAMS, *supra* note 52, at 259.

57. This correspondence is discussed in Chapter 3.

58. F. Dewey, *Thomas Jefferson's Notes on Divorce*, 39 WM. & MARY Q. 212, 216 (1982).

59. Thomas, *supra* note 55, at 52.

60. *Id.* at 18.

61. *Id.* at 3.

62. *Id.*

63. *Id.*

64. *Id.*

65. Williams, *supra* note 52, at 259.

66. *Id.* at 20.

67. Prior to 1867, when Maryland first sanctioned abortion by statute, the state followed the common law on abortion which punished the performance of an abortion only after quickening. Given the timing of the alleged abortion at only the two month mark, it is unlikely that Sarah was quick with child. For some of this history, *see* Hays v. State of Maryland, 40 Md. 633 (1874); Lamb v. State of Maryland, 67 Md. 524 (1887); Jones v. State of Maryland, 70 Md. 326 (1889); J. MOHR, ABORTION IN AMERICA: THE ORIGINS AND EVOLUTION OF NATIONAL POLICY 211–215 (1978).

68. Thomas, *supra* note 55, at 19–21.

69. *Id.* at 51. Though the court action could be filed and the bill served upon Sarah by publication in Maryland (*see* Section 3 of the divorce act of March 1, 1842, reprinted in Appendix 2), Sarah could simply allow the action to go foward without her presence.

70. In the 1846 session, one senator even moved to repeal the 1841 general act, presumably leaving divorce entirely in the hands of the legislature. 1846 SENATE JOURNAL at 169.

71. 1849 HOUSE JOURNAL at 57–58.

72. *Id.* at 289.

73. *Id.* at 290–291.

74. 1849 SENATE JOURNAL at 56.

75. It is also worth noting that women could still bring alimony cases under the 1777 act without suing for divorce. Although the grounds for obtaining alimony and a partial divorce were similar, cases for only alimony were still brought. *See, e.g.,* Dunnock v. Dunnock, 3 Md.Ch. 140 (1852).

76. *See* the discussion in Chapter 7.

77. In Mary McWilliams v. John McWilliams, Baltimore County Ct. Chancery Papers, MdHR 40, 200-4172, 2/15/14/40 (1850), Mary McWilliams ran a small store. She accused her violent husband of preparing to sell his considerable property in order to deprive her of her share and to take her inventory and household goods. She obtained injunctive relief against her husband pending the disposition of the case. The file does not reveal the final outcome. Such events are one of the reasons why access to *a vinculo* divorce on cruelty grounds was so important. No pretense of continuing legal connection would have existed in such cases.

78. Mary Harrington v. Otis Harrington, Ch. Ct. Chancery Papers, MdHR 17, 898-8433, S 512-8408, 1/38/4/25 (Baltimore City, 1847).

79. *See* Ricketts v. Ricketts, 4 Gill 105 (1846). The court affirmed an alimony award of $300 a year when the ex-husband's income was $900 a year. Though the amount awarded was within the discretion of the trial judge, the Court of Appeals noted that the award of a third, or sometimes a moiety, depending on the circumstances, was reasonable.

80. Amelia Tayman v. Levi Tayman, Ch. Ct. Chancery Papers, MdHR 17, 898-11423-1/2, S 512–11251, 1/39/4/16 (Anne Arundel, 1850).

81. Tayman v. Tayman, 2 Md.Ch. 393, 399 (1851).

82. *Id.* at 401.

83. *Id.* at 400.

84. *See* the discussion in Chapter 6.

85. *Tayman*, 2 Md.Ch. at 398.

86. *Daiger v. Daiger*, 2 Md.Ch. 335 (1850).

87. Gertrude Daiger v. Frederick Daiger, Ch. Ct. Chancery Papers, MdHR 17, 898-7370-1/4, S 512-7395, 1/37/5/32 (Baltimore City, 1850). The description of this case comes from the papers in this file unless a citation is made to the reported opinion.

88. Frederick Daiger did indeed file a petition in the Senate, rather than the House. It went nowhere. 1849 SENATE JOURNAL at 221, 238.

89. *Daiger*, 2 Md.Ch. at 335, 337–339.

90. This order was modified midway through the litigation so he could continue to carry on his business without constant interference from Gertrude or the court.

91. It is also a very early example of a practice, common in today's divorce law, to award costs and attorney fees to the party least able to afford to pay for them.

92. *Daiger*, 2 Md.Ch. at 335, 341.

93. THE CONSTITUTION OF THE STATE OF MARYLAND, *supra* note 3, at 78.

94. Use of private acts in marital property and family law related areas occurred in scattered fashion throughout the United States. R. Chused, *Married Women's Property Law: 1800–1850*, 71 GEO. L. J. 1359, 1369–1370 (1983). In addition to their use for divorces in many Southern states, private acts granted *feme sole* status, L. KERBER, WOMEN OF THE REPUBLIC: INTELLECT & IDEOLOGY IN REVOLUTIONARY AMERICA 150–151 (1980); J. SPRUILL, WOMEN'S LIFE AND WORK IN THE SOUTHERN COLONIES 361–362 (1938), and resolved legitimacy and adoption questions, Zainaldin, *The Emergence of a Modern American Family Law: Child Custody, Adoption and the Courts, 1796–1851*, 73 NW. L. REV. 1038, 1043–1044 (1979). A good history of private acts does not exist, though we do know that many state constitutions adopted after 1840 outlawed their use. The press of other business and the "privatization" of many matters previously resolved by private acts doomed the practice. C. BINNEY, RESTRICTIONS UPON LOCAL AND SPECIAL LEGISLATION IN STATE CONSTITUTIONS (1894).

9. Epilogue: The Long-Term Impact of the Legislative Divorce Process

The conservative coalition that finally led to the adoption of judicial divorce and the prohibition of legislative divorce in Maryland had long-term effects. The terms of divorce established by the statute of 1842 and the series of amendments adopted during the following decade were not changed in any significant way until well into this century. As Geoffrey May wrote in 1932:

> [T]he later legislation in Maryland has not, as in most other states, swept away the early divorce statute or amended it beyond recognition. The present law of divorce differs only in detail from the original law of 1842.[1]

The first major divorce reform of this century came in 1937 with the passage of a statute permitting divorce after voluntary separation for five years.[2] Divorce after a one-year separation is now available.[3]

The timing of Maryland's departure from the legislative divorce business guaranteed that further family law reform would be slow in coming. The years immediately following the adoption of the state constitution in 1851 were not conducive to further consideration of divorce issues in the legislature. The dramatic family controversies of the 1840s made the thought of further debate discomfiting. Malapportionment continued to dilute the influence of areas in the state most interested in divorce reform. The Civil War precluded any major alterations in civil law until the late 1860s. Once the war concluded, the entire country was hit by a wave of moral reform movements and mounting concern over increasing divorce rates.[4] The structural impediments to divorce reform that led to a very narrow divorce act in the 1840s thereby determined the basic tone of Maryland's formal family law code for almost a century.

Dissonance between the formal statutory divorce norms and the routine demands of families in distress was the result. The sorts of political and constituent pressures that led the General Assembly to reinvigorate the legislative divorce process between 1845 and 1850 eventually worked their will on the courts after legislative divorce was banned. This history is one many lawyers are intimately familiar with. Despite the moral overtones of the Victorian and Progressive eras, the demand for divorce grew. While traditionalists might have pined for the days of very limited access to divorce, moral censure could easily lead others to empathize with the victims of marital misbehavior. Consensual divorces, one-sided evidentiary hearings, and feigned testimony became common. The consensual divorce process visible in some of the early legislative divorces became the judicial norm rather than the exception. When the dissonance between the formal statements of divorce law in the statutes and the reality of everyday life in the divorce courts became too great, a new round of reform began.

Indeed, a study of the Maryland divorce process published in 1932 exhaustively explored the problem. Marshall and May, in a chapter entitled "The Mirage of Judicial Controversy," noted the contradictions between formal law and informal practice.[5] Widespread acceptance of the idea that divorce was "a dispute, an adversary proceeding,"[6] was debunked in the face of an extremely low rate of contested hearings and a widespread practice of tailoring allegations in complaints to the needs of the parties and the timing of the litigation. Thus the frequency of adultery complaints fell off dramatically after three years of separation when the abandonment ground became available to the litigants.[7] Five years after the study's publication, the consensual process was itself partially formalized when a separation ground was added to the statutes.

What is intriguing about this well-known history is how intimately linked it was to the nineteenth-century history of divorce. The legislative divorce process in Maryland displayed a mild degree of flexibility in dealing with the disheartening circumstances of individuals seeking government help, but a stubborn resistance to far-reaching general reform legislation. That paradox left Maryland's judges with a narrowly drawn statute unresponsive to the needs of many of the people parading through their courts. The response of some judges in the era shortly after judicial divorce became available was traditional; divorce complaints were simply dismissed if they fell outside the statute's scope. But by this century, many judges were responding as some of their legislative peers had before 1851—allowing uncontested divorce cases to go forward without much oversight and granting divorces if they could in order to avoid the anguish of maintaining destructive marriages. Surely this process repeated itself in many areas of the country. Even in those states with long histories of judicial divorce, dissonance between the terms of general divorce law and the realities of married lives became too large to ignore in this century. The seeds for adoption of present-day no-fault divorce statutes were sown long before by the differing reactions of nineteenth-century legislators and judges to individual stories of family disarray and general pleas for reform.

Notes

1. G. May, Divorce Law in Maryland, at 18 (Bulletin No. 4, Study of the Judicial System of Maryland, By the Judicial Council of Maryland and the Institute of Law of the Johns Hopkins University, 1932). *See also* H. Harlan, The Law of Domestic Relations in Maryland 32–35 (1909).
2. *See* Matysek v. Matysek, 128 A.2d 627, 631 (1957).
3. The present period is 12 months. Md. Ann. Code, Family Law §7–103(a)(3) (1991) permits a divorce on the ground of:

voluntary separation, if:
(i) the parties voluntarily have lived separate and apart without cohabitation for 12 months without interruption before the filing of the application for divorce; and
(ii) there is no reasonable expectation of reconciliation.

Another ground permits divorce after a two-year *involuntary* separation. Proof that there is no reasonable expectation of reconciliation is not required. Md. Ann. Code, Family Law §7–103(a)(5).
4. L. Friedman, A History of American Law 499–501 (1985).
5. L. C. Marshall & G. May, The Divorce Court 199–231(1932).
6. *Id.* at 199.
7. *Id.* at 300–304.

Appendix 1: Tables

Editorial Note

The era in all of the tables is determined by the date on which the legislative session actually began, not the date the private act was formally adopted. Most sessions began late in one year and continued into the following calendar year. Subsequent tables also include the three private annulment acts unless otherwise noted. Percentages in the tables are usually rounded to the nearest whole number. Some totals, therefore, will not add up to exactly 100 percent.

The various tables use somewhat different time period breakdowns. This reflects the fact that the first private act was not passed until 1790, even though petitions seeking divorces began appearing as early as 1782. In addition, many of the tables with data on private acts, rather than petitions, merge the 1782 or 1790 to 1804 time period with the 1805 to 1815 time period. This was usually done to provide enough data to make the tables statistically meaningful.

Where it was appropriate, the chi-square test was used to measure the statistical significance of the cross-tabulations used in much of this study. This commonly used test follows the general rule that if $p < .05$, then the data are considered statistically significant. When p is at the level of .05 or less, the likelihood that the events represented by the data occurred by chance is 5 percent or less.

TABLE 1. Major Result of Private Divorce Acts by Era of Session.

ERA OF SESSION	ACTS GRANTING A VINCULO DIVORCES	ACTS GRANTING BED AND BOARD DIVORCES	ACTS GRANTING ANNULMENTS	TOTAL PRIVATE DIVORCE ACTS
1790–1815	96% (48 of 50)	— (0 of 50)	4% (2 of 50)	100% (50 of 50)
1816–1825	— (0 of 102)	100% (102 of 102)	— (0 of 102)	100% (102 of 102)
1826–1836	53% (102 of 193)	47% (91 of 193)	— (0 of 193)	100% (193 of 193)
1837–1841	80% (135 of 168)	19% (32 of 168)	1% (1 of 168)	100% (168 of 168)
1842–1850	100% (52 of 52)	— (0 of 52)	— (0 of 52)	100% (52 of 52)
All Eras	61% (337 of 552)	38% (212 of 552)	1% (3 of 552)	100% (552 of 552)

Significance: The results of the chi-square test are $X^2 = 310.494$, $df = 8$ and $p < 10^{-4}$.

TABLE 2. Passage Rate of Divorce Bills by Residence of Petitioners.

PERCENT OF DIVORCE PETITIONS PASSED BY THE GENERAL ASSEMBLY:

ERA OF SESSION	When petitioner from Baltimore	When petitioner not from Baltimore	When residence not available[a]	Of total petitions filed
1782–1804	— (0 of 3)	21% (5 of 24)	— (0 of 6)	15% (5 of 33)
1805–1815	22% (15 of 67)	23% (28 of 123)	— (2 of 7)	23% (45 of 197)
1816–1825	37% (26 of 70)	44% (63 of 144)	— (0 of 12)	39% (89 of 226)
1826–1836	54% (83 of 154)	45% (107 of 236)	14% (3 of 21)	47% (193 of 411)
1837–1841	56% (82 of 146)	51% (80 of 158)	12% (6 of 52)	47% (168 of 356)
1842–1849	29% (17 of 58)	38% (29 of 76)	21% (6 of 29)	32% (52 of 163)
All Eras	45% (223 of 498)	41% (312 of 761)	13% (17 of 127)	40% (552 of 1386)

Significance: For the Baltimore data, $X^2 = 36.11$, $df = 5$ and $p < 10^{-4}$. For the data outside of Baltimore, $X^2 = 29.55$, $df = 5$ and $p < 10^{-4}$.

[a] This column includes cases in which the residence is unknown or in which both spouses filed petitions while one was living in Baltimore City and the other was not.

TABLE 3. Passage Rates of Divorce Bills by Gender of Petitioners.

ERA OF SESSION	PERCENT OF DIVORCE PETITIONS PASSED BY THE GENERAL ASSEMBLY:				
	When petitioner female	When petitioner male	When both spouses file[a]	When gender not available	OF TOTAL PETITIONS FILED
1782–1804	0% (0 of 11)	24% (5 of 21)	— (0 of 1)	— (0 of 0)	15% (5 of 33)
1805–1815	26% (31 of 118)	18% (11 of 62)	— (2 of 12)	— (1 of 5)	23% (45 of 197)
1816–1825	45% (61 of 136)	32% (20 of 63)	25% (4 of 16)	— (4 of 11)	39% (89 of 226)
1826–1836	54% (128 of 238)	33% (40 of 120)	39% (13 of 33)	60% (12 of 20)	47% (193 of 411)
1837–1841	48% (102 of 214)	47% (56 of 120)	— (2 of 13)	— (8 of 9)	47% (168 of 356)
1842–1849	33% (26 of 79)	27% (17 of 62)	— (2 of 10)	— (7 of 12)	32% (52 of 163)
All Eras	44% (348 of 796)	33% (149 of 448)	27% (23 of 85)	56% (32 of 57)	40% (552 of 1,386)

Significance: For the wives' data only, $X^2 = 38.11$, $df = 5$ and $p < 10^{-4}$. For the husbands' data, $X^2 = 18.31$, $df = 5$, and $p = .0026$.

[a]In a few cases, both spouses petitioned for divorces in the same legislative session.

TABLE 4. Issues Resolved in Divorce Acts by Era of Session.

ERA OF SESSION	PERCENT OF TOTAL ACTS WITH PROVISIONS ON:			TOTAL ACTS PASSED
	Custody	Name change	Property[a]	
1790–1815	— (0 of 50)	2% (1 of 50)	— (0 of 50)	100% (50 of 50)
1816–1825	15% (13 of 89)	— (0 of 89)	49% (44 of 89)	100% (89 of 89)
1826–1836	25% (49 of 193)	15% (29 of 193)	47% (91 of 193)	100% (193 of 193)
1837–1841	9% (15 of 168)	8% (13 of 168)	8% (14 of 168)	100% (168 of 168)
1842–1850	8% (4 of 52)	15% (8 of 52)	— (0 of 52)	100% (52 of 52)
All Eras	15% (81 of 552)	9% (51 of 552)	27% (149 of 552)	100% (552 of 552)

Significance: Each column represents a separate cross tabulation. For the custody data, $X^2 = 32.75$, $df = 4$ and $p < 10^{-4}$. For the name change data, $X^2 = 22.69$, $df = 4$ and $p = .00015$. For the property data, $X^2 = 129.94$, $df = 4$ and $p < 10^{-4}$.

[a] Many different sorts of property issues appeared in the bills. This table tabulates only the percentage of acts with provisions on the rights of husbands in property of wives. Note that the importance of these issues would by and large disappear after the adoption of married women's property acts in the 1840, 1841, and 1842 sessions of the General Assembly.

TABLE 5. Petitioners for Enacted Divorce Bills by Gender.

ERA OF SESSION	COMPLETE DIVORCE ACTS PETITIONED FOR BY:				
	Wife	Husband	Both	Not available	TOTAL ACTS[a]
1790–1815	65% (31 of 48)	29% (14 of 48)	4% (2 of 48)	2% (1 of 48)	100% (48 of 48)
1816–1825	— (0 of 0)	— (0 of 0)	— (0 of 0)	— (0 of 0)	— (0 of 0)
1826–1836	50% (51 of 102)	34% (35 of 102)	7% (7 of 102)	9% (9 of 102)	100% (102 of 102)
1837–1841	57% (77 of 135)	38% (51 of 135)	1% (2 of 135)	4% (5 of 135)	100% (135 of 135)
1842–1849	50% (26 of 52)	33% (17 of 52)	4% (2 of 52)	13% (7 of 52)	100% (52 of 52)
All Eras	55% (185 of 337)	35% (117 of 337)	4% (13 of 337)	7% (22 of 337)	100% (337 of 337)

ERA OF SESSION	PARTIAL DIVORCE ACTS PETITIONED FOR BY:				
	Wife	Husband	Both	Not available	TOTAL ACTS[a]
1790–1815	— (0 of 0)	— (0 of 0)	— (0 of 0)	— (0 of 0)	— (0 of 0)
1816–1825	69% (61 of 89)	22% (20 of 89)	4% (4 of 89)	4% (4 of 89)	100% (89 of 89)
1826–1836	85% (77 of 91)	5% (5 of 91)	7% (6 of 91)	3% (3 of 91)	100% (91 of 91)
1837–1841	78% (25 of 32)	13% (4 of 32)	— (0 of 32)	9% (3 of 32)	100% (32 of 32)
1842–1849	— (0 of 0)	— (0 of 0)	— (0 of 0)	— (0 of 0)	— (0 of 0)
All Eras	77% (163 of 212)	14% (29 of 212)	5% (10 of 212)	5% (10 of 212)	100% (212 of 212)

Significance: Treating the data as one table with six columns (excluding the "NA" data), $X^2 = 257.55$, $df = 20$ and $p < 10^{-4}$.

[a] The three annulments in the sample are not included in this table.

TABLE 6. Petitioners for Enacted Divorce Bills by Residence.

ERA OF SESSION	PERCENT OF PETITIONERS FOR ACTS FROM:			
	Baltimore	*Outside Baltimore*	*Not Available*	TOTAL ACTS
1790–1815	30% (15 of 50)	64% (32 of 50)	6% (3 of 50)	100% (50 of 50)
1816–1825	29% (26 of 89)	71% (63 of 89)	— (0 of 89)	100% (89 of 89)
1826–1836	43% (83 of 193)	55% (107 of 193)	2% (3 of 193)	100% (193 of 193)
1837–1841	49% (83 of 168)	48% (81 of 168)	2% (4 of 168)	100% (168 of 168)
1842–1849	33% (17 of 52)	56% (29 of 52)	12% (6 of 52)	100% (52 of 52)
All Eras	41% (224 of 552)	57% (312 of 552)	3% (16 of 552)	100% (552 of 522)

Significance: Excluding the "NA" column, $X^2 = 13.64$, $df = 4$ and $p = .0086$.

TABLE 7. Residence of Legislative Divorce Petitioners by Era.

ERA OF SESSION	PERCENT OF PETITIONERS FROM:			
	Baltimore	*Outside Baltimore*	*Not Available*	TOTAL PETITIONS
1782–1804	9% (3 of 33)	73% (24 of 33)	18% (6 of 33)	100% (33 of 33)
1805–1815	34% (67 of 197)	62% (123 of 197)	4% (7 of 197)	100% (197 of 197)
1816–1825	31% (70 of 226)	64% (144 of 226)	5% (12 of 226)	100% (226 of 226)
1826–1836	37% (154 of 411)	57% (236 of 411)	5% (21 of 411)	100% (411 of 411)
1837–1841	41% (146 of 356)	44% (158 of 356)	15% (52 of 356)	100% (356 of 356)
1842–1849	36% (58 of 163)	47% (76 of 163)	18% (29 of 163)	100% (163 of 163)
All Eras	36% (498 of 1,386)	55% (761 of 1,386)	9% (127 of 1,386)	100% (1,386 of 1,386)

Significance: Excluding the "NA" column, $X^2 = 24.70$, $df = 5$ and $p = .00016$.

TABLE 8.   Gender of Legislative Divorce Petitioners by Era.

| ERA OF SESSION | PERCENT OF PETITIONERS FILED BY: | | | | |
	Wives	Husbands	Both	Not available	TOTAL PETITIONS
1782–1804	33% (11 of 33)	64% (21 of 33)	3% (1 of 33)	— (0 of 33)	100% (33 of 33)
1805–1815	60% (118 of 197)	31% (62 of 197)	6% (12 of 197)	3% (5 of 197)	100% (197 of 197)
1816–1825	60% (136 of 226)	28% (63 of 226)	7% (16 of 226)	5% (11 of 226)	100% (226 of 226)
1826–1836	58% (238 of 411)	29% (120 of 411)	8% (33 of 411)	5% (20 of 411)	100% (411 of 411)
1837–1841	60% (214 of 356)	34% (120 of 356)	4% (13 of 356)	3% (9 of 356)	100% (356 of 356)
1842–1850	48% (79 of 163)	38% (62 of 163)	6% (10 of 163)	7% (12 of 163)	100% (163 of 163)
All Eras	57% (796 of 1,386)	32% (448 of 1,386)	6% (85 of 1,386)	4% (57 of 1,386)	100% (1,386 of 1,386)

Significance: Without the "NA" column, $X^2 = 27.07$, $df = 10$ and $p = .0025$.

TABLE 9. Divorce and Petition Rates in Maryland and Baltimore City.[a]

MARYLAND

Year	Population	Average number of petitions	Petitions per 100,000	Average number of divorces	Divorces per 100,000
1790	209,000	1.2	0.6	0.2	0.1
1800	216,000	2.2	1.0	0.3	0.1
1810	235,000	18.7	8.0	4.0	1.7
1820	260,000	20.8	8.0	7.8	3.0
1830	291,000	35.8	12.3	15.4	5.3
1840	318,000	66.3	20.8	21.2	6.7

BALTIMORE CITY

Year	Population	Average number of petitions	Petitions per 100,000	Average number of divorces	Divorces per 100,000
1790	12,000	0.1	0.8	0.0	—
1800	21,000	0.2	1.0	0.0	—
1810	36,000	6.6	18.3	1.3	3.6
1820	48,000	5.7	11.9	2.0	4.2
1830	62,000	13.8	22.3	6.9	11.1
1840	81,000	26.5	32.7	15.0	18.5

[a]These data are crude, but still helpful. Since data are not readily available on the female child-bearing age population, the entire *white* population for the state of Maryland is used as a base. *See* U.S. BUREAU OF THE CENSUS, HISTORICAL STATISTICS OF THE UNITED STATES: COLONIAL TIMES TO 1970, at 29 (1975). In order to even out the ups and downs in the number of petitions filed and divorces enacted each year, the numbers compared with the census populations for 1800, 1810, 1820 and 1830 are the average number of petitions or divorces per year for the period of four years before and after the census. Thus the 1810 divorce rate is the average number of divorces per year for the period 1806–1814 divided by the 1810 population. For 1840, inclusion of years after 1841 would significantly understate the petition and divorce rates. When the courts obtained divorce jurisdiction in 1842, legislative activity declined. No private divorces were passed during the 1842, 1843, and 1844 sessions. For the 1840 divorce rate, therefore, the period 1836–1841 is used. The stated divorce rate is for a population of 100,000.

TABLE 10. Legislative Controversy over Enacted Divorce Bills.[a]

ERA OF SESSION	PERCENT OF ACTS PASSED AFTER:		
	Roll call vote in House, Senate, or both	Amendment proposed on divorce type	Either roll call or amendment
1790–1804	— (0 of 5)	— (0 of 5)	— (0 of 5)
1805–1815	**44% (20 of 45)**[b]	— (0 of 45)	44% (20 of 45)
1816–1825	11% (10 of 89)	8% (7 of 89)	17% (15 of 89)
1826–1836	9% (17 of 193)	7% (13 of 193)	15% (29 of 193)
1837–1841	1% (2 of 168)	**17% (29 of 168)**[b]	18% (30 of 168)
1842–1849	17% (9 of 52)	6% (3 of 52)	23% (12 of 52)
All Eras	11% (58 of 552)	9% (52 of 552)	19% (107 of 552)

Significance: Each column represents a separate data set. For the roll call data, $X^2 = 72.98$, $df = 5$ and $p < 10^{-4}$. For the amendment data, $X^2 = 20.00$, $df = 5$ and $p = .0012$. For the last column, $X^2 = 19.218$, $df = 5$ and $p = .0018$.

[a] The entries in this table show the percent (and number) of debates on enacted divorce bills in which roll call votes were taken during floor debates, amendments were offered to change the bills from partial to complete or complete to partial divorces, and, in the last column, either or both of these events occurred. The numbers in the last column may be less than the sum of the other two since both events occurred during the debates on some bills.

[b] High controversy eras are in bold type.

TABLE II. Legislative Controversy over Nonenacted Divorce Bills.[a]

ERA OF SESSION	PERCENT OF UNSUCCESSFUL PETITIONS FAILING AFTER:			
	Roll call vote in House, Senate, or both	Amendment proposed on divorce type	House and Senate disagree	One or more of roll call, amendment or disagreement
1782–1804	14% (**4 of 28**)[b]	— (0 of 28)	11% (3 of 28)	21% (6 of 28)
1805–1815	7% (11 of 152)	1% (1 of 152)	5% (8 of 152)	12% (18 of 152)
1816–1825	4% (5 of 137)	1% (2 of 137)	25% (**34 of 137**)[b]	26% (36 of 137)
1826–1836	3% (7 of 218)	— (0 of 218)	13% (28 of 218)	13% (28 of 218)
1837–1841	2% (3 of 188)	3% (6 of 188)	22% (**41 of 188**)[b]	22% (42 of 188)
1842–1849	3% (3 of 111)	— (0 of 111)	13% (14 of 111)	14% (15 of 111)
All Eras	4% (33 of 834)	1% (9 of 834)	15% (128 of 834)	17% (145 of 834)

Significance: Each column represents a separate data set. For the roll call data, $X^2 = 15.73$, $df = 5$ and $p = .0076$. For the amendment data, $X^2 = 12.17$, $df = 5$ and $p = .0326$. For the disagree column, $X^2 = 29.43$, $df = 5$ and $p < 10^{-4}$. For the last column, $X^2 = 18.61$, $df = 5$ and $p = .0023$.

[a] The entries in this table show the percent (and number) of unsuccessful divorce bill debates in which roll call votes were taken, amendments were proffered to change the divorce from partial to complete or complete to partial, and disagreements occurred between the House of Delegates and Senate (one approving, the other not). The last column shows if one or more of these events occurred. The numbers in the last column may be less than the sum of the other three since more than one event occurred during debates on some bills.

[b] High controversy areas are in bold type.

TABLE 12. Degree of Malapportionment in the House of Delegates.

REGION[a]	PERCENT OF DELEGATES BEFORE 1838	PERCENT OF STATE POPULATION IN 1790	PERCENT OF STATE POPULATION IN 1810	PERCENT OF STATE POPULATION IN 1830	PERCENT OF DELEGATES AFTER 1837
Baltimore City	3% (2 of 80)	6%	15%	21%	6% (5 of 79)
Eastern Shore	40% (32 of 80)	31%	29%	23%	34% (27 of 79)
North Central	15% (12 of 80)	27%	27%	27%	23% (18 of 79)
South	33% (26 of 80)	27%	20%	17%	28% (22 of 79)
West	10% (8 of 80)	9%	9%	11%	9% (7 of 79)

[a]These data do not exactly mirror the regions described in the text since separate data for whites in Annapolis and the rest of Anne Arundel County were not available. Thus Baltimore City is the only urban area listed separately in this table. Annapolis is included in Anne Arundel County in the southern region. The population of Annapolis was not very large, so the basic thrust of the data is not disturbed. The Eastern Shore region includes Caroline, Cecil, Dorchester, Kent, Queen Annes, Somerset, Talbot, and Worcester Counties. North Central includes Baltimore, Frederick, and Harford Counties. South includes Anne Arundel, Calvert, Charles, Montgomery, Prince Georges, and Saint Marys Counties. West includes Allegany and Washington Counties. Areas in bold were overrepresented in the House of Delegates. Areas in italics were underrepresented. County population figures are based on data taken from J. MCSHERRY, A HISTORY OF MARYLAND 405–407 (1852). They are based on the white population only.

TABLE 13. Roll Call Voting Patterns in House of Delegates by Era.

			PERCENT OF VOTES CAST IN FAVOR OF:			
REGION[a]	1782–1804 private bills	1805–1815 private bills	1816–1825 private bills	1826–1836 private bills	1837–1849 private bills	1826–1841 general bills
Baltimore and Annapolis	— (2 of 8)	63% (45 of 71)	61% (14 of 23)	57% (16 of 28)	70% (14 of 20)	58% (15 of 26)
Eastern Shore	46% (39 of 85)	60% (348 of 578)	57% (82 of 144)	69% (157 of 229)	67% (94 of 140)	38% (61 of 161)
South	33% (23 of 69)	36% (147 of 406)	52% (61 of 117)	35% (55 of 157)	38% (35 of 92)	62% (64 of 103)
North Central	35% (17 of 48)	48% (142 of 297)	69% (61 of 89)	62% (73 of 118)	63% (64 of 102)	33% (33 of 101)
West	48% (12 of 25)	48% (79 of 165)	80% (35 of 44)	70% (43 of 61)	78% (32 of 41)	58% (25 of 43)
All Areas	40% (93 of 235)	50% (761 of 1,517)	61% (253 of 417)	58% (344 of 593)	61% (239 of 395)	46% (198 of 434)

Significance: The chi-square test was run on each column as a separate set, with five rows of data, one for each region. For 1782–1804, $X^2 = 4.39$, $df = 4$, and $p = .36$. This is not a significant result. Put another way, there is a 36% chance the data are random. For 1805–1815, $X^2 = 60.9$, $df = 4$, and $p < 10^{-4}$. For 1816–1825, $X^2 = 13.28$, $df = 4$, and $p = .01$. For the private bill 1826–1836 data, $X^2 = 49.12$, $df = 4$ and $p < 10^{-4}$. For the private bill 1837–1850 data, $X^2 = 28.25$, $df = 4$, and $p = .000011$. For the general bill 1826–1841 data, $X^2 = 26.27$, $df = 4$, and $p = .000028$.

[a]For the counties in each region, see the note under Table 12. In this table, the urban areas of Baltimore City and Annapolis are included as a region.

TABLE 14. Passage Rates for Divorce Petitions by Legislative Body and Era.

ERA OF SESSION	PERCENT OF PETITIONS:[a]						TOTAL PETITIONS
	Passed by both houses	Passed only by House	Passed only by Senate	Entertained only by House	Entertained only by Senate	Entertained in both houses	
1782–1804	15% (5 of 33)	9% (3 of 33)	— (0 of 33)	76% (25 of 33)	— (0 of 33)	— (0 of 33)	100% (33 of 33)
1805–1815	**23%[b]** (45 of 197)	4% (8 of 197)	— (0 of 197)	73% (143 of 197)	1% (1 of 197)	— (0 of 197)	100% (197 of 197)
1816–1825	**39%[b]** (89 of 226)	**15%[b]** (33 of 226)	0% (1 of 226)	43% (97 of 226)	1% (2 of 226)	2% (4 of 226)	100% (226 of 226)
1826–1836	**47%[b]** (193 of 411)	7% (27 of 411)	0% (1 of 411)	43% (175 of 411)	2% (10 of 411)	1% (5 of 411)	100% (411 of 411)
1837–1841	47% (168 of 356)	8% (30 of 356)	3% (11 of 356)	39% (139 of 356)	1% (4 of 356)	1% (4 of 356)	100% (356 of 356)
1842–1849	32% (52 of 163)	6% (10 of 163)	2% (4 of 163)	58% (94 of 163)	2% (3 of 163)	— (0 of 163)	100% (163 of 163)
All Eras	40% (552 of 1,386)	8% (111 of 1,386)	1% (17 of 1,386)	49% (673 of 1,386)	1% (20 of 1,386)	1% (13 of 1,386)	100% (1,386 of 1,386)

Significance: $X^2 = 122.86$, $df = 25$ and $p < 10^{-4}$.

[a] Data on petitions passed by both houses and enacted into law are displayed in the first column. The second and third columns include data on petitions passed either by the House of Delegates or the Senate but not by both. The fourth column contains cases entertained only in the House of Delegates, and not passed by that body. The fifth column includes petitions entertained only in the Senate and not passed by that body. The sixth column contains petitions entertained in both bodies and adopted in neither one.

[b] The historically most dramatic shifts are in bold type.

TABLE 15. Property Provisions in Divorce Acts by Petitioner and Era.

	PERCENT OF ACTS WITH WIFE AS PETITIONER:[a]			
Era of session and type of divorce	Having provisions limiting husband's rights in wife's property[b]	Having provisions limiting wife's rights in husband's property	Having limits on property of both spouses	Having no limits on property of either spouse
1816–1825 Partial Divorces	69% (42 of 61)	0% (0 of 61)	25% (15 of 61)	7% (4 of 61)
1826–1836 Partial Divorces	26% (20 of 77)	0% (0 of 77)	62% (48 of 77)	12% (9 of 77)
1826–1836 Complete Divorces	14% (7 of 51)	4% (2 of 51)	14% (7 of 51)	69% (35 of 51)
	PERCENT OF ACTS WITH HUSBAND AS PETITIONER:[a]			
Era of session and type of divorce	Having provisions limiting husband's rights in wife's property[b]	Having provisions limiting wife's rights in husband's property	Having limits on property of both spouses	Having no limits on property of either spouse
1816–1825 Partial Divorces	20% (4 of 20)	35% (7 of 20)	20% (4 of 20)	25% (5 of 20)
1826–1836 Partial Divorces	— (1 of 5)	— (1 of 5)	— (3 of 5)	— (0 of 5)
1826–1836 Complete Divorces	0% (0 of 35)	0% (0 of 35)	9% (3 of 35)	91% (32 of 35)

Significance: For the acts with wife as petitioner, $X^2 = 107.58$, $df = 6$ and $p < 10^{-4}$. For the acts with husband as petitioner, $X^2 = 38.49$, $df = 6$ and $p < 10^{-4}$.

[a] The three annulments are not included in this table. Cases in which both spouses petitioned for a divorce in the same session are also omitted.

[b] Provisions making a wife *feme sole* are included in this column.

TABLE 16. Roll Call Voting Patterns by Region and Political Party Affiliation.[a]

| | PERCENT OF ROLL CALL VOTES IN FAVOR OF: | | | |
| | PRIVATE BILLS | | GENERAL BILLS | |
REGION	Cast by Democrats[b]	Cast by Whigs[c]	Cast by Democrats[b]	Cast by Whigs[c]
North Central	80% (60 of 75)	67% (24 of 36)	14% (9 of 62)	— (8 of 15)
Eastern Shore	68% (40 of 59)	63% (109 of 173)	42% (22 of 53)	37% (28 of 76)
South	— (4 of 10)	38% (56 of 147)	— (8 of 17)	71% (60 of 85)
West	85% (29 of 34)	74% (17 of 23)	46% (12 of 26)	— (7 of 13)
Baltimore and Annapolis	86% (18 of 21)	— (4 of 11)	50% (9 of 18)	— (5 of 7)
All Regions	76% (151 of 199)	54% (210 of 390)	34% (60 of 176)	55% (108 of 196)

Significance: For column 1, Democrats voting on private bills, $X^2 = 12.59$, $df = 4$ and $p = .0135$. For column 2, $X^2 = 31.37$, $df = 4$ and $p = .000002$. For column 3, $X^2 = 16.85$, $df = 4$ and $p = .0021$. For column 4, $X^2 = 19.26$, $df = 4$ and $p = .0007$.

[a]Political party affiliations for this table from 1828 to 1834 were obtained from the NILES WEEKLY REGISTER issues in the following volumes, pages and dates: vol. 35, at 82 (Oct. 11, 1828); vol. 37, at 122 (Oct. 17, 1829); vol. 43, at 101–102 (Oct. 13, 1832); vol. 45, at 104–105 (Oct. 12, 1833); vol. 47, at 84–85 (Oct. 11, 1834). Political affiliations for 1836 to 1841 were provided by letter (on file with the author) from Lynne Brown, an archivist at the Maryland State Archives.

[b]The Democrat columns include votes from those called Jackson supporters, Van Buren supporters, and Democrats.

[c]The Whig columns include votes from those called anti-Jacksonians and Whigs.

Appendix 2: Process Proposals, General Bill Proposals, and Statutes

Private Divorce Bill Process Proposals[a]

SESSION YEAR	MEMBER INTRODUCING PROPOSAL	PROPOSAL	RESULT
1811	Emerson (Calvert)	Establish standing divorce committee	Failed
1817	Wilson (Worcester)	Establish standing divorce committee	Passed
1818	Kell (Baltimore City)	Establish standing divorce committee	Failed
1820	Not known	Refer one private dispute to court for taking evidence	Passed
1822	Kennedy (Baltimore City)	Establish standing divorce committee	Passed[b]
1822	Millard (Saint Marys)	Require divorce committee to give notice to and opportunity for filing of counter affidavits by nonpetitioning spouse	Failed
1823	Millard (Saint Marys)	Establish standing divorce committee	Passed
1823	Millard (Saint Marys)	Require petitioner to publish notice in newspaper for three weeks and require divorce committee to provide opportunity for filing of counter affidavits	Failed
1825	Millard (Saint Marys)	Require petitioner to publish notice in newspaper for three weeks	Failed
1826	None	McCoy petition committee report unfavorable because "there is no proof of the respectability of witnesses"	No action

SESSION YEAR	MEMBER INTRODUCING PROPOSAL	PROPOSAL	RESULT
1828	Not known	Require thirty days' notice in a newspaper before filing any petition for private relief	Failed (Senate)
1829	Not known	Allow petitioners to seek the appointment of a commissioner by a county court to take testimony for use by General Assembly in deciding a petition for a private divorce	Passed
1833	Johns (Harford)	Grant divorce committee authority to send for persons, papers, and evidence at expense of petitioner	Failed
1833	Handy (Somerset)	Grant divorce committee authority to examine witnesses	Passed
1833	Not known	Require compliance with 1829 statute on appointment of court commissioner before entertaining private petition	Failed (Senate)
1835	Jones (Somerset)	Amend constitution to require two-thirds vote on any private divorce bill	Passed first time
1836	Not known	Amend constitution to require two-thirds vote on any private divorce bill	Passed Senate; failed House, 38–24
1837	Pitts (Baltimore City)	Require compliance with 1829 statute on appointment of court commissioner before entertaining private petition	Failed
1838	Risteau (Baltimore County)	Require divorce committee to receive only testimony taken according to regular form in law	Failed
1839	Risteau (Baltimore County)	Regulate form of testimony to Divorce Committee	Passed House; failed Senate
1840	Causin (Saint Marys)	Refuse to entertain any more divorce petitions	Failed
1840	Frazier (Dorchester)	Supplement to 1829 court commission legislation	Passed

SESSION YEAR	MEMBER INTRODUCING PROPOSAL	PROPOSAL	RESULT
1840	Scott (Senate)	Refuse to entertain divorce unless fulfills court testimony statutes	Passed Senate
1843	Semmes (Prince Georges)	Abolish Divorce Committee	Failed

[a] All proposals were in the House of Delegates unless otherwise noted.
[b] This attempt succeeded, but only after two other attempts to establish a standing committee failed. A later attempt to abolish the committee also failed.
[c] Amending the constitution required approval by both houses of the General Assembly in two successive sessions. This proposal was passed by both houses during this session.

General Bill Proposals[a]

SESSION YEAR	MEMBER INTRODUCING PROPOSAL	PROPOSAL	RESULT
1809	Worthington (Baltimore City)	General divorce bill	Refer to next General Assembly
1811	Not known	Two general divorce bills (Senate)	No committee action
1815	Stoddert (Charles) Hebb (Senate)	Two general divorce bills (one House, one Senate)	Refer to next General Assembly
1816	Hands (Talbot) Winder (Senate)	Two general divorce bills (one House, one Senate)	No committee action
1818	Forrest (Montgomery)	General divorce bill	No committee action
1819	Key (Saint Marys)	General divorce bill	Refer to next General Assembly
1821	Semmes (Prince Georges)	General divorce bill	No committee action
1822	Allen (Harford) Millard (Saint Marys)	Two general divorce bills	No committee action
1822	Pratt (Senate)	Amend constitution	No committee action

SESSION YEAR	MEMBER INTRODUCING PROPOSAL	PROPOSAL	RESULT
1823	Millard (Saint Marys) Price (Senate)	Two general divorce bills (one House, one Senate)	Refer to next General Assembly
1824	Millard (Saint Marys)	General divorce bill	No committee action
1824	Merrick (Washington)	General divorce bill	Passed House; failed Senate
1825	Millard (Saint Marys)	General divorce bill	No committee action
1826	Buchanan (Baltimore County)	General divorce bill	Tabled
1826	Thomas (Cecil)	General divorce bill for Baltimore City only	Tabled
1826	Heath (Senate)	General divorce bill	No committee action
1827	Hooper (Worcester)	General divorce bill	Recommitted
1827	Linthicum (Anne Arundel)	General divorce bill	Failed
1828	Phelps (Dorchester)	General divorce bill	Failed, 37–30
1829	Buchanan (Baltimore City)	General divorce bill	Failed, 38–35
1832	Mudd (Charles)	Bill to protect *feme coverts* and avoid need for bed and board divorces	Refer to next General Assembly
1833	Palmer (Frederick)	General divorce bill	Failed, 31–29
1833	Mayer (Senate)	General divorce bill	Refer to next General Assembly
1834	Dulaney (Charles)	General divorce bill	No committee action
1834	Mayer (Senate)	General divorce bill	Refer to next General Assembly
1835	Wharton (Washington)	General divorce bill	Refuse to refer to committee
1836	Fooks (Worcester)	General divorce bill	Unfavorable committee report

SESSION YEAR	MEMBER INTRODUCING PROPOSAL	PROPOSAL	RESULT
1837	Jump (Caroline)	General divorce bill	Failed
1838	Pitts (Baltimore City)	General divorce bill	No committee action
1838	Not known (Senate)	General divorce bill	Passed Senate; failed House
1839	Sprigg (Prince Georges)	Imposition of tax on divorce	No committee action
1839	Not known (Senate)	General divorce bill	Passed Senate, 12–4; failed House, 31–27
1840	Scott (Senate)	General divorce bill	Passed Senate, 12–5; failed House, 33–26
1841	Scott (Senate)	General divorce bill	Passed Senate; passed House, 37–35

ᵃAll proposals were in the House of Delegates unless otherwise noted.

Statutes

CHAPTER 202
(Passed February 27, 1830)

An act for taking testimony in cases of applications for divorce.

SEC. 1. *Be it enacted by the General Assembly of Maryland,* That it shall be lawful for any person who may intend to apply to the Legislature for a divorce, to file a petition, stating the grounds of his application in the court of the county in which the person from whom he desires to be divorced resides; and, upon the filing of such a petition, a subpoena shall issue to the party implicated, to appear and answer the same; and, upon such appearance, it shall be the duty of the court to issue a commission to a person or persons therein to be named, to take such testimony as the respective parties require to be taken; which testimony, after twenty days notice to the parties, of the time and place of meeting, shall be received and reduced to writing, and be returned to the clerk of the court in which such proceedings have been had, whose duty it shall be to forward to the

Legislature, the petition, answer, testimony, and all other the proceedings had under said application.

SEC. 2. *And be it enacted*, That the clerk shall receive the sum of two dollars, for receiving, filing, and forwarding, said proceedings; that the sheriff shall receive one dollar for serving the subpoena on the party, and fifty cents for each subpoena served by him on any witness that shall be summoned by him; and that every commissioner shall receive three dollars, for each and every day he shall be employed in receiving and reducing to writing, the testimony of the witnesses; all of which costs and charges shall be paid by the party petitioning.

CHAPTER 238
(Passed March 9, 1841)

A bill supplementary to an act passed December session, eighteen hundred and twenty-nine, chapter two hundred and two, relative to the taking of Testimony in all applications for Divorce.

SEC. 1. *Be it enacted by the General Assembly of Maryland*, That in all applications for divorce, the party so applying shall make application to some justice of the peace, who shall thereupon issue a subpoena directed to some constable or other person, who shall serve the same on the person from whom the divorce is sought; and the person serving the same shall make an affidavit of the fact of the service of the same.

SEC. 2. *And be it enacted*, That after the subpoena shall have been served and returned to the justice issuing the same, either party may proceed to take testimony after the lapse of thirty days, before a justice of the peace in the county or city where they reside, if they both reside in the same county or city; but if they should not reside in the same county or city, then either party may take the depositions of such witnesses as they may think proper in the county or city where they may reside, and transmit the same to the Legislature at its next annual session.

SEC. 3. *And be it enacted*, That if the person from whom the divorce is sought be a non-resident of the State, or shall be absent from the same, the person applying shall give at least three months notice in some newspaper published in the city of Baltimore, of their intention to apply for a divorce at the next session of the General Assembly; and at the expiration of such time may proceed to take the testimony of such witnesses as they may think proper before a justice of the peace, on oath; and transmit the same to the next Legislature for their action, to be judged of by them.

SEC. 4. *And be it enacted,* That the justice of the peace issuing a summons or summonses, and the constable or other person serving the same, shall be allowed the same fees as are now allowed by law for similar services; each party to pay their own costs.

SEC. 5. *And be it enacted,* That all acts or parts of acts inconsistent with this act, be and the same are hereby repealed.

CHAPTER 262
(Passed March 1, 1842)

An act to give to the Chancellor and the County Courts as Courts of Equity, jurisdiction in cases of Divorce

SECTION 1. *Be it enacted by the General Assembly of Maryland,* That from and after the passage of this act, the chancellor or any county court of this State as a court of equity, shall have jurisdiction of all applications for divorces and any person desiring a divorce shall file his or her petition or bill to the chancellor or in the county court as a court of equity, where the party resides against whom the petition is filed, or if the party against whom the petition is filed, be a non resident, then such petition may be filed in the high court of chancery or county court as a court of equity where the petitioner resides, and upon such petition the same process by summons, notice or otherwise, shall be had to procure the answer and appearance of a defendant as is now had to a bill in chancery, and in all cases where, from the default of the defendant a bill in chancery might be taken pro confesso, the county court as a court of equity or chancellor on a petition for a divorce shall order a commission to take testimony to issue exparte, and shall decide the case upon the proof taken under such commission.

SEC. 2: *And be it enacted,* That upon hearing of any petition for divorce, the chancellor or the county court as a court of equity, as the case may be, may decree a divorce a vinculo matrimonii, for the following causes, to wit: first, the impotence of either party at the time of the marriage; secondly, for any cause which by the laws of this State renders a marriage null and void ab initio; thirdly, for adultery; fourthly, where the party complained against has abandoned the party complaining, and has remained absent from the State for five years.

SEC. 3. *And be it enacted*, That upon such petitions as aforesaid, divorces, a mensa et thoro, may be decreed for the following causes, to wit: first, cruelty of treatment; secondly, excessively vicious conduct, abandonment and desertion, and the chancellor or any county court, as a court of equity, may decree a divorce, a mensa et thoro, in cases where a divorce a vinculo matrimonii is prayed, if the causes proven be sufficient to entitle the party to the same under the provisions of this act, and in all cases where a divorce is decreed, the court passing the same shall have full power to award alimony to the wife and to award to the wife such property or estate, as she had when married or the value of the same or of such part thereof as may have been sold or converted by the husband, having regard to the circumstances of the husband at the time of the divorce, or such party of any such property as the court or chancellor may deem reasonable, and also have power to order and direct who shall have the guardianship and custody of the children and be charged with their support and maintenance.

SEC. 4. *And be it enacted*, That in all cases where the facts are disputed, the same proceeding shall be had to procure testimony which are now used in suits in chancery.

SEC. 5. *And be it enacted*, That no person shall be entitled to make application for a divorce under this act where the causes for divorce occurred in another State, unless such person so applying shall have resided within this State for two years next preceding his or her application.

CHAPTER 198
(Passed March 6, 1843)

A supplement to an act entitled, An act to give to the Chancellor and the County Courts as Courts of Equity, jurisdiction in cases of Divorce

SEC. 1. *Be it enacted by the General Assembly of Maryland*, That when an application is made to any court in this State having jurisdiction over the subject of divorce *a vinculo matrimonii*, the fact that the parties have been divorced, *a mensa et thoro* shall not be taken to interfere with the jurisdiction of the court over the subject, and that any bill dismissed for such reason shall be reinstated and be acted upon *de novo*.

SEC. 2. *And be it enacted,* That the admission of respondent of the facts charged in a bill for a divorce, who consents to the application, shall not be taken of itself as conclusive proof of the facts charged, as the ground of application.

CHAPTER 287
(Passed March 7, 1844)

A supplement to an act entitled an act to give to the Chancellor, and the County Courts as Courts of Equity, jurisdiction in cases of Divorce.

SEC. 1. *Be it enacted by the General Assembly of Maryland,* That no person shall be entitled to make application for a divorce, under the provisions of the act to which this is a supplement, where the cause or causes for divorce occurred in another State, District or Territory, or without the jurisdiction of this State, unless the person so applying shall have resided in this State, for two years next preceding his or her application.

CHAPTER 306
(Passed March 10, 1845)

A further supplement to an act entitled, an act to give to the Chancellor, and the County Courts as Courts of Equity, jurisdiction in cases of Divorce, passed at December session, eighteen hundred and forty-one, chapter two hundred and sixty-two.

SEC 1. *Be it enacted by the General Assembly of Maryland,* That all such parts of the second section of the act to which this is a supplement, as require absence from the State for five years on the part of the party complained against, as a cause for divorce a vinculo matrimonii, be and the same is hereby repealed; *provided however,* that the chancellor and the county courts, as courts of equity, shall in no case decree a divorce a vinculo matrimonii, on account of abandonment on the part of the party complained against, unless they shall be satisfied by competent testimony, that such abandonment has continued uninterruptedly for at least three years, and is deliberate and final, and the separation of the parties beyond any reasonable expectation of reconciliation.

CHAPTER 330
(Passed March 10, 1846)

A further supplement to an act to give to the Chancellor, and the County Courts as Courts of Equity, jurisdiction in cases of Divorce, passed at December session, eighteen hundred and forty-one, chapter two hundred and sixty-two.

WHEREAS, the act passed at December session, eighteen hundred and forty-one, chapter two hundred and sixty two, requires that where a party sues for a divorce in the county court as a court of equity, he or she shall file his or her petition or bill in the court of the county where the party against whom the divorce is sought resides; *and whereas* instances may occur in which it would be conducive to the interest and convenience of the party petitioning, to have the right to petition in the county in which he or she may reside—therefore,

SEC 1. *Be it enacted by the General Assembly of Maryland,* That from and after the passage of this act, in all cases of application to the county courts of this State for divorce, it shall and may be lawful for the party applying, to file his or her petition or bill, either in the court of the county where he or she may reside, or in the court of the county where the party against thom the divorce is sought may reside, at the option of the applicant or petitioner.

SEC. 2. *And be it enacted,* That all acts and parts of acts inconsistent with the provisions of this act, be and the same are hereby repealed.

CHAPTER 340
(Passed March 10, 1847)

A supplement to an act entitled, an act to give to the Chancellor and the County Courts as Courts of Equity, jurisdiction in cases of Divorce.

SEC 1. *Be it enacted by the General Assembly of Maryland,* That the jurisdiction of the chancellor and of the county courts, as courts of equity, to decree divorces, shall extend to all cases in which before the marriage, the female shall be guilty of illicit carnal intercourse with another man, the same being unknown to the husband at the time of the marriage, and when such carnal connection shall be proved to the satisfaction of the chancellor or any of the said county courts as courts of equity, the court shall grant a divorce a vinculo matrimonii.

CHAPTER 245
(Passed March 4, 1850)

A further supplement to an act entitled, an act passed at December session, eighteen hundred and forty-one, chapter two hundred and sixty-two, entitled an act to give jurisdiction to the Chancellor and County Courts, as Courts of Equity, in cases of Divorce.

SEC 1. *Be it enacted by the General Assembly of Maryland,* That the chancellor and the county courts, sitting in equity, shall have power to decree divorces, a vinculo matrimonii, as provided for in the acts of December session, eighteen hundred and forty-one, chapter two hundred and sixty-two, and the supplement passed at December session, eighteen hundred and forty-four, chapter three hundred and six, as well where the parties have lived separate and apart, without any reasonable expectation of reconciliation, in the State, as where the party complained against has lived out of it.

SEC. 2. *And be it enacted,* That this act shall go into effect from after the passage thereof.

Appendix 3: The Warfield v. Warfield *and* Thomas v. Thomas *Pamphlets*

The *Warfield v. Warfield* Pamphlet

EDITORIAL NOTE

This twenty-page printed pamphlet was assembled by Charles Warfield and filed on February 2, 1825, with his answer in an alimony proceeding brought by his wife Sarah in the Chancery Court in Annapolis, Maryland. The records of this case are in the Chancery Court Chancery Papers at the Maryland Hall of Records, No.12108, MSA S512, MdHR 17, 898–12108, 1/39/5/5. The date at the end of the document suggests it was printed on January 25, the week before it was filed. Page breaks in the document are denoted by bracketed page numbers that mark the beginning of each new page.

COPY OF LETTERS,

Some general remarks, etc. for the perusal of Charles Warfields friends.

Baltimore, Dec. 7th, 1823.

JOHN GODDARD, Esq.
Dear Sir,
It must be known, that at the time I married your sister, I was actuated by sentiments of compassion. Previous to our marriage, I observed to an acquaintance, I did not wish to be the means of rendering any person miserable; and, as I had rashly, as things turned out, entered into an engagement, and your sister insisted on a compliance, I would marry her. Since, there has been a succession of circumstances, calculated to render a mans life uncomfortable.
My views in relation to this life—provide the means for a decent

support, and live in an unassuming manner, in the discharge of the respective duties, looking for the hope, revealed in Christ.

Some short time since, I thought it best for Mrs. W. and myself to divide our habitation, to lodge and eat separate; we seldom eat our meals in peace, and beside, there is other circumstances, in my judgment, that makes such a course an act of prudence. I did not contemplate extending the breach further; and hoped these means would be a corrective, that in a short time they might be dispensed with.

Circumstances that occurred in relation to me, last evening, makes it necessary I should take another step; I do not say in special relation to Mrs. W. but in relation to my small family, which consists of one grown woman, a boy and girl, your sister and myself. That you may at once distinctly see the purport, as far as it may be necessary to communicate, I will give you a concise history of the affair.

In the morning, I rose rather earlier than common, just as it was getting light. Soon after I took a walk, as I frequently do; returned, eat my breakfast, which consisted of two cups of coffee and [p. 2] one full slice of toast, and sat down by my fire to read the newspaper. In about one hour, I left my dwelling, called at Aldrige and Higdons and at my property on Pratt street, on business, then repaired to the Exchange building; I spent one hour in the reading room, went to Market street, called at four different places, and then returned home. After some time, dinner was prepared, I sat down and dined on two slices of boiled beef, some vegetables, a glass of brandy and water, and two small apples, a kind of dinner I am this season of the year fond of, and is favourable to my health. A short time after dinner, say at three o'clock, I brought my store books and and [sic] other account books from my counting room, which is over the kitchen, placed them in the back parlour, and commenced examining and adjusting them; at which business I continued with little interruption till near nine o'clock. About half past five o'clock, I drank two cups of tea, and ate a small slice of bread; during the time, sundry persons were in the room where I was; at nine o'clock, I called for my supper, which the girl brought me, as usual; I drank a small glass of brandy and water, eat three of Jemiesons crackers, two links of sausages, and one apple: during all of which, I enjoyed myself comfortably, and believed that I enjoyed good health. When at supper, or about that time, I requested that the newspaper might be brought from Mrs. W's apartment; intending after supper to read until about ten o'clock, my usual time for going to bed. After supper I felt very stupid; in most cases, after eating in this way, I am refreshed; in this instance, I felt drowsy and stupefied. In this condition I remained seated by the fire, with the newspaper on my knee, until about ten o'clock; when I rang the bell and requested the servant to put out the fire, preparatory to retiring to bed: feeling duller than common, I declined reading of the Scriptures and praying with my family as my custom has been. When the servant came in to put out the fire, with some difficulty I arose, and commenced walking the room; my indisposition increased, I repaired to the sideboard and drank a glass of Madeira wine, commenced walking again, and the servant retired. My indisposition continued to increase; with difficulty, leaning on the sideboard, I obtained another glass of wine, and endeavoured to resume my walks. I felt a strong motion to action, a giddiness in the head, a very great dis-[p. 3]tress arising from my stomach, and a prostration of my strength. In attempting to continue my walks, I soon fell prostrate on the floor; the unusual exertions made, and expressions of distress uttered, influenced Mrs. W. and the coloured woman to come into the room. They appeared to be much agitated and alarmed; my countenance, naturally dark, became exceeding so, and covered with a cold clammy sweat, which dropped freely in very large drops. My coloured woman assisted me up from the floor, and up the stair steps towards my lodging room: on the first flight, I fell prostrate on my face, when Mrs. W. came to my assistance with some mint water; with assistance I seated myself on one of the steps, drank the mint water, my affliction continued to increase. My distress was very great; yet, I retained my judgment so far, as to know my situation, and judge of the course proper to be pursued; farther than this, and the knowledge of persons and things around me, my mind was buried in distress. This state of things increased, until I believed myself to be in a very dangerous situation, thought of sending for a physician; when I was fortunately relieved by a discharge of my *supper* from my stomach, on the stair steps; otherwise, in a few minutes, I would have been in another world. After the discharge, I felt feeble, but relieved from distress; I rested myself, then repaired to my lodging room and went to bed, and rested comfortably. This morning, when I awoke, I felt very tranquil, although not as much life as usual. It is now half past one o'clock, P. M; I would not wish to enjoy more comfortable [sic] health, than I now enjoy. I usually drink two glasses brandy and water a day, and nothing more in the character of ardent spirits; one when I eat my dinner, the other when I eat my supper.

Under existing circumstances, I believe the proper course for me to pursue, for the present, is to eat at the Fountain Inn Tavern, where I am now just going to get my dinner. I have requested Mrs. W. to give me the keys of the pantries and sideboard.—While she may remain under the roof of my house, she will have two rooms to occupy, and good boarding. I cannot consent to have any further intercourse with her, than I have with my acquaintances generally.

[p. 4] You are now prepared to judge of my situation, and the course that ought to be persued; I have no disposition to act otherwise, than as prudence may direct, and you placed in my situation would adopt. Although Mrs. W. and myself, have never lived in that harmony that should mark a matrimonial relation; hitherto, I have not consented to the propriety of a separation, for example sake: now, I am decidedly of the opinion, that an entire separation ought to take place.

After dining as above, I have examined the contents stated; so far, there is not a full representation of facts; my face and head was as wet, as, if there had been a bucket of water thrown over me, and my appearance as shocking and death-like, as any, that ever recovered their health. It is not my wish to bring accusations against your sister, or in any manner to render the present state of things more unpleasant, than circumstances make it absolutely necessary. My confidence is so far lost, and suspicions hightened; I can never think of eating at home while your sister remains under the roof of my house. Is it not an extreme hard case, in a Christian country; for a man, who has wrought hard to acquire a home, and is not permitted to enjoy it. For a length of time, say about two years, I have been so teazed and tormented, that it has, literally been the means of almost destroying my life. When I arise in the morning, it has been my first calculation to meet, during the day, those that are either seeking my Property, or subjugation to some religious party. Sometimes lovers of head are exhibited, linen sheets, old green carpets, etc. are hung out in full length at the windows of Mrs. C. and Mr. B—dwelling houses; Hugh B—is exceedingly officious, as all weak men are, when there is a prospect of their being noticed; the black boy opposite, I have no doubt was employed to treat me with ridicule: the black man next door, shook a carpet in my *face*, apparently with design; when I have been walking the streets, I have been insulted; I am watched and have been for a length of time on every side, and almost at all hours, as well when I go to the privy as when I go to my dwelling house. This is a mere hint at the afflictions I am called in the providence of God to sustain. Hitherto, the Lord has preserved me. In all, I am more than conqueror; my health is improved, my mind enlarged, strengthened and established in the [p. 5] grace of God. I entertained some remote thoughts of leaving Baltimore, at present I have none; my distress and afflictions have been great; a good God has turned them all to my account, and I trust to his glory. When this sight of persecutions commenced, I had but few friends and they of the weaker sort; now I have many friends, and those of the most powerful order; their number is increasing daily.

I intend, until I get my difficulties so far arranged as to be protected in my rights, according to the constitution of the United States, which is all I claim; to board at some public Inn. I will lodge at home, but eat nothing, and drink very cautiously in my dwelling.

You will perceive I write, as to a friend; you need not calculate on any modification of the above. Under these circumstances, it would be best for yourself and me to come to some amicable terms of settlement. I would be willing to give something, but not much; for me and my estate to be entirely freed from your sister. It is far from my wish to injure your sister or your family; I purchased for her a great variety of flower pots and every thing else that ought to make any reasonable person contented.

I have told my acquaintances, the greatest favour I desired of them, is for them not officiously to concern themselves about me or mine; then I could be contented and happy: providence has give me all that I need in this life. Genuine love, never degenerates into servile obedience—Justice and Love, is the two great points, in matters moral and divine; those that believe this, have no grounds to persecute me. What is to be done, let it be done immediately, that things may be quiet. Unless we come to some terms immediately, I expect my dwelling will be closed, and I will take lodgings for your sister, for it is impossible for us to live together, and maintain the christian character.

I do not know that I have in my possession a single paper, that has not been examined; neither do I know of a place in my house, where I can with confidence place a single paper for twenty four hours, without having it examined. This I consider a great [p. 6] grievance, and one that has for a long time been the theme of my complaints. I have altered my locks, replaced them; yet I have no confidence in the security of my secretary: if this is violated, I see no reason why my counting room should not, also. In the neighbourhood, where I was born, every negro was allowed a box to himself; to have concerned therewith, it was regarded disgraceful. *My rights ought to be respected as much as a Negroes.* I believe most persons would prefer death, rather than have their private affairs constantly exposed to public view. The will of the Lord be done, and may his name be glorified; I now suspect the grounds of my long indisposition.

I do not wish to join any association of Christians; but remain as I am, and do what good I can; of which, I believe myself fully competent to judge. If I am compelled to join any association; I prefer the Friends. I have tried the Episcopal church, am pleased with most of the people as acquaintances, but as it relates to religious matters, they are too gay for me: although I respect them, nothing in this world, my opinion and judgment, would influence me to join them; I do not wish to alter any habits.

Much is said about friendship; it is notorious great attention and interest is entertained about my property: Now let it be seen if there is such a thing as real candour or love. If there is, let my professed friends, who are solicitous about my property, afford me protection in rights that I am entitled to, being a citizen; then I may place my papers and books away with confidence.

You will excuse the length of this letter, acknowledge the receipt thereof, and as soon as possible, let me have your reply, as far as your sister is concerned. Please to present my best respects to Mrs. Goddard; and accept for yourself the assurances of my best wishes.

CHARLES WARFIELD.

Being frequently in custody, by the Sheriff, I deem it prudent to have these documents printed: for, it seems to me, my opposers are disposed to lay hold of an opportunity, when my strength is exhausted by labours that devolve, to vex me. Therefore, they are printed, that I may be prepared to afford my friends some information, if need be; otherwise, I am not desirous to circulate any impressions that I may hold.

[p. 7] [Editor's Note: The next document is a bill of complaint requesting issuance of a subpoena for Charles Warfield's appearance in the chancery court.]

To the Honourable John Johnson,
Chancellor of Maryland.

The bill of complaint of Sarah Warfield, by her next friend and brother John Goddard, humbly sheweth, that on the twenty-ninth day of January, eighteen hundred and eleven, the complainant intermarried with a certain Charles Warfield, of the city of Baltimore; then a merchant and in comparatively humble circumstances, to his present condition. That not long after the marriage, the said Charles began to discover a morose and sullen disposition, and to observe a course of conduct unbecoming in a man, and disgraceful and dishonourable in a husband; in his conversations he applied epithets of the basest kind to the complainant, and her family; and before the expiration of one year from the time of her marriage, actually inflicted violence on her person, and for several years past, indulged himself in abuse and violence, almost without the intermission of a day; every thing which the ingenuity of malice could suggest, was resorted to by the said Warfield, to torture and injure the complainant. While setting at her own table, she dare not ask for, or touch any thing upon it, and when supplied with whatever he thought proper to give her: if she presumed to ask for more, it almost invariably produced some violence, such as throwing a cup of coffee or tumbler, and frequently a pitcher of water into her face; and indeed, at a later period of their intercourse, it was his constant practice, to supply himself with a pitcher of water when setting down to his meals, which, with or without pretext, was invariably discharged upon her; not content with his own tyranny, he encouraged his servants in disobedience and abuse; and finally, would not permit her to set at the table, and ordered her to the kitchen, while he eat his meals; he frequently locked her up without food, and she was compelled to escape through the kitchen, to obtain from her mother necessary food. Your complainant begs leave further to state, that she has borne with these indignities and sufferings for a long while, from a faint hope that some change in his conduct would take place; and from that reluctance which [p. 8] every delicate mind must feel at the exposition of such circumstance to the world—but forbearance on her part seemed but to increase his unkindness and cruelty. He seemed very desirous that she should leave his house, and frequently ordered her to do so, with threats of his determination to enforce the order by violence. Your orator begs leave further to state that on the thirtieth of December, eighteen hundred and twenty three, the said Charles Warfield delivered in person a letter, addressed by himself to your orator in the following words:

Maddam. This is *decisively* to inform you that a separation between yourself and me must take place. This note may be understood in the same *lites* and points of interest as though I had expelled you from my dwelling and board. You will have until the close of to morrow to remove from my dwelling house, after which time you not be accommodated by me in my dwelling house with boarding.

Mrs. *Sarah* Warfield.　　　　　I am respectfully yrs.
Presented in person after three o'clock. CHAS. WARFIELD.

The original of which your *orator* has now in her possession ready to be produced before this Honorable Court whenever it may be necessary so to do.

Your orator begs leave further to state that on the fourth of January, eighteen hundred and twenty four, after her return from church, she found the front door locked and the said Charles Warfield walking the room, who, upon application, refused admission to her. The attention of some of the neighbours being drawn toward the door, he, in their presence, refused to admit her to enter: after some time however he said she might enter for the night, but no longer.

Your orator was therefore compelled to seek shelter and protection from her relations, by whom she is now supported, without the slightest aid from the said Charles Warfield.

Your orator begs leave further to state, that the conduct of the said Charles Warfield is wholly without cause or justification, as she most solemnly avers, and will prove to the entire satisfaction of your honor that she has in all things faithfully discharged her duty as a wife, and her reputation is without blemish or reproach: nor [p. 9] has even the said Charles Warfield ventured to allege any thing in her character or conduct justifying this treatment of her.

Your orator begs leave to state that the said Charles Warfield has forcibly turned her out of his house without the means of subsistence, and that she hath no separate estate or property of her own to enable her to live, and she is now supported by her relations, and must continue to be so, unless relief should be offorded [sic] by this Honorable court.

Your orator begs leave to state that the said Charles Warfield is seized of a large real and personal estate, and that they are without children.

Your orator cannot state particularly of what his estate consists, but knows it to be very large, and estimated at or about $150,000, (one hundred and fifty thousand dollars.) Of his real estate your orator knows that he is seized or possessed of a large farm near Elk Ridge Landing which cost him about $16,000, (sixteen thousand dollars:) of several tenements about the corner of Charles and Pratt streets, which produce an annual rent of about one thousand dollars; a large stone house in Market street rented for seven hundred dollars per annum; of a house in Chatham street rented for two hundred and fifty dollars per annum; a valuable dwelling house in Tammany street, occupied by himself, which would rent for four or five hundred dollars per annum; and also of a ground rent on the lot adjoining, producing an annuity of one hundred and fifty dollars. And your orator believes that he is seized of other real estate and of personal estate in stocks, debts and other effects which would make his estate amount to the sum of one hundred and fifty thousand dollars or more; out of said estate your orator is advised she is entitled to an adequate maintenance and allowance in proportion to her condition in life and the estate of her husband.

And now, inasmuch as your orator is wholly without remedy in the premises unless by the aid of this Honorable court, where claim for Alimony can alone be entertained and decreed upon.

To the end therefore, that the said Charles Warfield may true, full and perfect, make answer to all, and singular the matters and facts herein set forth, as fully as if particularly interrogated there-[p. 10]to; and especially whether the said Charles and *Sarah*, did not intermarry as stated in said bill—and he did not insult, abuse and strike her as stated. Whether he hath not often ordered her to leave his house, and locked out as stated.

Also, whether he did not write and deliver to the said Sarah, the letter dated thirteenth December, eighteen hundred and twenty three, a copy of which, is set forth in the said bill of complaint. Whether he the said Charles, is not seized or possessed of the property mentioned in the said bill, and what is the value of thereof, and how much doth it produce annually; and also to the end, that he the said Charles Warfield, may discover and disclose. Whether hath any real and personal estate, and where the same is situated, and of what does it consist, and what is the amount and value thereof, and the annual produce thereof. And that by a decree of this Honourable Court your orator, may be allowed and decreed alimony, according to the usage and practice of this court, and the act of Assembly in such cases made and provided.

And that she may have, such other and further remedy in the premises, as the nature of the case may require, and to your honour may seem just and right. May it please your Honour, to grant unto your orator, the State of Maryland's writ of Subpoena, to be directed to the said Charles Warfield, commanding him to be and appear before this Honourable court, on a day therein named, to answer the premises, and soforth.

GEORGE WINCHESTER
Solr. for Complt.
True Copy.
Test.
RAMSEY WATERS,
Reg. Cur. Can.

Answer

Charles Warfield, acknowledges to have married Sarah Goddard, as set forth in her bill of complaints to the Chancellor of Maryland, Spring 1824; no date to the copy received from the Chancellor's office.

C. W's property, when he married, was worth 10,000 dollars.

When they went to house keeping, Mrs. W. furnished a bed and other articles of small value; afterwards, her brother made [p. 11] her a present of some china; all, and exceeding in value, have been returned, with a large quantity of clothing—Mrs. Slater, witness.

As C. W's affairs improved he increased his dwelling establishment; his annual expenditures, were from $2000 to 2750; excepting, not more than two years, then $1500 to 1600; soon after marriage, Mrs. W. had every commodity that ought to have been expected.

Before and after marriage, C.W. was subjected to bad health; often much fatigued by attending to business: and remembers, Mrs. W. exhibited a very unhappy disposition. He has generally been in public walks of life, and now lives near the place of his birth; his character is known to many.

Some time after marriage, in the evening, C. W. struck Mrs. W. with his hand; the reason, Mrs. W. called him a liar: C. W. does not justify his conduct in this, it was the effect of abhorrence, suddenly excited: otherwise, after much forbearance, he knows of no acts of violence, by him, on his wife, unjustifiable.—In many instances, he has laid his hand on Mrs. W's mouth to stop her insulting language, and took her by the hand and led her out of the room; having no object in view, other than peace.

C. W. is ignorant of the epithets about her relations. It is recollected, Mrs. W. frequently spoke of the dignity of her family, and contemptibly of things about the dwelling; and, that she was occasionally reminded of her improved external condition: C. W. entertained no intention, hostile to Mrs. W's relations.

C. W. was disposed to promote domestic peace; frequently reflected on means that might lead that way; sundry measures were tried; the dwelling establishment increased, a pew in St. Peter's church, in the most eligible situation, purchased, etc.

Mrs. W. behaved rudely at her meals: C. W. was not disposed to deny Mrs. W. any thing about the dwelling, or at her meals, it was proper for her to have. Some time after the marriage, say two years, C. W. was compelled to take possession of the key of the liquor case; it was used too freely: Mrs. W. held in her possession keys of the other apartments connected with the dwelling, and used things in the house as she was disposed, until a short time before, excluded. Mrs. W. at her meals, helped herself to any [p. 12] she wanted, near her; it was C. W's wish to exchange civilities of this sort: Mrs. W. was by C. W. furnished with such articles near him as wanted, a very few instances, on account of bad behaviour, excepted: after being served in a respectful and friendly manner, Mrs. W. would frequently rise in a rage and put the articles from whence they were taken; and in a childish manner, exhibited much bad feelings, by complaints and accusations;—J. Merriman knows the family; Mrs. John Brice, Jacob Baltzell and McHenry, of that they said about Mr. Merriman.

C. W. frequently used persuasion, this generally produced insolence and impudence: yet, Mrs. W. could behave herself with propriety, when she chose to do it. By experience, he was disposed to believe, the most prudent course; to excite a degree of fear, mixed with kind treatment. Means adopted, were intended to effect reformation; that harmony and cordiality might be realized: no intentions to separate were entertained, until December 7th, 1823. He threw several tumblers of water and cups of coffee in her face; and for a short time before their separation, did supply himself with a pitcher of water, when at his meals; he found it to be necessary; without, there was much bad feeling displayed, seemingly with an intention to vex and irritate: He did not invariably discharge the contents of the pitcher on Mrs. W. it was reluctantly done, and not more than about two or three times; Mrs. W. returned the compliment about as often. C. W. firmly believes, it was Mrs. W's wish and intention to excite a course of procedure of this sort.

C. W. did frequently request Mrs. W. to go and live with her sister, and offered to pay as far as was necessary to her subsistence: this was repeated a short time before she was expelled.

C. W. did not encourage the servants to disobey and abuse Mrs. W. at Mr. W's request, he has chastised the servants, and frequently told them he would not allow them to be impudent to Mrs. W. also cautioned Mrs. W. about her behaviour to the servants; by her familiarity, she gave occasion to take liberties, to which, a quarrel and sometimes a fight ensued. C. W. saw Mrs. W. when they lived on Liberty street, on its commencing to rain, threw open the window shutters, then get in a great rage about the ser-[p. 13]vants not shutting them; other similar examples might be mentioned.

In some very few instances, C. W. refused to let Mrs. W. eat with him; it was seldom and always because of bad behaviour. When going together, about May 1815, to Church; Mrs. W. accused C. W. with having unlawful intercourse with the cook: C. W. immediately separated from Mrs. W. by different routs, both reached the Church. If Mrs. W. had not indulged in vulgar language, they would have harmoniously went together to religious worship: an accommodating disposition, would have produced the same effect in the domestic arrangements generally; for C. W. married to promote his happiness. C. W. does not recollect, ordering Mrs. W, at any time into the kitchen. A short time before, C. W. received with his supper a large portion of poison, as he believes; he requested, that Mrs. W. should occupy different apartments: this was done with intentions as expressed; the former, having failed of the end derived, this measure was resorted to. In this arrangement Mrs. W. was supplied with needful commodities, and her brother John Goddard informed thereof. During the latter part of Mrs. W's stay in C. W. house, for about two days and not more; and at two different times; C. W. locked the doors between her apartments and the back building.

Mrs. W. was never locked up; always had full liberty to go out at the front door: if a different condition existed, C. W. declares, he has no recollection of it. Mrs. W. was always furnished with good boarding, except about two days at different times, the servants were requested not to supply her with victuals, yet, then she had victuals in her room: this course was adopted to induce her to return to her relations, and took place a short time before their separation. C. W. frequently expostulated with Mrs. W. about sending from his residence, bundles to the city and county residence of her relations; and requested that all intercourse be without appearance of mistery.

C. W. acknowledges to have wrote the letter alluded to, under date December 30th, 1823; also, that he refused Mrs. W. admittance into his house, on her return from church, soon after [p. 14] he wrote the letter referred to: Elias Glenn, Esq. was present and heard the conversation between Mr. and Mrs. W. C. W. letter to John Goddard, December 7th, 1823, gives the reasons for this procedure. C. W. believes there has existed a conspiracy, contemplating his ruin, (originating, *it may be*, about Religion;) and that Mrs. W. united therein.

C. W. appeals to those that have known him for his general character. Why should he be disposed to treat his wife improperly, or expel her from his house without sufficient cause.

C. W. believes that Mrs. W. improperly exposed his books and papers, and united with others, when at C. W's house, in a course of hostility; thereby, C. W. was in a great measure deprived from the enjoyment of his property. Mrs. W. winked at and exhibited such imprudent behaviour; that, this world does not contain a consideration that would induce him to live with her; beside, he verily believes that he would thereby endanger his life. C. W. now resides in the country with a few servant, has comfortable health; is contented and happy; being in possession of that portion of good, allotted to man.

Mrs. W. apparently, wished C. W. to support her mother and sister. It was C. W. wish, as far as circumstances rendered fit, to promote a friendly intercourse; Mrs. W's mother being frequently deranged, he would not consent to board her in his family. If Mrs. W. can obtain a considerable amount in the way of Alimony; she will in some measure have realized her wishes.—She does not appear to regard C. W. character or interest; her behaviour has the marks of exaggeration and misrepresentation.

C. W. having no object in view, other than recognized by the laws of the State; did not think of adopting any means of defence, until a copy of the bill filed by Mrs. W. was received; then, materials to answer the bill was handed to a lawyer, and nothing more.

Mr. Joseph Owens visited C. W. the 19th June, in the afternoon of the Sabbath; Mr. Glenn saw C. W. as stated above: in both instances he had been alone during the respective days; of the dispositions exhibited, they can testify.

Circumstances connected with his marriage, are known.

[p. 15] If C. W. is actuated by improper motives, or acted improperly; let it be proven in a manner, to accord with his general proceedings in life.

C. W. paid in settlement of a debt for a farm near Elk Ridge Landing, $13,000: about which time the property was offered at public sale; Mr. Oliver, was the only person present that wished to purchase; he offered $12,000, with a view to accommodate the former proprietor. The property is not productive to C. W. it is however valuable, money has been expended in the way of improving; the property is in the market for sale.

The estimation made of C. W's property, is in character with other specifications in the bill: C. W. is willing to take less than half the amount named in the bill, for his property: he believes he never owned more property at any one time, than he now possesses; neither has he ever desired to have his estate much increased: with a moderate estate, he feels himself somewhat secure; a large estate might be the means of his destruction. C. W. is not willing to make any estimation of his property on oath; he is ready and willing if ordered by the chancellor, to exhibit on oath, all his external wealth to commissioners, with *every species* of property books and papers that he possesses: his account books are posted and in readiness.

C. W. in his letter to J. Goddard, Dec. 7th, 1823, proposed a compromise; he was so disposed to satisfy all parties, until wearied by vexations: although he firmly believes he is not bound either by the laws of God or of the state, to afford Mrs. W. any sort of support; provided the case can be fully and fairly developed. C. W. requested Mrs. W. previous to her leaving his house, to take with her a servant girl: this she declined.

Immediately on being informed of the bill; C. W. obtained a copy, provided materials for an answer, and wished it answered forthwith: he has frequently called on his council, and as often been informed that it would be attended to in due time; also, that he had conversed with the opposite council, and assured him that he would not be put to any inconvenience on account thereof.

Should it be determined that Mrs. W. is entitled to an interest in C. W. estate; it would be better that a division of property take place: believing, that this and other means is the effect of per-[p. 16]secution, C. W. cannot consent, voluntary to give Mrs. W. any support; therefore, it is believed, a final settlement is better for all parties concerned.

That C. W. possesses, is by much care and considerable labour; if Mrs. W. will attend to business, as C. W. is daily in the habit of doing; she will have whereof, to supply her wants. Moreover, if she possessed an accommodating disposition, by taking the oversight of C. W. dwelling; her services would be worth more than the amount necessary to her personal expenses; beside the felicities that might be enjoyed in domestic arrangements.

FINIS

Baltimore, July 5, 1824

JOHN PURVIANCE, ESQ.

Sir—In your presence I have freely expressed my feelings in relation to afflictions I have sustained; and it may be intrudes on your patience. On a view of the past, believing, that the advocates for Religion have been the principle cause of the difficulties; next thereto, a desire to obtain my property: I am induced to express in writing, the course of procedure I intend adopting.

If the opinions I have formed are correct, it appears to me, it would be improper to use great exertions or spend large sums of money in opposing the bill filed by Mrs. Warfield; it is a matter in which the public are concerned, with whom I am willing, as I conceive in duty bound, to rest the case; believing that it does not become a man, conscious of being injured, *and has a right to remuneration*, to act otherwise. I have adopted no means other than communicate the notes in reply to the bill, as requested by you.

I wish the bill answered according to the notes, with those alterations; I have returned to Mrs. W. the whole of her property; also, I believe, the principle cause of separation, originated in an improper interference about religion.

I take the liberty to hand to you, herewith $200; this with money expended by me about this affair, makes $460, which is as much as I feel myself authorized to expend; except I obtain a di[p. 17]vorce, then I would be willing to expend eight hundred dollars more, in the way of compensation and for expenses that might accrue. Further than herein expressed, I do not intend to concern, other than give any information that may be reasonably requested, and to have the documents connected herewith, printed and published. I do not entertain the remotest disposition to resist the contributed authorities: my wish is that the attention of the public may be called to the subject, and that they may correctly judge of the merits thereof.

I am respectfully, your obd't. servant,

CHARLES WARFIELD

Baltimore, October 13th, 1824

Charles Warfield wishes to be informed of the present condition of the case, in relation to her, formerly his wife, with any information deemed interesting; such as, whether she has a legal claim on his estate, or whether he will obtain a divorce, etc. Mr. Warfield would have waited in person, but perceiving at this time, there is a press of business; he solicits a reply by the Post Office, as soon as convenient.

To John Purviance, Esq.
Charles Warfield has not received an answer to this note.

SOME HINTS.

Messrs. Mitchell and Hope, lived near C. W.'s residence. David Winchester has known C. W. since a youth. Has not John McCabe been visited by Lott Warfield and James Kemp, in relation to C. W. Mr. Briscoe, about locks and keys. Doctor Birckheads behaviour in the office of the Savings Bank of Baltimore, in the presence of John Ogston and Thomas Phenix. Captain Youngs and others, testimony about the Savings Bank. Were not persons employed to watch C. W. at St. Peters Church—Messrs. Jackson, Williamson, Alex. Browns testimony. Was not Judge Dorsey requested to attend on church to see of his behaviour. Respecting the Orphans court— Perrion and the honorable Judges; Was not J. Purviance called in, in relation thereto, etc. Has not C. W.'s papers been removed from his dwelling without his consent. Jacob Snether, Jacob Landess, and Thomas Harwood, of Fre-[p. 18]derick County, has known C. W. from his childhood:—Stephen Williams. Has not attempts been made to deprive him of his property. Has not his letters been opened in the Post Office without his consent. Was not Doctors Alexander and Birckhead requested to attend at Owen Dorseys office, to notice his behaviour. Has not his warehouse been entered without his consent? inquire of Mr. Henshaw, Doctor Baker, B. Randle, and Judge Brice. David Hines, and Wm. Bergess, have been clerks to C. W. and lived in his family. Did not a meeting exist about C. W. when he was viewing Jones paintings, at the corner of Market and Charles streets? inquire of W. W. Taylor. James Campbell, seems to have been officious about C. W. C. W. is in the habit of dwelling with Mr. Wheelan. Mr. Woodard saw of Hu. Birkheads behaviour to C. W. while passing him in the street, early in the morning. Has not persons been employed to watch and look after C. W. when attending to his business, and walking the streets?—inquire of Fridge & Morris. Was not Mr. Laurenson requested to call and see C. W. Mr. Jessop knows of C. Ws. behaviour in church. Mr. King seen of B. H. Mullikins insulting behaviour in church. Mr. King seen of B. H. Mullikins insulting behaviour, at C. Ws warehouse. door. For what purpose did Ridgley and Warner carry a cow-hide with them in Market street? C. W. has for a long time been acquainted with Fielder Israel. Mr. Stewart has frequently called on C. W. Rev. Mr. Duncan dined once at C. Ws house. Mrs. W. bought a pair of lamps of Mr. Gould. Has not C. W. been accused of insanity, and great exertions made to establish this point? Has not opportunities been looked after, to that end? Has C. Ws opposers, in any instance, been able to prove it. Is C. W. to be subjected to this sort of persecution? Has he not equal rights with any other, in relation his person and property? Was not Mr. Carroll requested to visit C. W.? Has not *penitentiary acts*, been performed by persons in conspicuous situations? If so, are not such persons equally responsible to the law, as C. W. or is he only bound. These hints, are not noted in the way of accusations, but to elicit information. During his affliction, he attended to several concerns, wrote many letters, copies of which are recorded.

It is C. W. wish to have this business settled. If Mr. Purviance will have the above notes put in due form, C. W. will swear in the [p. 19] truth thereof, in form as prescribed Rev. X. C. W. is in the city every week, a paper of this sort presented to him, will have his immediate attention.

If it is desired C. W. will forthwith present himself before the Chancellor. With this explanation C. W. believes, he is entitled to be protected in his person. C. W. wishes it also to be understood, that he does not intend willingly to expend any more money about this affair.

N. B.—C. W. by reason of delay, at intervals, really believed, the opposition had subsided, and that the bill would be withdrawn: had he been privileged, it would have been forthwith answered by himself. Previous to the case being decided; C. W. wishes all the names mentioned, and others, summoned before the Chancellor, and the matter fully sifted in all its bearings and relations, and noted; that his fellow citizens may determine of the merits thereof. If the *woman* is entitled to a part of his property; she is welcome to it, in the way the law has or may prescribe: nothing more than the clear fair thing is desired. In cases where lawyers do not attend to their duties; it seems, there ought to be some means devised to compel them to return fees, also to prevent them from practising; good laws have general bearings; and protect the rights of all. C. W. is inclined to believe, by appearances, if he would change his religious principles, there are many, that would use their influence to obtain for him a divorce; which he believes he is entitled to. C. W. again repeats, it is his wish, that the business be settled as soon as the nature thereof will admit; as soon as Mr. Purviance will furnish him with an answer, he will attend to it; or, if the Chancellor believes he is bound thereto, he will endeavour to get some one else to answer the bill.

If details are examined, Charles Warfield requests, he may be permitted to attend to this part of the case.

Baltimore, January 25th, 1825.

[p. Back Cover][Editor's Note: There is a handwritten notation on the back cover of the pamphlet which reads as follows: "Filed 2 Feb.y 1825 with answer."]

The *Thomas v. Thomas* Pamphlet

EDITORIAL NOTE

This fifty-two-page pamphlet was published by Governor Francis Thomas on February 19, 1845. The pamphlet is in the Maryland Hall of Records collection (*A Statement of Francis Thomas Concerning His Domestic Grievances*, MSA L1055T, 9/4/4.). Much of it reprints correspondence between Thomas and various members and acquaintances of his wife's family. Only selected portions of the pamphlet written by Thomas himself are reprinted here. As with the Warfield pamphlet, page breaks are noted by bracketed page numbers.

[p.3]

TO THE PUBLIC

Montevue, Frederick County, Maryland,
February 19, 1845

Conspicuous calumniators, who have labored to forestall and pervert public sentiment, have left me no alternative but this, to me exquisitely painful, publication. Sensible of the partial success of their contrivances, for a long period of time I submitted almost in silence to the shocking and disgusting slanders of me, which they disseminated. For a woman was involved; and even if I had not tenderly and desperately loved her, sex alone was sacred in my consideration. If not my wife, even if a stranger, I could not, without infinite reluctance, expose her frailties, or soil her character. Never have I taken a liberty with, spoken ill of, or given umbrage to any virtuous female. At now past life's meridian, I can with perfect truth aver, that the chastity, privacy, or society, the name or character of a woman, of any woman of character, never was invaded or disparaged by any act or word of mine. Having lived, until somewhat advanced in years, a life of study and ambition, little familiar with female society, I may have seemed wanting in that respect and attention for ladies which no doubt refines and improves man. But to degrade one, as has become the stern duty and only alternative of my self-preservation, is a resort to which I could be driven only by the daggers of the men of her family, aimed at the only portion in life I have left, dearer to me than life itself—a character till now unblemished, and which must and shall be vindicated, at whatever cost.

When the horrible doubts of Mrs. Thomas' fidelity flashed on my mind, lacerated my affections, disordered, distracted, unmanned me, even my reproaches were never harsh—my conduct was not cruel or arbitrary—I exercised no overruling authority, I did not repudiate or drive her from my dwelling. I did not, could not, even yield positively my belief to the evidences against her. I still alternately doubted, hoped and confided, and long felt the excruciating agony of one who doubts, yet doubts, and fondly loves.

During several months of anguish, my constant endeavor was to prevail on her to leave me and return to her father's house, without public scandal; to separate at least till we might, if pos-[p. 4]sible, come together again, with my belief in her fidelity restored by her proofs of it made good. I dreaded public scandal for her sake and for mine too. I desired, that her parents and friends might interpose, and either reconciliation or separation be brought about, without the world's malign intermeddling. To her and her family alone were my distrusts intimated. The public saw no outbreak, they had no evidence of estrangement. She continued apparently unconcerned and sociable in the world as ever. I repressed bitter feelings by, at any rate, no act or word of violence, betrayed them to others. I sought her family and besought their mediation. With great difficulty I prevailed on them to take part in my distress. They avoided; I insisted on interference. I offered every explanation and facility of intercourse with Mrs. Thomas and with myself. I unbossomed to them, and to them alone, my griefs, which, though unavoidably reproachful, were never uttered in indignant or reproachful language. They cannot deny, that my expostulations were often in tears; and that I earnestly entreated a domestic investigation and family judgment, of the complaints I was constrained to prefer, and proofs I submitted.

One of the calumnies attempted to be fastened on me, is harsh treatment, violence of conjugal sway, debarring Mrs. Thomas from the liberties of a wife. This mere calumny is without even pretext. I never confined her or deprived her of any liberty she could claim; and defy proof of it. Never did I upbraid her with any such terms, as the following disclosures will satisfy every one, I might have justifiably used. On the contrary, I treated her uniformly with tenderness. In the presence of her parents in Baltimore I claimed the right to make this solemn averment; she did not even contest it. In all the fitful moods of distracted affection, which I own almost unsettled my understanding, nothing violent, cruel or ungenerous ever marked my deportment, or fell in the utmost paroxysm of grief from my lips. For I repeat, I am incapable of wantonly wounding any woman; and the one whom this narrative must expose, I have had the misfortune to love with the fondest, truest, best devotion.

I own therefore anxiety, that they to whom this appeal is addressed, wrung from me by dire necessity, when all other redress is denied, I own much anxiety that it may be received as my only alternative from a life of dishonor, worse than death. I premise this statement with the assurance, that it never would have been published if any other resort were left for me. After mildly entreating an infatuated wife to return to her parents for domestic trial of my accusations, surrounded and supported by her best friends, after explaining to them that accusation, and repeating my prayer for such a trial, and consenting to her leaving me and going home, as will be hereafter explained, I still and constantly persevered in a reserve as near as possible to absolute silence; waiting and hoping for refutal of my fears and restoration of my wife. In anguish and ill concealed distraction I waited, if not patiently, at [p. 5] least forbearingly in silence, till roused from it by the infernal calumnies of the men of her family, who have endeavored to acquit her by defaming me. Mrs. Thomas left me and returned to her father's house with the fruits of marriage in her bosom; yet did members of her family propagate gross and false imputations against me, which, if true, branded her with adultery and her child as illegitimate! Yes; while I was living alone in the solitude of the large Governor's mansion at Annapolis, shrinking from all association with the world, chief magistrate of the State of Maryland, for many years before a faithful and not an unknown member of the Congress of the United States; a man till then of fair report, whom even party violence had not attacked in his private character; living thus in such miserable constrained silence, and subjugation of feeling, as affected me at times almost to insanity on one subject, the cunning and savage champions of a rash wife, filled the ears of all who would hear them with vulgar, blackguard aspersions on my person, character and reputation. They defamed not me alone, but the woman they were to vindicate by their vile tactics, and even assailed the child she bore in her bosom, by the most detestable and intolerable of all detractions. They mortified and distressed my venerable and venerated father, with whose name dishonor, during a life of near eighty winters, has never been connected; a father who received the portionless daughter of Gov. McDowell as his own, and provided for her every comfort. They disgusted and dismayed my excellent and irreproachable sisters in their unobtrusive spheres of respectable life; my brother, my nephews, my nieces; a large family to whom till then, I had been familiar only as a man worthy of that which it had been always my ambition to gain, their esteem and affection. They tried to blast the public and private hopes of one not unambitious of, or unknown to public distinctions, or indifferent to individual esteem. They tried to make a monster of me, by that common rule of aggressors to anticipate attack by being assailants; and have hoped possible that false pride would forbid me to expose them and defend myself.

Thus goaded, I yet preserved so much self-possession as to seek for justice in a form that would have less exposed the parties concerned, than that to which I am now about to resort. By sending to Governor McDowell two copies of the following circular, I invited a judicial investigation. [Editor's Note: The circular, dated December 5, 1843, is omitted.]

* * *

[p. 6]I have never feared the utmost publicity on my own account. But I have preferred judicial investigation, because in courts proof may be taken under solemn obligations of oaths and affirmation, and in some seclusion from public scorn. I sought domestic trial. When that seemed to be hopeless, as the next best tribunal, I asked for judicial arbitrament. I was reluctant to print and publish the abominations that must stain this paper. I respect too much and sincerely, the sanctity of the sex. I did love too fondly, even an unfaithful wife. I hugged, let me confess, too sensitively my own pride, to appeal to public determination, while any chance or hope, without that, remained of either private or judicial scrutiny and decision. And I yield now to the necessities that constrain me, much more on account of respect for the rights and wishes of others, than from any considerations affecting myself alone.

Finding that Gov. McDowell would not notice my invitation for an appeal, by all parties, to the justice of the courts, in a moment of irritation, which may be perhaps pardoned, provoked at such a man as Col. Benton; gravely volunteering, as he did in his Texas letter, to teach the public, morals, I addressed to him, on the 3rd day of May, 1844, a note, intended, if possible, to provoke if [p. 7] nothing else, at least, the measure Gov. McDowell had declined. . . .

Several months have now elapsed, and no notice has been taken of this letter. I am thus inevitably brought at last to a stage in this most painful affair, when all must see, that dishonored and dishonorable life, or this appeal to public justice, are the only alternatives I have left. I have understood, and believe, the eminent and reckless defamers of whom I complain, deterred by the general abhorrence at their first main charges against me, now shelter themselves, and the woman they have undertaken to justify, under the more decent, as well as more compendious assertion, that I am only insane. I am, it is said, an honorable man, but labouring under a monomania. My assailants are therefore not bound to notice me. They would now leave me to the contempt of the world, instead of its execration. I was insane, it is said, when married; went armed to the marriage couch; and with maniac suspicions took pistols to bed with my wife, designed to take the lives of some of her family. This story, fabricated by one with whom she was too intimate, and then put in circulation by her father, part of the shield they now throw around her, will be shown clearly to be false whenever it assumes such a shape as to be entitled to further notice. Whether I am bereft of reason, will appear in the vindication of my much abused conduct, which I am with infinite reluctance about to undertake—disclosing not all the particulars, they could not be put on paper, but under the solemn injunction in a court of justice, to tell the whole truth—but such outline of them as I flatter myself will carry conviction, that I am not so insane but that I can be forced to convince all right-minded persons, that I have been a true-hearted and faithful husband.

Since Mrs. Thomas has joined in attempts to destroy me, I feel less reluctance to vindicate my own character at her expense. Far, however, from the intention of passing judgment against, or the most distant desire of establishing the actual guilt of one I have loved, the first wish of my heart still is, that her innocence, if possible, may be made clear. I wish to vindicate myself without condemning her. In this publication, therefore, I shall go so far only as my own vindication requires. Let her crafty counsellors, if they dare, afford the opportunity I seek, to unveil all I know, and all I have heard, and they shall look upon it all. Let those who craftily put aside the domestic forum, and haughtily dispise judicial appeal, now take their course. I am prepared for any alternative they or any of them may think proper to choose.

In the spring of the year 1836, when I had been many years, and had attained to a respectable station in the House of Representatives of the

United States, boarding in the same house with Col. Benton and his family, the eldest daughter of Gov. McDowell, then a promising young girl of only fifteen years of age, was sent [p. 8] to Washington in order to be put to boarding school at Georgetown. The young lady instead of going to school, for which purpose she was sent from home, spent the whole of the session of 1836 which transpired after her arrival, and nearly the whole of the session of 1836–'7, in the mess at the same boarding house where we were; and at a very early period of our acquaintance, I quote her own words, told me that "she had set her cap for me." Being then thirty-seven years of age, without having ever seriously turned my attention towards marriage, I answered, with perhaps too much plainness, but with perfect sincerity, "it will be time enough for you to think of such things two years hence, after you have completed your education." In saying this, I spoke like an older brother, who, disliked mixed boarding houses for young ladies, would have spoken to an interesting and inexperienced sister. This, it is to be observed, occurred after others of the mess had said to me, that they had discovered, that Col. and Mrs. Benton were anxious to make a match between their niece and myself. With this, I was flattered, and at that early day was perhaps more pleased than I was conscious of, with the prospects of such a destiny. Nevertheless, at her tender age, I felt it would be ungenerous to take advantage of the influence of her friends, and desired to see her go to her boarding school. Her uncle and family, however, had determined otherwise. I cannot lengthen this narrative by introducing proofs of their extreme solicitude, to prevent any occurrence that might unfavorably interpose with their design to promote our union. These could be adduced to abundance, in the course of a courtship frequently interrupted on my part, and as often renewed by the immediate interposition of Col. Benton and her friends. . . . No one was more conspicuous than Gov. and Mrs. McDowell at some stages of this affair, in the furthering, as far as they could, what seemed to be to their daughter and her friends a favorite purpose. Imputing, at the time, these proceedings to generous attempts to overcome my extreme diffidence, and guard against my want of address, they had the effect to create in me for the daughter and [p. 9] niece a most passionate love, and for her friends a devoted attachment.

In the summer of 1841,[1] all arrangements being made for the marriage, it took place on the *eighth of June* of that year, at Gov. McDowell's residence in Virginia. After a few days, passed at her father's residence, she was confided to me to be taken home to the residence provided for her in

Maryland. Young and inexperienced as Mrs. Thomas was, I solicited her sister and her cousins to accompany her to her new home. Not one of them could be prevailed upon to be of our party, and she came amongst strangers without a female friend, to whose society she has been accustomed; and no one of the many young ladies of her large family connexion, ever entered my dwelling during the five months she was an inmate. To repel one of the impudent charges afterwards made against me, that I had not furnished her with a suitable wardrobe, I must be excused here for declaring, that Gov. McDowell's daughter came from her father's house to mine, with a wardrobe so scanty as to afford me ample opportunity to gratify, as I did gratify, my affection for her, by adding liberally to its variety, exceeding her own wishes in that respect.

During our stay at her father's house, she told me of her having kissed a young man of her acquaintance at one of the parties we attended. I made no comment, but on our way home, in consequence of this communication, in connexion with other occurrences, I took care to make her understand she was about to be introduced into a society, where such familiarities were not customary. In the same conversation, I condemned the conduct of her cousin; which had come under my own observation in Virginia—a young man whom at her instance, I had, before our marriage and after our engagement, invited from his residence there, and established in Maryland. I had seen him attempt what I deemed gross liberties with a young lady, who was entitled to his particular respect. This slight circumstance is here mentioned because it had an influence in subsequent occurrences. A few days after our establishment in Frederick, at the hotel, this person, who was at our wedding, returned to that place. Familiar, as he had a right to be in my family, I soon perceived an intimacy between him and Mrs. Thomas which I did not like, on account of my knowledge of his want of delicacy towards another lady, which I had communicated to her. There were apparently contrived interviews, out of my presence, which could not but attract my notice. Predisposed to put a favorable construction on her conduct, I could not cherish the slightest suspicion of her honor, and looked upon her participation in these proceedings, as perhaps attempts to make me jealous. After several disagreeable occurrences, which elicited no comment from me, on the 17th of July, one of those concerted interviews took place, of which I thought proper to speak. After breakfast, on the morning of that day, she said to me, go up street and do not return till dinner-time, I intend to pass the forenoon in [p. 10] my bed-chamber. As soon as he became aware of my absence, he hastened

to her, for when I returned unexpectedly in a few moments, I found them
together, in our parlor, at the hotel, alone, so seated that she changed her
position as soon as I entered. When we were alone, I cautioned her against
what might be said by any casual observer of such apparent familiarity in
my absence. My admonition was as kind as possible. It was received in a
temper and with a tone of defiance. Shortly before this, when her cousin
was riding in my carriage with us, and she amusing herself and him with
a defect in my dress, I checked him for joining afterwards in her jeer, when
she turned upon me with passion and said, "you are neither a gentleman
nor a man of truth." This was the first harsh word that ever passed between
us. At the moment I said nothing, and continued the conversation as if
nothing unusual had passed. But subsequent occurrences convinced me,
as I think they will others, that her defending him passionately from my
reproof, proved, that even then he shared her strong regard. On the 22nd
of July, we changed our residence, at her instance, from the hotel in the
town to my house one mile and a half in the country. That evening we
were together at a party in town, where we met her cousin, when her
language and deportment concerning him were more than ever remarkable. In the afternoon of the 23rd, as we were riding alone, and talking of
the occurrences of the night before, she petulantly said to me, "mind I
have not yet broken my marriage vow," to which my reply was, an exclamation of surprise and regret at her use of such language. Shortly after
our return home, about twilight, I had reason to believe she had a clan-
destine interview with some one, and that night the suspicion was much
strengthened. The next morning, after discovering additional proof that
some one had been secretly at my residence, I did not hesitate to make
known to her my apprehension of the fact. And then, for the first time, I
told her that my confidence was impaired, and urged her with much earnestness to go with me to her friends. She protested her innocence, con-
fessing that her cousin had promised to come to my house the evening
before, but declared that he had not come, or at least she had not seen
him. I still insisting we should separate, she proposed, as a means of con-
vincing me of her fidelity and attachment, that she would require him to
leave that part of the country. Throughout the 24th and 25th, this painful
contest continued, until at last I yielded to her entreaty. Harassed with
doubts, and still incapable of believing what seemed to be extremely im-
probable, I was not unwilling to submit the matter to further investigation. I had no positive proof to found an opinion upon; the scene of
the interview, if it occurred, was out of the house: one of the parties a

woman but six weeks married, and the other a young relative, then living on my bounty. There was nothing in my own heart, that did not teach me to resist the conclusions to which a chain of circumstances directly led, and to [p. 11] enquire further before I acted into this unnatural affair. As soon as I consented to her arrangement, she went into an adjoining room and forthwith brought to me the . . . letter, intended for him . . . .

[Editor's Note: The correspondence, the cousin's reply, and Thomas's reactions to it at pages 11–14 are omitted. Suffice it to say that the contents of Sarah Thomas's first draft of the letter, in which she accused her cousin of entertaining "wrong designs and polluting wishes" toward her, only added to Francis Thomas's suspicions. The draft was so forward that Francis rewrote it. It is possible, of course, that Sarah wrote a truthful document; it is also possible she wrote an outrageous one knowing any reader would laugh it off. The cousin, claiming correctly that the letter he received was drafted by Francis, rejected the charge that his behavior risked "exciting criticism all around." The cousin, nonetheless, left.]

*   *   *

[p. 14]Although I had so far yielded to her entreaties as to adopt her plan for getting rid of her cousin, of whom she said to me when I was leaving home for that purpose, "beat him Mr. Thomas, but dont kill him," I still persisted in my determination to take her home to her family, and should probably have had the heart to firmly but mildly execute my purpose, if it had not been that within a few days she gave me to understand she bore the fruit of our marriage, as would appear in the course of nature; and insisted with great earnestness, that time would show this had been her condition a month before.[2] Then it was that affection, struggling with suspicions, and ignorant as I was on such subjects, believing that conception could not be the result of promiscuous intercourse, I postponed the intention of taking her home, and undertook to learn, if possible, the true character of the woman I had married.

[Editor's Note: A section at pages 14–18, which is omitted, contains copies of correspondence over an allegation that in 1837 Sarah McDowell, before her marriage to Thomas, carried on a serious flirtation with the husband and in the presence of a well-known and highly respected woman. The letters were in the possession of Mrs. Benton, who turned them over to Thomas. With some persistence, the letters suggest, Mrs. Benton eventually gained a retraction of the charges and an apology.

Thomas, of course, refused to believe the retraction, preferring to view it as obtained under the coercive influence of the powerful Benton family.]

*   *   *

[p. 18][T]here can be no doubt that, no human agency, no persuasion, no covert appeals to my gallantry or generosity, could have led me deliberately to court and marry any woman to whom such a letter as this first letter, had ever been addressed, if that fact had come to my knowledge before the courtship had commenced.

*   *   *

[p. 19]The frightful and disgusting details I am next obliged to expose to public animadversion, I think proper to give as much as possible in the very language of all the parties to them, as well for the purpose of presenting the precise facts, as for relieving myself from the torment of any particular statement of my own.

I returned in the course of my electioneering tour, and passed a night at my father's with my wife, about the 29th of September. The next day, happening to be in the office of a physician in Frederick, he inquired how is Mrs. Thomas? My answer was, she is very well. To my great surprise, he asked, did you not hear of the accident that happened to her on the 21st of September? I said, no sir. He went on to say, an accident had happened to her on that day, which her attending physician said, was a case of eight weeks. In the course of a conversation on other subjects, he repeated, the Doctor says it was a case of eight weeks. Of which communication, whatever my feelings at the moment were, I took no other notice, than to rejoin, I suppose Mrs. Thomas did not like to speak with me on such a subject. I must acknowledge, however, that the shocking feelings which immediately followed my marriage, and were renewed on the 23rd of July, recurred at this time with infinite force, from the evident coincidence of their being just eight weeks between the occurrence of the 23rd of July, and the accident of the 21st of September, which directly conflicted with her own statement in August preceding, the truth of which she appealed to time to prove.³ With a heavy heart I completed my electioneering tour, going again to my father's on the day after the election. During the several weeks of my absence, Mrs. Thomas had passed part of the time with one of my relations, living near Charlestown, in Virginia, and part of it with other members of my family, in Maryland. While in my father's house, I subdued my feelings so far, as not to say one word upon what was agonizing to me. Within a day or so, I took Mrs. Thomas to our home, near Frederick. And then immediately communed with her of the deep-seated anxiety which the communication of the physician in Frederick, had awakened. My tone, language, and manner, were as delicate as they could be, consistently, with my desire to be understood. With this guard upon my feelings, I intimated to her my distress, at the before mentioned coincidence, of the eight weeks between the 23rd of July and the 21st of September, and reminding her of her own statement in August, appealed to her to say, what had produced the accident. Inasmuch as she had before taken pains to satisfy me, that the change in her situation, made known to me early in August, had preceded the 23rd of July by some weeks, as would appear, if I would wait until she became a mother, I was desirous of ascertaining whether the occurrence was truly accidental. It is painful to confess that I could be brought to entertain such thoughts, but [p. 20] it is due to truth to make the acknowledgement. And it was equally painful to me, that she to whom they were divulged, would not voluntarily separate. For some time her persisting answer was, that she could not tell what had caused it; but before our conversation on the painful subject closed, she stated, to my utter astonishment and incredulity, she had procured the means to produce it at Charlestown. What, said I, took drops? No, she replied, it was a powder. Incapable of believing any such statement, I, insisting upon testing the truth of it by further enquiry as to the agents used to procure such means, said to her, did you employ the servants for that purpose, or obtain it in person yourself? To these enquiries she gave no satisfactory answer. They were renewed the next day, but not in a manner to extort an answer. Throughout all these scenes, her manner was perfectly self-possessed and collected, which made me incredulous. In this state of our feelings, she varied her first confession, by saying that the drug had been furnished by another, whom she named. My exclamation was, great God do you know what you are saying, it is a penitentiary offense! Upon which she said, I have not told the truth, I do not know what caused it. The utter incongruity of these monstrous statements, with what I had thought of her and her friends, and the improbability, as I thought, of the person named being her agent, bewildered and confounded me,

I recurred with more earnestness than ever to my entreaties, that she would go with me to her family, promising that if she would go, what had occurred should never transpire. I felt the utmost horror of exposing her, of being connected myself, or of mixing any of the members of my own unsullied family before the public, with this monstrous transaction; and desired, even if her statements were true, to separate and bury the whole in oblivion. Of this engagement I reminded Mrs. Thomas, and said it would be a sufficient excuse for her going home, without exciting suspicion. She persisted in refusing to go, and stated, what I cannot but think remarkable, that during my absence, her mother had released her from the engagement to visit her father's family, and advised her not to come home. Finding all my entreaties vain, during several days of expostulation, I gave up endeavoring to prevail upon Mrs. Thomas to go, and substituted attempts to bring her mother to my residence, in which I was altogether unsuccessful. During all the months of November and December, I was in vain entreating her mother, through letters from her daughter and myself, to come to Maryland. And it is a fact, which I have since ascertained, that at this time Gov. McDowell was perfectly aware of the reason why I had compelled his nephew to leave my neighborhood, and return to his.

Long after this, in March 1842, . . . after many of my [p. 21] open hearted confidential letters were written, which Col. Benton and Gov. Mc-Dowell shamefully exposed, hideous circumstances which I am not at liberty to withhold, came to my knowledge. I must now indicate them, in order to give the true character of the accident of the 21st of September. My information is derived from sources beyond the reach of refutation or reproach. But as my informants are ladies they shall not be named, unless my persecutors think proper to put them on their oaths, in any judicial proceeding they may desire to dissolve the marriage. Then, though it may be a terrible alternative, as one of them in her written statement now before me declares, they will appear and tell the whole truth.

On that night of the 21st of September Mrs. Thomas slept in a room with another lady, in different beds. During the night the lady was awakened by the groans and complaints of Mrs. Thomas. Kindly enquiring to as [sic] the cause and offering her assistance for relief, she was told, in substance, by Mrs. Thomas, it is only the toothache, to which I am accustomed, go to sleep, I know how to manage it. I recoil from setting forth the details of what followed, unless judicially compelled to do it. The written evidence lies now before me of what I must indicate, but I shall do so with as much regard to delicacy as possible. In brief then the embryo was found next morning, under the head of the bed wrapped in her under clothing. And so far was concealment carried, that after washing, and particularly the feet in cold water; when left alone in the room in the morning, she dressed and prepared to descend to the breakfast table as if nothing had happened, and was only prevented by the remonstrances [sic] of a lady who learned what had occurred. It is wholly unnecessary to add a comment. Let others decide whether it is not calculated to aggravate the feelings with which I have been harrassed. This occurrence, in itself so revolting, necessarily and effectually destroyed the means of testing the truth of her declaration made in August, when she appealed to time to prove the date of her condition.

[Editor's Note: Thomas then goes on for thirty more pages, charging that his wife had another affair on December 18 and 27, 1841; that the man charging him with taking pistols to bed spent a long time in the bed chamber of Mrs. Thomas in January 1842; that until January 30, 1842, the McDowell and Benton families blocked every attempt he made to send his wife back to her original home; that on January 30 he made a sudden recantation and apology to his wife under the influence of physicians who convinced him his impression of the September 21 "accident" was erroneous, only to have the McDowell family then decline to return their daughter to his household; that calculated attempts were made to convince Thomas his wife would return if he continued to recant his allegations and profess his love, when the McDowells actually intended to use such letters only to vindicate their daughter; and that he was constantly being vilified in political and other public circles.]

*   *   *

[p. 50][S]he was co-operating with her friends. By inculcating the contrary belief many of my friends and some of her friends, it will be perceived, had kept me silent and passive, while other friends of her's were warring mercilessly on my reputation. It was in truth a state of profound and generous peace on my part; of incessant and cruel vituperation on theirs. This . . . has dissipated all my delusions as to the possibility of her affection, and left me at full liberty to enter upon my own defence.

*   *   *

If any further insult had been necessary to restore gradually my independence, it was not long before it was offered. At a fair in Lexington . . . , Mrs. Thomas made her appearance, bringing with her a figure dressed in boy's clothing, on the collar of which was pinned the word "Governor," and to other parts of the dress of which were attached scraps of dogrel rhyme, all in her own hand writing, and offered it for sale to the highest bidder, while she herself flaunted about the room, boasting of her youth, health, and good spirits. This indecent and unfeeling attempt to make a man ridiculous, who from an unwillingness to wound her sensibilities was enduring a mountain of unremitted obloquy in silence, served to satisfy me that I need not postpone my own vindication, under an apprehension that her mortification would be very poignant even at exposures like this. My bitter reluctance to mortify her mother was diminished somewhat by this same proceeding, as it must have had her sanction, and was par-[p. 51]ticularly discreditable to the parties concerned, as they well knew that of the young persons of both sexes who were to be present at the fair, there would be several to whom I am nearly related, and whose enjoyments could not but have been interrupted by this wanton and vulgar exhibition.

*   *   *

For many tedious months have I sought gentler redress; elucidation which would not hold up a female to public criticism. Mrs. Thomas and her friends being non-residents of the State, and beyond the jurisdiction of the courts where I reside, every lawyer knows I cannot, as plaintiff or complainant, before those tribunals, force them to answer my bill or interrogatories. Without their consent therefore, I cannot make that full and perfect record indispensable to such an adjudication of this horrible case, as would do justice to all the parties concerned. Without such means of vindicating my character from the aspersions of that malicious host of both sexes who have united in this ruthless assault, I am compelled, by this most reluctant publication, to unveil my domestic misfortunes, and stand in that respect uncovered before the world.

*   *   *

Driven to this last and most painful resort of publication, not one word have I set down in malice, or uttered in wantonness; much have I withheld, and in all that I publish, have endeavored to use language as mild as I can consistently, with a fair and intel-[p. 52]ligent statement. And reiterate here an earnest hope, notwithstanding all that has passed, for her acquittal. Moreover, if she was not, and is not now, I shall rejoice with a joy unspeakable, when she has become, as she can become, all that my glowing fancy painted her.

The blackguard catastrophe to which Gov. McDowell brought the drama . . . , which I most conscientiously sought to settle amicably and peacefully . . . , by an honorable reunion, or a decent and dignified separation, has at any rate roused me to self-defence, restored my independence of thought and action, struck the film away which blinded me, and I think all must acknowledge, would justify my using much stronger language than I have done. Divulging some, but withholding much of the dreadful details forced from me, my oath is always at the call of Mrs. Thomas' friends for the *whole* truth. What I have told is submitted with a clear conscience to all honorable men and virtuous women, as the reluctant, but indispensable vindication of one much abused, long forbearing, but now ready for any contest, and all events.

This expose, preliminary to one of graver import, is made under a deep and solemn conviction, that it is due, to the memory of my mother, who could not have nurtured a son capable of wronging a woman, to the honest pride of a gray-haired father, whom dishonor never touched, to the good name of a large and respectable family, whose hitherto very happy and still unsullied circle has been by these atrocious proceedings so cruelly disturbed, to a generous host of political friends, who have repeatedly clothed me with high public honor; and let me add, it is due to the honor of a man, without fear, with self-respect unimpaired, resolved to live without reproach, armed with the fortitude to repel wrong, prevent ignominy, and resent aggression.

FRANCIS THOMAS.

Notes

1. Making the participants approximately 42 and 19.
2. "[A] month before" was early July 1841.
3. This recalls Francis's recollection, *supra*, that early in August Sarah had claimed she was one month pregnant, making her pregnancy the product of the marriage's first month.

Bibliography

BOOKS AND MONOGRAPHS

BASCH, N., IN THE EYES OF THE LAW: MARRIAGE AND PROPERTY IN NINE-
  TEENTH-CENTURY NEW YORK (1982).
BILHARTZ, T. D., URBAN RELIGION AND THE SECOND GREAT AWAKENING:
  CHURCH AND SOCIETY IN EARLY NATIONAL BALTIMORE (1986).
BINNEY, C., RESTRICTIONS UPON LOCAL AND SPECIAL LEGISLATION IN STATE
  CONSTITUTIONS (1894).
BISHOP, J. P., COMMENTARIES ON THE LAW OF MARRIAGE AND DIVORCE (1852).
BLACKSTONE'S COMMENTARIES (1765).
BLAKE, N. M., ROAD TO RENO: A HISTORY OF DIVORCE IN THE UNITED STATES
  (1962).
BROWN, D. M., PARTY BATTLES AND BEGINNINGS IN MARYLAND (1961) (Thesis,
  Georgetown U.).
BRUGGER, R., MARYLAND: A MIDDLE TEMPERAMENT, 1634–1980 (1988).
CHESLER, E., WOMAN OF VALOR: MARGARET SANGER AND THE BIRTH CON-
  TROL MOVEMENT IN AMERICA (1992).
CONGRESSIONAL QUARTERLY, GUIDE TO ELECTIONS (1975).
THE CONSTITUTION OF THE STATE OF MARYLAND, REPORTED AND ADOPTED
  BY THE CONVENTION OF DELEGATES ASSEMBLED AT THE CITY OF ANNAP-
  OLIS, NOVEMBER 4TH, 1850, AND SUBMITTED TO AND RATIFIED BY THE
  PEOPLE ON THE FIRST WEDNESDAY OF JUNE, 1851 (Hinkley, E. O., ed., 1855).
COTT, N., THE BONDS OF WOMANHOOD: "WOMAN'S SPHERE" IN NEW EN-
  GLAND, 1780–1835 (1977).
DAYTON, C., WOMEN BEFORE THE BAR: GENDER, LAW, AND SOCIETY IN CON-
  NECTICUT, 1710–1790 (1986) (Thesis, Princeton U.).
DEGLER, C., AT ODDS: WOMEN AND THE FAMILY IN AMERICA FROM THE
  REVOLUTION TO THE PRESENT (1980).
DEMAREE, L. S., MARYLAND DURING THE FIRST PARTY SYSTEM: A ROLL-CALL
  ANALYSIS OF THE HOUSE OF DELEGATES, 1789–1824 (1984) (Thesis, U. Mo.
  Columbia).
DOUGLAS, A., THE FEMINIZATION OF AMERICAN CULTURE (1977).
EVANS, S. M., BORN FOR LIBERTY: A HISTORY OF WOMEN IN AMERICA (1989).
EVERSTINE, C. N., THE GENERAL ASSEMBLY OF MARYLAND 1776–1850 (1982).
FORD, B. L., WOMEN, MARRIAGE AND DIVORCE IN CALIFORNIA, 1849–1872
  (1985) (Thesis, U. Cal. Davis).
FRIEDMAN, L., A HISTORY OF AMERICAN LAW (1985).

GRISWOLD, R., FAMILY AND DIVORCE IN CALIFORNIA, 1850–1890 (1982).

GROSSBERG, M., GOVERNING THE HEARTH: LAW AND THE FAMILY IN NINE-TEENTH CENTURY AMERICA (1985).

HALEM, L. C., DIVORCE REFORM: CHANGING LEGAL AND SOCIAL PERSPEC-TIVES (1980).

HARLAN, H., THE LAW OF DOMESTIC RELATIONS IN MARYLAND (1909).

KENT, J., COMMENTARIES ON AMERICAN LAW (4 vols. 1826–1830)

KERBER, L., WOMEN OF THE REPUBLIC: INTELLECT & IDEOLOGY IN REVOLU-TIONARY AMERICA (1980).

KOHL, L. F., THE POLITICS OF INDIVIDUALISM: PARTIES AND THE AMERICAN CHARACTER IN THE JACKSONIAN ERA (1989).

LEIPHEIMER, R. E., MARYLAND POLITICAL LEADERSHIP, 1789–1860 (1969) (The-sis, U. Md.).

LEVI, E., AN INTRODUCTION TO LEGAL REASONING (1948).

LUKER, K., ABORTION AND THE POLITICS OF MOTHERHOOD (1984).

MARSHALL, L. C. & G. MAY, THE DIVORCE COURT (1932).

MAY, DIVORCE LAW IN MARYLAND: INTERIM REPORT OF THE STUDY OF DI-VORCE LITIGATION IN OHIO AND MARYLAND (1932).

MAY, G., DIVORCE LAW IN MARYLAND (Bulletin No. 4, Study of the Judicial System of Maryland, By the Judicial Council of Maryland and the Institute of Law of the Johns Hopkins University, 1932).

MAYFIELD, J., THE NEW NATION 1800–1845 (1961).

MCPHERSON, J. M., ORDEAL BY FIRE: THE CIVIL WAR AND RECONSTRUCTION (1982).

MEYER, M. K., DIVORCES AND NAMES CHANGED IN MARYLAND BY ACT OF THE LEGISLATURE, 1634–1854 (1970).

MOHR, J., ABORTION IN AMERICA: THE ORIGINS AND EVOLUTION OF NA-TIONAL POLICY (1978).

PETRIK, P., NO STEP BACKWARD: WOMEN AND FAMILY ON THE ROCKY MOUN-TAIN MINING FRONTIER, HELENA, MONTANA, 1865–1900 (1987).

PHILLIPS, R., PUTTING ASUNDER: A HISTORY OF DIVORCE IN WESTERN SOCI-ETY (1988).

REEVE, T., LAW OF BARON AND FEMME (1816).

RENZULLI, L. M., MARYLAND: THE FEDERALIST YEARS (1972).

RIDGWAY, W. H., COMMUNITY LEADERSHIP IN MARYLAND, 1790–1840: A COM-PARATIVE ANALYSIS OF POWER IN SOCIETY (1979).

RILEY, G., DIVORCE: AN AMERICAN TRADITION (1991).

RISJORD, N., CHESAPEAKE POLITICS, 1781–1800 (1978).

RUBIN, E. R., ABORTION, POLITICS, AND THE COURTS: ROE V. WADE AND ITS AFTERMATH (1982).

RYAN, M., CRADLE OF THE MIDDLE CLASS: THE FAMILY IN ONEIDA COUNTY, NEW YORK, 1790–1865 (1981).

SALMON, M., WOMEN AND THE LAW OF PROPERTY IN EARLY AMERICA (1988).

SEMMES, J. E., JOHN H. B. LATROBE AND HIS TIME 1803–1891 (1917).

SMITH, W. W., ANTI-JACKSONIAN POLITICS ALONG THE CHESAPEAKE (1989).

———, THE WHIG PARTY IN MARYLAND, 1826–1856 (1967) (Thesis, U. Md.).

Spruill, J., Women's Life and Work in the Southern Colonies (1938).
Steiner, B. C., Life of Roger Brooke Taney: Chief Justice of the United States Supreme Court (1922).
Story, J., Commentaries on Equity Jurisprudence as Administered in England and America (2 vols. 1835–1836).
Swisher, C. B., Roger B. Taney (1935).
Warbasse, E., The Changing Legal Rights of Married Women, 1800–1861 (1960) (Thesis, Harvard U.).
White, F. F., The Governors of Maryland: 1777–1970 (1970).
Wiebe, R. H., The Opening of American Society (1984).
Williams, T. J. C., History of Frederick County Maryland (Vol. 1, 1910).
Williams, W. H., The Garden of American Methodism: The Delmarva Peninsula, 1769–1820 (1984).

Journals and Newspapers

Basch, N., *Relief in the Premises: Divorce as a Women's Remedy in New York and Indiana, 1815–1870*, 8 Law & Hist. Rev. 1 (1990).
Censer, J., *"Smiling Through Her Tears": Ante-Bellum Southern Women and Divorce*, 25 Am. J. Leg. Hist. 1 (1981).
Chused, R., *Married Women's Property Law: 1800–1850*, 73 Geo. L. J. 1359 (1983).
———, *Married Women's Property and Inheritance by Widows in Massachusetts: A Study of Wills Probated Between 1800 and 1850*, 2 Berkeley Women's L. J. 42 (1986).
———, *The Oregon Donation Act of 1850 and Nineteenth Century Federal Married Women's Property Law*, 2 Law & Hist. Rev. 44 (1984).
Clark, E., *Matrimonial Bonds: Slavery and Divorce in Nineteenth Century America*, 8 Law & Hist. Rev. 26 (1990).
Cohen, S., *The Broken Bond: Divorce in Providence County, 1749–1809*, 44 R.I. Hist. 67 (1985).
———, *"To Parts of the World Unknown": The Circumstances of Divorce in Connecticut, 1750–1797*, 11 Can. Rev. Am. Stud. 275 (1980).
Cott, N., *Divorce and the Changing Status of Women in Eighteenth-Century Massachusetts*, 33 Wm. & Mary Q. 586 (1976).
———, *Eighteenth Century Family and Social Life Revealed in Massachusetts Divorce Records*, 10 J. Soc. Hist. 20 (1976).
Dewey, F., *Thomas Jefferson's Notes on Divorce*, 39 Wm. & Mary Q. 212 (1982).
McKenna, C., *Women, Welfare and Work in Maryland: A Historical Survey of the First Two Hundred Years* (1982) (Student paper on file with author).
Meehan, T., *"Not Made Out of Levity": Evolution of Divorce in Early Pennsylvania*, 92 Pa. Mag. Hist. & Bio. 441 (1968).
Niles National Register.
Niles Weekly Register.
Rasmussen, W., *The Mechanization of Agriculture*, 247 Sci. Am. 76 (1982).

Schultz, M., *Divorce in Early America: Origins and Patterns in Three North Central States*, 25 SOCIOLOGICAL Q. 511 (1984).

———, *Divorce in the South Atlantic States: Origins, Historical Patterns, and Recent Trends*, 16 INT'L J. SOC. FAM. 225 (1986).

Steinfeld, R., *Property and Suffrage in the Early American Republic*, 41 STAN. L. REV. 335 (1989).

Tarka, D., *Thalidomide: The Drug Companies' Fallacy* (1991) (Student paper on file with author).

Zainaldin, J., *The Emergence of a Modern American Family Law: Child Custody, Adoption and the Courts, 1796–1851*, 73 NW. L. REV. 1038 (1979).

MANUSCRIPT COLLECTIONS

Collection of the Archives of the Episcopal Church of Maryland in Baltimore.

Md. Hall of Records, Baltimore County Court Chancery Papers, Document Group 40.

———, Chancery Court Chancery Papers, Document Group 17.

———, JOURNAL OF A CONVENTION OF THE PROTESTANT EPISCOPAL CHURCH IN THE STATE OF MARYLAND HELD IN THE CITY OF BALTIMORE FROM MAY 20, TO MAY 22, 1807.

———, Saint Marys County Court Equity Papers, Document Group 19.

———, Sharf Collection.

———, Thomas, Francis, *A Statement of Francis Thomas Concerning His Domestic Grievances* (1845).

Md. Hist. Soc'y., Dielman-Hayward File, Baltimore.

LEGISLATIVE MATERIALS

Md. Laws (1789–1851).

VOTES AND PROCEEDINGS OF THE HOUSE OF DELEGATES OF THE STATE OF MARYLAND.

VOTES AND PROCEEDINGS OF THE SENATE OF THE STATE OF MARYLAND.

JUDICIAL MATERIALS

Bayly v. Bayly, 2 Md.Ch. 326 (1847).

Bowie v. Bowie, 3 Md.Ch. 51 (1850).

Coles v. Coles, 2 Md.Ch. 341 (1951).

Daiger v. Daiger, 2 Md.Ch. 335 (1850).

Dunnock v. Dunnock, 3 Md.Ch. 140 (1852).

Hays v. State of Maryland, 40 Md. 633 (1874).

Helms v. Franciscus, 2 Bland Ch. 519 (1830).

Hewitt v. Hewitt, 1 Bland Ch. 101 (1825).

Jones v. State of Maryland, 70 Md. 326 (1889).
Lamb v. State of Maryland, 67 Md. 524 (1887).
Matysek v. Matysek, 128 A.2d 627 (1957).
Ricketts v. Ricketts, 4 Gill 105 (1846).
Tayman v. Tayman, 2 Md.Ch. 393 (1851).
Wallingsford v. Wallingsford, 10 Md. (6 H. & J.) 398 (1825).

Index

This book has been set in Linotron Galliard. Galliard was designed for Mergenthaler in 1978 by Matthew Carter. Galliard retains many of the features of a sixteenth-century typeface cut by Robert Granjon but has some modifications that give it a more contemporary look.

Printed on acid-free paper.